Economic Appraisal of Transport Projects

 EDI Series in Economic Development

Economic Appraisal of Transport Projects
A Manual with Case Studies

Revised and Expanded Edition

Hans A. Adler

Published for The World Bank
The Johns Hopkins University Press
Baltimore and London

The Johns Hopkins University Press
Baltimore, Maryland 21211, U.S.A.

The findings, interpretations, and conclusions expressed
in this study are the results of research supported by
the World Bank, but they are entirely those of the
author and should not be attributed in any manner
to the World Bank, to its affiliated organizations, or
to members of its Board of Executive Directors or
the countries they represent.

First printing   January 1987

Library of Congress Cataloging-in-Publication Data

Adler, Hans A.
  Economic appraisal of transport projects.

  (EDI series in economic development)
  "Published for the Economic Development Institute
of the World Bank."
  Bibliography: p.
  Includes index.
  1. Transportation—Cost effectiveness.
2. Transportation—Cost effectiveness—Case studies.
I. Economic Development Institute (Washington, D.C.)
II. Title. III. Series.
HE151.A32   1986   380.5′068′1   86-21348
ISBN 0-8018-3411-2
ISBN 0-8018-3429-5 (pbk.)

Contents

Preface

A TRANSPORT INFRASTRUCTURE is a prerequisite—though by no means a guarantee—of economic development. The intensive efforts of many developing countries to expand agricultural output, for example, require the timely availability of seeds, fertilizers, and other inputs and the reasonable access of farmers to markets. Expanded industrial output requires the efficient transport of raw materials, for example, as well as the distribution of finished products. Transport of exports requires adequate port facilities and land transport connections to the port. The costs of imports are increased if ships are delayed unduly in the ports.

Since in the early stages of economic development it is not unusual for traffic growth to be two to three times as large as the rise in national income, and since the ratio of capital to output is high, investments in the transport sector often account for as much as 15 to 30 percent of public investments. Transport investments in the private sector, primarily for motor vehicles, also tend to be sizable.

The importance of transport investments is underscored by the fact that a significant part of these investments in developing countries involves foreign exchange expenditures. The extent varies, depending primarily on the degree of a country's industrialization and the type of investment, but foreign exchange components ranging from 30 to 60 percent of transport investments are not uncommon. In addition, operating costs often require continuing foreign exchange expenditures for spare parts, maintenance equipment, tires, and fuel.

In view of the strategic role of transport in a country's economic development, the large investments required, and the heavy foreign exchange costs that are frequently involved, a careful economic appraisal of these investments is particularly important. An increasing number of planning agencies, highway departments, railways, port authorities, and other agencies in developing countries are therefore establishing staffs that specialize in project appraisal. Effective transport coordination requires that these agencies apply common investment criteria;

otherwise, railway investments, for example, might be undertaken where road transport would serve more economically, or vice versa. The purpose of this manual is to serve as a guide to all agencies responsible for the planning of investments in the transport sector.

The manual deals with the appraisal of transport projects in developing countries. Although there are many similarities between appraisal in developed and appraisal in developing countries, there are also important differences. First, shadow pricing, which is applied only rarely in industrial countries, is frequently used in developing countries (for reasons explained in chapter 2). Second, while one of the main purposes of transport improvements in developing countries is to reduce the operating costs of transport, in industrial countries the emphasis is now on time saving, particularly for individuals, and, to a somewhat lesser extent, on accident reduction. Third, the importance of opening up new lands with rural roads is much greater in developing countries. In most developing countries rural roads account for about 80 percent of the total length of roads, and only a small proportion of them have been improved above the level of basic tracks and trails (Carapetis, Beenhakker, and Howe 1984, p. 3). Fourth, while the external costs of transport, such as noise and pollution, are glaring in industrial countries, the governments of developing countries are giving higher priority to increased production of tangible goods and services, such as food and housing, than to environmental improvements, in part because the environmental effects are uncertain and are frequently felt only in the long term.

The emphasis in this manual is on the practical application of economic analysis, and for this reason Part II contains fifteen case studies for the principle modes of transport. Since there are many types of transport investments and the range of their benefits is very wide, not every situation could be covered. But Part I provides background on the methodology of economic appraisal so that it can be applied to the many cases which are not specifically illustrated. In addition, the bibliography makes suggestions for those who wish to pursue specific subjects in greater depth. The manual is not intended to deal with urban transport improvements since this involves broad and complex issues in urban planning and usually large external costs and benefits. Many of the concepts used in the appraisal of intercity transport, however, such as savings in transport costs or in passenger time, also have applicability to urban transport, and the bibliography suggests some readings on urban transport.

Similarly, this manual does not deal with the appraisal of environmental factors such as noise, air pollution, visual intrusion, and severance of communities; it does, however, cover the valuation of accident reduction, and some regard accidents as the most serious of the social costs of transport. The science of appraising environmental factors quantitatively, both the costs and the benefits, is still at an early stage, and their evaluation has to be supplemented by other methods. Moreover, most of the environmental effects of transport arise in urban areas. (Roads in rural areas can also have detrimental environmental effects if, for example, they cause an expansion of agricultural land or the exploitation of timber for firewood and building lumber that leads to deforestation, soil erosion, lowering of water tables, or the elimination of wildlife [Devres 1980].) As suggested above, developing countries are not yet willing to give environmental improvements the same priority as increases in production. This is particularly true of environmental improvements, such as noise reduction, which are regarded as contributing to human welfare less than does the production of goods and services. Environmental considerations are becoming increasingly important, however, because economic growth is leading to an increase in the environmental costs of transport. For readers who want to explore environmental factors, the bibliography lists a number of references.

The analytical methods suggested in this manual are not a substitute for the exercise of judgment, but a tool for the more disciplined and systematic formulation of such judgment. The appraisal of projects is not a mechanical process; a high degree of analytical ability and a broad imagination are required. The consequences of a project's being appraised must be clearly understood and formulated, and the feasible alternatives must be fully considered. The most serious mistakes in project appraisal do not arise from the application of erroneous statistical techniques, but from inadequate analysis of alternatives and results.

The first edition of this manual was prepared in 1968–69 while I served as economic adviser to the Pakistan Planning Commission under the auspices of the Harvard University Development Advisory Services. The author is grateful to both organizations because the stay in Pakistan presented the opportunity to test the manual in the field with both planning and operating agencies. In general, the tests were eminently successful in that economists in these agencies, as well as engineers with some economic training or sympathy for economic analysis, were able to understand it; some, in fact, started to apply its concepts to actual projects.

In the meantime, there have been opportunities to further test the manual in courses on transport sponsored by the World Bank's

Economic Development Institute. The manual has been translated into several foreign languages and has been used extensively in developing countries. The second revised edition takes into account the lessons of experience accumulated with the prior edition, the literature of the past fifteen years on more sophisticated methodologies (shadow pricing, for example), and empirical work on measuring some of the benefits of transport improvements. In addition, the revised edition puts greater emphasis on transport sector planning as a prerequisite to the appraisal of individual projects, on the analysis of rural roads, and on the applicability of cost-benefit analysis not only to investments, but also to operations and maintenance. It also includes an extensive bibliography.

Meekal Ahmad of the Pakistan Planning Commission and Angeline Rajendra of the World Bank assisted in the preparation of the case studies. Henri Beenhakker, Prem Garg, Vincent Hogg, and Jan de Weille of the World Bank and others contributed valuable comments. I also wish to thank the World Bank for the opportunity to appraise a large number of transport projects in a broad range of developing countries. It goes without saying that none of these individuals or organizations necessarily endorses the views presented herein.

Part I

Appraisal Methodology

Introduction

PROJECT APPRAISAL is the process whereby a public agency or private enterprise determines whether a project meets the country's economic and social objectives and whether it meets these objectives efficiently. Appraisal provides a comprehensive review of all aspects of the project and lays the foundation for its implementation after it has been approved and for its evaluation after it has been completed.

Aspects of Project Appraisal

Appraisal involves the investigation of six different aspects of a project:

- Economic appraisal has to do with the identification and measurement of the economic costs of the project and the size and distribution of benefits.
- Technical appraisal is concerned, for example, with engineering, design, and environmental matters and with estimates of capital and operating costs as they relate to the construction process and the operation of the project after it is completed.
- Institutional appraisal deals with the multitude of management, organizational, and staffing problems involved in the construction and operation of the project.
- Financial appraisal is used to determine what funds will be required and whether the enterprise is likely to be financially viable—that is, whether it can meet its financial obligations, produce a reasonable return on the capital invested, and, in appropriate cases, make a contribution from earnings toward the cost of future investments. The financial analysis focuses on the costs and revenues of the enterprise responsible for the project and is usually summarized in the enterprise's income and cash flow statements and balance sheets.

- Commercial appraisal deals with the procurement of goods and services to implement and operate the project and with the marketing arrangements for the sale of its output.
- Social appraisal addresses the social objectives of the project, such as a more equal income distribution or improved nutrition and health, and the social, cultural, and human variables affecting the project, such as involuntary population resettlement or the role of women in development.

The basic purpose of the economic appraisal of a project is to measure its economic costs and benefits from the point of view of the country as a whole to determine whether the net benefits are at least as great as those obtainable from other marginal investment opportunities. As illustrated in this manual, these costs and benefits may differ substantially from the financial costs and revenues of the enterprise operating the project.[1] Greater mobility does, of course, offer many benefits other than economic ones—such as cultural opportunities and military and adminstrative advantages—and sometimes disadvantages as well. Although such factors may influence project decisions, they are not explicitly considered here—though the bibliography lists a number of references—because they are not directly related to economic development. To the extent that these purposes lead to increased demand for transport, however, they do become, in effect, part of the economic appraisal.[2]

The six elements of project appraisal summarized above are closely related. If, for example, the engineer underestimates costs, the enterprise's financial situation will suffer and the project may no longer be economically justified. If the project is mismanaged, its costs will be higher and its revenues and benefits may be less than anticipated. Forecasts of revenues and benefits are closely related since consumers will not pay more than the value of the benefits they receive. This willingness-to-pay, as expressed in revenues, can be an important indicator of a project's benefits. Although substantial progress has been made in many developing countries in the various aspects of project appraisal, economic analysis is still often neglected. This manual deals only with economic appraisal, but does so with the recognition that without adequate technical, institutional, financial, commercial, and social analyses, the economic evaluation cannot be satisfactory.

Definition of Project

There is no accepted, uniform definition of a project. The World Bank, for example, looks upon a project as a set of interrelated expenditures, actions, and policies designed to achieve a country's specific objectives for economic and social development within a specific (usually medium) time period. This is a useful concept since World Bank financing of projects is accompanied by appropriate institutional and policy conditions. Gittinger (1982, p. 5) defines a project as "an activity for which money will be spent in expectation of returns and which logically seems to lend itself to planning, financing, and implementing as a unit. It is the smallest operational element prepared and implemented as a separate entity in a national plan." Although a project is usually regarded as an investment in capital assets, the concept in fact applies equally to the abandonment of an existing asset (see case study 9, "Discontinuing Service on a Railway Line") and to resources used for operation and maintenance (see case study 6, "A Highway Maintenance Program").

For the purpose of project appraisal, a project is the minimum investment which is economically and technically feasible. Building or improving a road from Delhi to Calcutta, for example, is not a single project, but a considerable number of projects which need to be analyzed separately. Traffic densities on different sections of a road vary widely, so that the types of improvement needed would differ. From the standpoint of technical construction, there are also no reasons for regarding it as one project. It is, however, quite likely that an improvement of one section of the road could, by stimulating new traffic, affect other sections, and these interrelationships must be allowed for in the appraisal. In contrast, a new railway line from Rawalpindi to Islamabad would be only one project, since all traffic would have to move from one end of the line to the other.

The proper division of a proposed investment into meaningful projects for analytical purposes must rely heavily on practical experience and judgment. Obviously, not every minimum investment possibility can be analyzed; the costs of doing so would exceed the benefits. Nevertheless, if investments are not sufficiently broken down into projects, it is quite possible that the very large benefits of one component of an investment may hide the insufficient benefits of another. For example, in the case of a port expansion project, the engineers recommended the construction of two new berths. The economic analysis indicated a return on the investment of about 12 percent, which was satisfactory. But when separate analyses were made for each berth, it turned out that the rate of return on the first berth was nearly 20 percent, whereas that on the second was only about 4 percent, even after allowance was made for the extra cost of building it separately; the second berth was clearly not justified. The same principle applies in the case of highways, especially when various degrees of improvements can be made or, frequently, when the highway can be constructed in sections.[3]

As already suggested, project appraisal applies not only to new investments, but also to expenditures for the rehabilitation or maintenance of existing investments—that is, economic resources used for capital or operating purposes, including maintenance. Cost-benefit analysis can be a guide in deciding on the optimum level, composition, and timing of highway maintenance activities, or in deciding whether a particular railway line should be maintained or abandoned (see case studies 6 and 9). A study of road maintenance in developing countries found that "minimum levels of highway maintenance, generally well in excess of current levels in most African countries, yield extremely high economic returns"—returns which are frequently considerably higher than those on new investments (Harral and Fossberg 1977, p. 70). A study of twenty road projects financed by the World Bank found that the rate of return for maintenance components averaged about 60 percent, compared with 20 percent for new construction. Such findings indicate that maintenance is given inadequate priority in many developing countries compared with new construction.

Role of the Transport Sector Program

Before a transport project of significant size can be properly evaluated, it is highly desirable and usually essential that two preliminary steps be taken so as to reduce the number of alternatives to the project that have to be considered. The first step consists of a general economic survey of the country. Such a survey has two major functions: (1) to establish the country's overall transportation needs by exploring, for example, the rate of economic growth and the resultant expansion in traffic; and (2) to provide a basis for weighing transport needs against the requirements of other sectors of the economy. This is not something that can be done precisely, and it depends heavily on qualitative judgments. Several surveys have suggested that too much was being spent on transport investments. A survey of a South American country, for example, found that investments in education, housing, and health deserved a greater priority than marginal investments in transport. General economic surveys are also needed to help decide whether by changes in the location of industries the total demand for transport can be reduced, and, if so, at what cost. Failure to make such surveys has in some countries led to transport investments, as well as recommendations for additional investments, which were out of line with the total investment resources of the country and with the priorities of other sectors. Five-year plans and longer range plans which exist in many developing countries can serve as general guides in this respect.

The second desirable step is a detailed survey of the conditions of the country's transport system and policies so that priorities within the sector can be determined.[4] Project analysis alone is frequently not sufficient because in the transport sector individual projects tend to be closely related. For example, the success of a particular railway investment may depend on whether a competing road is improved; the effectiveness of a port investment may depend not only on improvements in competing ports but also on rail and road connections to the port; and the justification for a road improvement may depend on what is done to parallel or feeder roads. The function of the sector program is to identify promising projects, to relate them properly to one another, to determine their priorities, and to relate all projects together properly to the macroeconomic plan.

The preparation of transport sector programs is particularly important because in developing countries a transport infrastructure is usually a prerequisite—though by no means a guarantee—of economic growth. In addition, transport requirements tend to grow at a rate which may be two to four times as large as the growth in economic activity. As a result, and because the ratio of capital to output is high for transport, especially in its early stages, transport investments often account for a large part of public investments, and a significant part of these involves foreign exchange expenditures.

Transport sector planning is also important in developing countries because governments own or control nearly all transport facilities. Railways, roads, ports, inland waterways, airfields, and airlines tend to be exclusively public investments, and the major private investments, such as motor vehicles, are usually controlled by production licenses, import restrictions, and foreign exchange controls. Governments, therefore, generally have the instruments to ensure that the program can be carried out.

An effective transport survey requires an understanding of the broad transport policies which a government plans to pursue. Wasteful policies are prevalent, and a transport survey needs to address the following:

- *The rationality of the criteria used in deciding on new investments.* The systematic application of cost-benefit techniques is essential to minimize poor investments.

- *The relation of transport tariffs to the costs of services provided.* The efficient allocation of funds to transport in relation to other sectors and an optimum distribution of traffic among competing transport modes require that rates and fares reflect the costs of transport. The survey should identify all transport tariffs that are above or below costs and the resultant distortions in traffic and investments, and should ascertain whether adequate freedom exists in fixing and adjusting tariffs.

- *The adequacy of user charges.* In developing countries governments frequently do not charge adequately for the use of roads, ports, airports, and so on, through fuel taxes, license fees, tolls, or other charges. It is not unusual for the users of roads to pay less than half of the road costs. As in the case of subsidized tariffs, this leads to distortions among different transport modes, overinvestment in transport as a whole, inefficient location of new industries, and an undue burden on tax systems and public savings. These are particularly serious bottlenecks to economic growth in nearly all developing countries.

- *The nature of the regulatory system.* The transport survey should also review government policies toward regulation of the sector, particularly trucking and bus services. The review should cover licensing requirements, route and distance restrictions, limitations on rates and fares, and weight and other controls, as well as the enforcement of all these regulations. Some developing countries still retain the regulatory systems developed in Europe and the United States to protect railway monopolies or to meet the special problems of the depression of the 1930s. Such systems usually have little application to the transport problems of developing countries.

Because governments can develop and administer their transport policies only when properly organized to do so, a transport survey must also review the institutional arrangements. It must ask whether a central transport organization exists at all, and if one does, analyze the scope of its authority—that is, determine whether it includes all modes and methods of coordination, whether it is properly staffed, and whether adequate statistics are available—so that policies can be established and applied intelligently.

Relevance of Transport Prices

If the economic benefits and costs of transport projects are to be measured and compared with other investment opportunities, they must be expressed in monetary terms—the only practical common denominator. This presents a problem since market prices do not reflect economic costs to the country in the absence of workable competition in major sectors of the economy. In addition to any limitations on competition in developing countries, two special problems exist in the transport field. The first arises from the fact that some transport services by their very nature are oligopolistic or even monopolistic, and thus the prices charged for these services frequently have no direct relation to costs. The most obvious example is the historic practice of setting railway freight rates for particular commodities not on the basis of the costs of transporting these commodities but on the basis of the value of the commodity carried. A second problem arises from the direct and indirect subsidization of many transport services by governments. A common example is the provision of highways. In many developing countries gasoline taxes and other charges on the beneficiaries do not cover the costs of highways (including capital costs, maintenance, and administration); even where they may cover overall costs, there is usually no direct relation between specific user charges and the differing costs of the various transport services—such as those of trucks, buses, and passenger cars—or between user charges collected on particular roads and the cost of these roads.

In spite of these difficulties, monetary terms are the only practical common denominator, and they can be made more useful by the use of "shadow prices," which reflect real economic costs and benefits more closely; this is discussed in greater detail in chapter 2.

Adequacy of Statistics

The degree of accuracy and refinement which is possible in the economic appraisal of a project depends heavily on the availability of reliable data and other information. Better appraisal must be accompanied by better statistics. For example, most developing countries have only recently begun to collect highway traffic data on a systematic basis. Most of the statistics are limited to simple traffic counts; data on the origin and destination of traffic or on the types of commodities carried on highways are frequently not available. Information about vehicle operating costs on different types of roads or about road maintenance costs on different types of surfaces is often limited, although considerable progress has been made in recent years. As a result, new road investments and the allocation of maintenance expenditures have frequently been made without detailed analyses of priorities. Railway companies usually do not know the operating costs for different lines and for carrying different commodities; furthermore, the traffic data by line tend to be incomplete, and the systematic collection and analysis of origin and destination data are quite rare. As a result it is difficult to know what part of the railway network is unprofitable and whether the traffic could be carried at lower cost by alternative modes, such as roads or inland waterways.

In the past some investment decisions could be made simply by looking at a map and at the location of major industries and population centers or by observing or anticipating bottlenecks. But this is becoming less and less true as railway networks become more or less complete, as the most obviously needed highways are built, and as the most important cities are connected by air service. Furthermore, such a simple approach does not permit an adequate judgment about priorities over time among the modes of transport or between transport and investments in other fields. The systematic economic appraisal of transport projects, based on greatly improved statistics, is therefore becoming increasingly urgent.

Notes

1. See "Economic versus Financial Appraisal" in chapter 5 for a discussion of what should be the guiding criterion when projects are justified financially but not economically, or vice versa.

2. See the discussion of secondary benefits in chapter 4.

3. For illustrations see case studies 11 and 12. Number 11 is similar to the above illustration on berths. In case study 12 the appraisal of a port as a whole fails to indicate that the offshore oil terminal would not be justified at the new port.

4. For a more detailed discussion, see "Preparing Transport Sector Programs" in Adler (1967, pp. 3–31).

Economic Costs

MEASURING THE ECONOMIC COSTS of a project involves adjusting the actual expenditures on inputs where the prices paid do not properly reflect the real scarcity value of the inputs. Such adjustments of market prices involve the determination of "shadow prices," or, as they are also called, "economic accounting prices."[1]

The Use of Shadow Prices

Shadow pricing is more often discussed and applied in the context of developing countries than in the industrial countries, where it is used only in exceptional cases. One reason for the difference is the greater incidence of subsistence farming in the developing countries; in subsistence farming, market prices for costs and outputs do not exist. In addition, market prices are thought to be subject to greater distortion in the developing countries, where rapid inflation, government controls, over-valuation of the domestic currency, and imperfect market conditions, including low labor mobility and large underemployment of labor, are common. Because shadow pricing requires large quantities of data and judgments and forecasts that are difficult to make—and because the results cannot be very accurate in any case—it should be applied only in relation to the most serious price distortions. Four types of costs for which shadow price corrections are sometimes necessary are discussed in this section: foreign exchange, taxes, wages, and interest.

Foreign Exchange

The official exchange rates of many developing countries do not properly reflect the scarcity value of foreign exchange. As a result the costs of imports are held artificially low and the demand for them is high. Rationing devices such as tariffs and quotas are therefore required to keep the demand for foreign exchange in balance with the supply. To estimate shadow exchange rates which reflect the scarcity value of foreign exchange, a recommended approach is to use conversion factors which establish the correct relationship between the prices of internationally traded goods and services relevant to a project and the prices of goods and services which are not so traded.[2] Distortions arise from many sources, such as import or export taxes or subsidies, quantitative restrictions on trade, and so on. Because the distortions affect different goods differently, conversion factors are, in theory, needed for each commodity involved in a project. Since this is not practical, conversion factors are sometimes calculated for groups of commodities, such as investment goods and consumption goods, or for sectors, such as construction or transport. A single conversion factor, referred to as the standard conversion factor, corresponds to the economywide shadow exchange rate. It is a summary indicator of trade distortions that are expected to prevail in the future.[3]

To ensure a proper economic appraisal of the projects illustrated in this manual, a rate of 1.75 times the official rate has been used in calculating the economic costs of foreign expenditures; in practice the figure to use may be quite different. The 1.75 rate has been applied to all foreign costs—not merely to the items procured abroad but also to the foreign exchange component of items procured locally, such as gasoline produced by the local refinery from imported crude oil. Where the shadow price for foreign exchange is known only within a wide range, it may be necessary to appraise the project at different shadow prices to determine the sensitivity of the conclusion to different rates. If a project involves foreign exchange revenues, the adjustment required is the same as for foreign costs.

Taxes

Sales and other indirect taxes should not be included in the calculation of economic costs. The tax on gasoline, for example, is a financial cost to those who pay the tax, but it does not necessarily reflect economic costs to the country as a whole, for an increase in the tax does not mean that more economic resources are required to produce a given volume of gasoline. Similarly, license fees and import duties should be excluded from the calculation of economic costs.

Wages

Because of minimum wage laws, regulations, and other inflexibilities, wages actually paid may not be a correct measure of the real costs of labor—the value of the marginal output of labor forgone elsewhere because of its use in the project. In an economy marked by extensive unemployment or underemployment, the real costs of labor used in the project may be less than actual wage rates. When this is a widely prevailing condition that is likely to remain for some time, as in parts of India, Pakistan, and Africa, the cost of unskilled labor should be calculated at less than actual wage payments. In other instances, the real costs of skilled labor may be greater than the wages paid, and shadow pricing should be applied accordingly.

Such adjustments in wages, however, should be made only after careful investigation of the labor situation in the area of the project. Studies have shown that agricultural unemployment is often highly seasonal and that the movement of agricultural labor to construction work can interfere with agricultural operations unless the construction of the project and the agricultural operations are properly synchronized. This is frequently difficult to do and leads to undue delays in the completion of projects. Moreover, because of the low mobility of unskilled labor, unemployment in some parts of the country can coexist with a labor shortage in other areas; if the project is in an area with a shortage of labor, shadow pricing would not be justified. Other studies indicate that whether people are willing to work for low wages depends on their income situation while unemployed, the value of leisure time and of nonwage activities (such as fishing or repairing their homes), and the nature of the employment offered by the project.

Where shortages of skilled labor lead to the employment of less-skilled workers who are then trained on the job, no shadow price adjustment of wages is needed, provided the costs of the training and the lower output of such labor are adequately allowed for in the cost and output estimates.

Subject to these limitations, it may be assumed that the economic costs of skilled labor in many developing countries may be up to 25 percent higher than actual wages paid and the economic costs of unskilled labor up to 50 percent lower than wages.[4] Because these estimates are not based on any detailed studies, and for the reasons already explained, they should be used with caution and only for projects where the proportion of skilled or unskilled labor is unusually large (for example, case study 4, "Construction of a Development Road"). In many cases the use of shadow wages can safely be omitted. The same considerations are also applicable on the benefit side. For example, the real benefit derived from using labor-saving equipment is substantially less if the replaced labor remains unemployed for a significant period during the economic life of the equipment. (This point is illustrated in case studies 9, "Discontinuing Service on a Railway Line," and 13, "Cargo-

Handling Equipment for a Port.") The shadow price for labor used on the benefit side has no necessary relation to the shadow price used on the cost side because different types of labor and different periods of time may be involved.

The proper pricing of labor is also relevant to the choice of construction methods that may be employed, that is, the balance between labor and equipment in the construction of roads and other civil works. Studies by the World Bank (Coukis and others 1983, p. 25) indicate that labor-based methods are *technically* feasible for a wide range of construction activities and that they can generally produce a quality comparable to that obtained with capital-based methods. Labor-based methods can also compete *economically* for many civil works projects in labor-abundant and capital-scarce countries, particularly if labor productivity is increased by organizational, managerial, and mechanical improvements. The studies show that if the cost of unskilled labor is US $1.00 a day (at 1980 prices), the cost of building rural roads would be $4,350 a kilometer with equipment-based methods, but only $3,500 with labor-based methods (Coukis and others 1983, p. 35).[5] If, however, the government sets the minimum wage at $4.00 a day, the situation would be reversed: the costs of the labor-based methods would rise to $8,000 a kilometer, compared with $5,700 for equipment-based methods. If economic (shadow) wage costs are $2.00 a day and foreign exchange costs are shadow priced at a 50 percent premium, the labor-based methods would be $875 a kilometer cheaper than the equipment-based methods. A review of more than thirty types of civil works indicates that all would be less costly with labor-based construction methods at labor costs of $1.00 a day, depending on local factors (Coukis and others 1983, p. 40). These studies conclude that if the wages actually paid exceed that economic cost of labor, it may not be profitable to use labor-based methods even though they are more economic.

Interest

The financial cost of capital—that is, the interest actually paid for funds borrowed to carry out the project—frequently has no relation to its economic cost, the opportunity cost of capital. Investment funds for the transportation sector are often made available by governments at rates below the cost to the government. What is more, if the government obtained these funds through taxation or by requiring banks to lend it the money at below-market rates, even its costs do not reflect the economic costs to the country. Funds obtained from foreign aid sources frequently carry interest rates substantially below the opportunity cost of capital in developing countries.

The economic cost, or opportunity cost, of capital is difficult to determine in the absence of free markets, since prevailing interest rates also reflect such factors as inflation and risk. It appears likely, however, that the opportunity cost of capital in many developing countries is quite high, frequently 12 percent or higher. A rate of 12 percent has been used for illustrative purposes in the case studies (subject to certain modifications suggested in chapter 5 under "Methods of Comparison").

To ensure consistency in cost-benefit analysis within sectors and among sectors or subsectors, a central finance or planning ministry should provide guidelines on the use of common shadow prices which are uniformly applied to all projects. If the determination of shadow prices is left to individual ministries or project analysts, comparability among sectors and projects becomes difficult, if not impossible.[6]

Other Types of Adjustments

In addition to the use of shadow prices, other types of adjustments may be necessary for an economic appraisal. The examples that follow illustrate mistakes which occur frequently.

Contingencies and Inflation

In estimating the costs of a project, engineers usually include a contingency for unforeseen expenses. The expenses are of two types. First, costs may be greater than anticipated because the work turns out to be more difficult or more extensive than expected; for example, more earth may have to be moved or the soil conditions may be less favorable than indicated by the sample data on which the cost estimate was based.[7] Second, costs may be greater because general inflation increases wages and prices. For the purpose of economic analysis, it is a mistake to include a contingency allowance for a general rise in costs. Similarly, no allowance should be made for a general inflation in the prices of benefits. A general price rise does not affect the economic value of the resources used or saved in connection with the project. Costs and benefits should be measured at constant prices: all prices should be deflated to correct for general increases in prices. Even if domestic and foreign prices increase at different rates, there would be no effect on constant prices, since the differential increases would be reflected in the shadow rate for foreign exchange.

If, however, changes in the prices of specific project items are expected to differ significantly from changes in the general price level, such changes in relative prices must be reflected in the valuation of costs and benefits over the life of the project. For example, if the price of fuel is estimated to increase by 8 percent annually while inflation is expected to be only 5 percent, the real price of fuel would rise by 3 percent annually. In practice, however, it is very difficult to forecast relative price changes, and the record of past forecasts is poor. In general, therefore, changes in relative prices should be assumed only if there is convincing evidence for them and if they form a significant item of costs or benefits. An example might be large increases in the price of urban land, which should be allowed for to the extent that they are foreseeable and likely to affect costs and benefits differently. If relative price changes are expected, it is useful to apply sensitivity analysis to such forecasts (see the discussion under "Risk and Uncertainty" in chapter 5).

Interest during Construction

Interest during the construction period is usually included in the financial costs of projects financed by loans, such as new equipment for a railway or the construction of a toll road, but it is frequently excluded when the project is financed by grants from general revenues, as in the case of most highways. This important financial distinction has no significance as far as the economic costs of the project are concerned since the real resources used—labor, material, equipment, and so on—are the same regardless of the source of financing. Money is the means of procuring these real economic resources, and thus interest should not be included in the economic costs of the project.

Interest is relevant in quite a different sense, however. Since the benefits of a project do not begin until sometime after the project has been started and costs have been incurred, it becomes necessary to compare costs and benefits that begin in different years and have different time streams. Regardless of the financing method used, the timing of costs is an important element since a cost incurred this year has a different economic value than the same cost incurred sometime in the future. To measure the difference, future costs can be expressed in terms of present values by use of an appropriate discount rate. The proper method of comparing benefits and costs with different time streams is to discount all future costs and benefits as of the time a cost is first incurred (for a more detailed discussion of this, see "Methods of Comparison" in chapter 5). Under this method, interest (as well as depreciation) is implicitly allowed for, so that adding it to the costs would result in double counting.

An alternative method which is sometimes used includes interest during construction and discounts benefits as of the first year they begin, which is generally sometime after the first costs are incurred. While this alternative is theoretically feasible, it tends to confuse the financial analysis with the economic analysis since the interest usually included in costs is the interest actually paid. In most cases this has no direct relation to the opportunity cost of capital, the internal rate of return, or any other relevant rate by which the benefits should be discounted, so that, in effect, the costs are discounted by a rate different from that used for benefits. Moreover, this method actually overstates costs where benefits begin before the project is completed, something that occurs quite frequently in highway construction. There seems to be no particular advantage to discounting costs and benefits to a year other than the year in which work on the project starts and costs are incurred.

Scope of the Project

When the scope of a project is not defined properly, certain costs that are relevant may be overlooked, a mistake which occurs quite often in economic appraisal. For example, in estimating the costs of a new port, a port authority included only the expenses for which it would be responsible; no allowance was made for the improvement of access roads. Because the improvement of access roads was essential for the effective utilization of the port, the costs involved should have been included in the total project costs for the purpose of economic appraisal, even though they could properly be excluded from an analysis of the authority's financial position. Since in this particular instance it was probable that the access roads would have been improved in time in any case, it became necessary to establish the additional costs of (1) making the improvements earlier than would otherwise have been the case and (2) employing the higher standards of design needed to accommodate the increased volume of traffic the new port would bring.

Finally, sunk costs—costs which have been incurred in the past—should be excluded unless the assets involved can be used for other purposes. For example, the costs of feasibility studies should be excluded once they have been incurred since they presumably have no value for any alternative use. If work on a project was abandoned and the question is whether the project should be completed, only future costs—the costs of items needed to complete the project—are relevant for the economic analysis, if the assets reflected in sunk costs have no alternative uses. In contrast, as illustrated in case study 10, "Construction of an Oil Pipeline," the value of surplus railway rolling stock previously procured must be taken into account since the equipment could be used for other purposes.

Foreign Loans

A special problem arises in connection with the timing of costs for projects financed by foreign loans. For projects financed by either foreign or domestic credits, the financial costs to the executing agency occur in the year in which interest and debt payments are actually made. If the project is financed domestically, the financing arrangements are irrelevant in determining the economic costs to the country since it is the year in which the resources are used—and thus cannot be used for other projects—which is the relevant time period. With foreign loans, however, the costs to the country depend on whether a similar amount of foreign financing would have become available for other purposes had the loans not been used to finance the project in question. This is a factual matter, and the facts differ from country to country and could even vary over time in the same country. In most cases, however, the lending countries are prepared to provide a given volume of aid and allow some flexibility in the type of capital, service, or commodity financed. As for the borrowers, the volume of loans which the developing countries can prudently accept on commercial terms is limited by their anticipated balance of payments situation. Under these circumstances, it would be better to regard the economic costs as having been incurred in the year the project is undertaken. Neither domestic nor international financing arrangements, regardless of their terms, need be taken into account in the calculation of economic costs. For countries where these assumptions do not apply, the costs of the project are incurred at the time that foreign loans are repaid and interest is paid.

Notes

1. For a more extensive discussion, see the publications listed in section II of the bibliography, particularly Little and Mirrlees (1974); Marglin, Sen, and Dasgupta (1972); Squire and van der Tak (1975); and Ray (1984). Pearce and Nash (1981) compared various approaches and found little difference among them in practice if they are properly applied (p. 174). The World Bank has undertaken studies of shadow prices in Egypt (Page 1982), Pakistan (Squire and Little 1979), Thailand (Ahmed 1983), and Turkey (Mashayekhi 1980); other countries are covered in Little and Scott (1976), Bruce (1976), McDiarmid (1977), Lal (1980), and Powers (1981).

2. See Squire and van der Tak (1975), especially chap. 12, pp. 122–32.

3. Dickey and Miller (1984) find that most World Bank projects use a shadow exchange rate to convert the foreign exchange price of traded items into domestic currency terms. The conversion factor approach reduces domestic currency values for nontraded items in order to correct the over- or undervaluation. They conclude that "since road projects by themselves produce no direct exports, the former approach would involve fewer calculations. Moreover, if the latter approach were utilized, nontraded items (like labor) would have to be shadow priced twice (once for internal value in the country and again for foreign exchange equivalency)" (pp. 119–120).

4. McDiarmid (1977) finds that the economic cost of unskilled agricultural labor is about 75 percent of the money wage of industrial labor in Taiwan and about 60 percent in the Philippines. The difference reflects Taiwan's lower level of unemployment, more rapid economic growth, and greater mobility of labor. Page (1982) puts the economic cost of unskilled labor in Egypt at about one-half the relevant money wage; that of skilled labor 8 percent above. Mashayekhi (1980) suggests an economic cost of labor in Turkey of two-thirds of wages. A study by the Ministry of Overseas Development (Great Britain 1977) of shadow wages in eleven developing countries suggests rates ranging mainly from 0.5 to 0.8 of wages paid.

5. Dollar figures throughout this manual are in U.S. dollars.

6. The costs discussed in this section are not necessarily the only ones for which shadow pricing may be necessary. Other examples include land, which is sometimes provided free or at low cost by the government or made artificially expensive by speculation. The value of land now used for agriculture but to be used for a road or airport project is measured by the value of the agricultural output forgone. Similarly, the value of raw materials (such as natural gas, oil, or coal) in alternative uses may not be properly reflected in market prices.

7. The proper size of the physical contingency depends on the degree of refinement to which the costs have been estimated. For example, a road construction project based merely on a feasibility study should have a contingency of at least 25 percent; if the project is based on final engineering, this can be reduced to 10 percent. For procurement of more or less standard items, such as freight cars, a contingency of 10 percent might also be sufficent.

3

Forecasting Traffic

THE FIRST STEP in measuring the benefits of a transport investment is to estimate its future use, that is, the traffic it will have to carry or serve during its useful life.[1] Estimating future traffic is an imprecise—but unavoidable—art. Since many transport investments have potentially long lives—some as long as twenty years or more—the decision to make such investments rests inherently on long-term forecasts. It is clearly preferable to be explicit about the underlying assumptions than to leave them unstated.

Methods of Forecasting

The simplest method of traffic forecasting is to extrapolate from past trends, making whatever adjustments may be necessary to take into account changes that are likely to modify these trends. Extrapolation is rather crude, but it is relatively inexpensive and gives reasonable results under stable conditions. It should not be used, however, when the factors determining traffic flows are changing rapidly or will be modified by the transport improvement itself, as with the construction of a road to open up a new area.[2] In these situations, traffic forecasting falls into three stages. The first involves estimating the volume and location of future agricultural, industrial, and mining output and consumption, including exports and imports; analogous estimates of future population are also needed. In the second stage, the output and population data are translated into traffic—both by volume and by origin and destination. In the third stage, the traffic is distributed to the transport mode which can carry it most efficiently.[3] The three steps are related since regional outputs and traffic flows depend in part on transport costs.

Because future traffic depends on developments in the industrial, agricultural, mining, and other sectors of the economy and on population developments, traffic forecasts can be no better than forecasts of developments in these areas. Unfortunately, it is not sufficient to estimate outputs merely in macroeconomic terms, since such transport investments as roads, railway lines, and ports are fixed at definite locations and cannot be moved to other areas. It is therefore necessary to estimate not only future production and consumption as a whole, but also their specific location. For mobile equipment, such as motor vehicles and railway rolling stock, this refinement is less necessary.

After estimates have been made of future production and consumption, these must be translated into traffic. This is generally done on the basis of past relationships between output and consumption and traffic requirements, with adjustments for foreseeable future changes, such as a possible decline in the railway's share of a particular type of traffic, changes in relative costs, and so on.

The relation between production and consumption on the one hand and traffic on the other also depends on the rates and fares charged for transport. Little is known, however, about the price elasticity of the demand for transport. In general, changes in freight rates have less effect in the case of high-value commodities than in the case of low-value commodities because transport costs for the former are a smaller proportion of the final delivered price. There is also a difference in the price elasticity over time, since in the long-run changes in freight rates could affect the location of new industries. The price elasticity of demand for a particular mode of transport also depends on the prices charged by competing modes. Moreover, the rates charged may be less important than other distribution costs, such as those which arise from delays and damage to freight. (This will be discussed more fully later in the chapter.) The demand for passenger traffic is probably quite inelastic for the narrow range within which fare adjustments tend to be made. But if a project reduces transport costs sharply, informed guesses about the effect on demand cannot be avoided (see, for example, case study 5, "Construction of a Bridge").

Since the 1960s, numerous attempts have been made to build transport models which express the mathematical relations between the magnitude of traffic-generating factors and the volume of the resulting traffic. Most of these models have been developed in industrialized countries in connection with the preparation of urban transport plans. But such models are of limited use in developing countries, where incomes and land uses change frequently and rapidly, particularly in the cities, and where the data are often inadequate. In addition, the models cannot easily handle major changes in transport policies, such as changes in transport prices, and they tend to be weak in incorporating feedback on the number of trips made when the supply of transport is changed. Their cost may be high—as much as a million dollars or more; they take considerable time to become operative; and they require massive quantities of data on the population and its distribution over time, data which may have only limited use where changes are rapid and uncertain.

Even for intercity traffic, the factors that determine flows are frequently complex and the construction of the model difficult and time-consuming. For example, an initial model for coal transportation in a certain region was able to explain only about one-half of the actual coal traffic. Because coal is not a homogeneous commodity, it had to be broken down into various types, such as coking and noncoking coal. In addition, some of the coal originating from captive mines was not being moved in accordance with the lowest distribution costs because these mines evidently offered certain advantages, such as the assured availability of supplies, which offset the higher transport costs. It would no doubt have been possible to build a model allowing for these factors, but this would have required substantially more time and staff than were available.

A related problem arose in a case where the model indicated impossibly high increases in future air traffic. The value of passenger time, which is an essential ingredient in aviation demand, was not known, and the value used was based on experience in the United States, which was inapplicable to the developing country under study. In both these cases it became necessary to return to the standard technique of extrapolating from past traffic trends and adjusting for specific foreseeable developments. Further research will no doubt lead to improved models, but in the meantime project analysts will have to rely on the more traditional methods of traffic forecasting.

Once the total volume of traffic has been estimated, the final step is to estimate its division among the various transport modes. In principle, the traffic should be allocated to the mode which can carry it at lowest cost. In this connection, three problems deserve mention. First, it may be difficult to determine costs because key data are lacking or because the costs to the economy differ from the financial costs of the public agency or private enterprise carrying out the project. The types of adjustment necessary, primarily in the prices of labor, capital, and foreign exchange, have already been discussed.

Second, traffic is unlikely to move via the low-cost carrier if the rates charged do not reflect transport costs. This is frequently the case, especially with rail transport. Freight rates for rail cargo take into account the value of the commodity and tend to be uniform among different lines despite cost differences. User charges for roads and ports also rarely reflect costs properly. Although relative economic costs must be taken into account in estimating economic benefits for the purpose of project appraisal, actual or expected rates and fares must be employed when estimating future traffic distribution among various transport modes.

Third, there are important qualitative differences among the various modes of transport, and some of these are difficult to quantify in terms of costs. Road transport, for example, provides a door-to-door service, usually with substantial savings in time, greater frequency and reliability, lower breakage and losses, quicker settlement of claims, and other similar advantages over railway service. These advantages account for a large part of the trend to road transport, especially for general cargo, even though the direct transport charges by road may in fact be higher than those by rail. The ultimate aim is not lowest transport cost, but lowest total distribution cost for the delivered goods. Neglect of total distribution costs in some appraisals accounts for unduly optimistic forecasts for rail and coastal shipping potentials and underestimates for road transport. With respect to passenger traffic, too, there are not only differences in the money costs of transport, but also in the cost of time, comfort, convenience, and probability of accident.

Fortunately, several practical considerations make long-term traffic forecasting more manageable than it might appear. First, because a few bulk commodities, such as coal, ores, and grain, often account for most of the traffic of many railways and ports, the analysis can largely be limited to these items.

Second, many transport investments are relatively lumpy. A port berth that might be economically justified for 80,000 tons of general cargo a year might also handle 150,000 tons efficiently, so that a refinement of whether the traffic will be 80,000 or 125,000 tons may not be needed for a decision; for bulk cargo, the range might be as much as 300,000 to 1 million tons, or even more. Similarly, a paved two-lane road may handle as many as 5,000 vehicles a day, so that estimates of 3,000 or 4,000 vehicles may still lead to the same investment. Lumpiness presents a particularly difficult issue if the traffic forecast is at the margin of, say, one or two berths or a two- or four-lane road. For this and other reasons it is important to try to reduce the consequence of lumpiness by, for example, stage construction of roads. (For an example of stage construction of berths, see case study 11.)

Third, much of the future traffic, especially in the short and medium term, exists already, and basic patterns in the location of industry, agriculture, and population do not tend to change drastically overnight. Fourth, in many cases the forecast need not extend beyond the time when traffic reaches the project's capacity, provided it can be assumed that traffic will not decline thereafter; this is frequently the case, especially for roads. Fifth, because future benefits are discounted by opportunity costs of capital or by other discount rates which in developing countries are relatively high, the correctness of forecasts in the more distant future is substantially less important than it would be at lower discount rates. Sixth, because the demand for transport, and especially road transport, is nearly always growing rapidly in developing countries, an overestimate of traffic might be made up in a short time, so that the cost of the mistake would be less than if the estimated traffic level were never reached; from this point of view, investments in railway lines tend to be much riskier because traffic for most railways has been growing less rapidly than that for roads, but the life of railway track and equipment tends to be very long.

Types of Traffic

For purposes of measuring the benefits of a transport project, future traffic should be divided into three basic types: normal, diverted, and generated. Normal traffic is that which would have taken place on the existing facility in any case, even without the new investment. This type of traffic benefits by the full reduction in operating costs made possible by the new facility, since, by definition, this traffic would have traveled even at the higher (and perhaps steadily increasing) costs of the existing facility.

The second type of traffic is that which is diverted to the new or improved facility either from other modes or from other facilities of the same mode. Typical examples are traffic diverted from a railway to an improved parallel road (case study 3) or to a pipeline (case study 10), traffic diverted from an existing port to a new port (case study 12), coastal shipping diverted to lower-cost rail transport, inland water traffic diverted to road or rail (case study 4), and bus traffic diverted to private car. As discussed more fully below, the benefit to diverted traffic is measured by the difference between future transport costs on the old route or mode of transport and future transport costs on the new facility. The amount of traffic diversion, however, does not depend on relative economic costs but on the actual financial charges. In the case of passenger traffic, since many people make decisions about driving largely on the basis of out-of-pocket costs, the difference between these and the railway rates actually charged (regardles of costs) will largely decide the amount of passenger traffic which will be diverted from a railway to a highway. Since, as discussed above, it is the difference not merely in transport charges but in total distribution costs which determines the amount of diversion, such factors as time saving, reduced breakage, and lower insurance rates must also be considered. Many traffic studies tend to underestimate the importance of such factors, especially for high-value cargo. These costs are, however, much less relevant for shipments of bulk traffic, such as coal or iron ore.

The third type of traffic is that which is generated as a result of the lowering of transport costs and which previously did not exist at all (see case studies 3, 4, and 5). This includes traffic resulting from increased industrial or agricultural production caused by the cheaper transport as well as the transport of commodities previously sold locally but now transported to markets where better prices can be obtained. It is not possible to generalize about the volume of traffic likely to be generated by a specific transport investment. In some cases a transport improvement generated large volumes of new traffic, but in others hardly any new traffic materialized. Each project must therefore be examined individually in the light of information about demand elasticities and similar experiences in the country or region concerned.

Notes

1. The useful life of a facility is sometimes determined by its physical life, but more often it is limited by economic change and technical obsolescence, such as new or improved processes and changes in markets.

2. For a useful discussion, see Heggie (1972, chap. 8, "Forecasting the Volume and Composition of Future Traffic Flows").

3. If, however, financial charges do not reflect economic costs, the financial charges will govern the distribution of traffic. This is discussed in more detail later in the chapter.

4

Economic Benefits

MEASURING THE ECONOMIC BENEFITS of transport projects usually involves more complex conceptual and practical problems than does measuring their economic costs. There are a number of reasons for this. First, some benefits, even though direct—such as the increased comfort and convenience made possible when a road is improved or the time savings made possible when a bridge replaces ferry service—are difficult to express in monetary terms since there are usually no market prices to indicate what people are willing to pay for them. Second, benefits in the form of reduced transport costs accrue to a wide range and a great number of people over a long period of time; this makes it difficult to forecast and trace their impact. Third, many benefits from improved transport are indirect, such as the stimulation of the economy; for these benefits to materialize, investments in fields other than transport are often necessary, but they are not always assured.

General Issues

Measuring the benefits of a proposed project involves not only a comparison with the situation without the project, but also a comparison with the next best alternative to make sure that the project is the best alternative. If the project is compared with the third or fourth best alternative, the benefits will be overstated. Complex conceptual problems, however, sometimes make identification of the next best alternative difficult. For example, if passenger trains are overcrowded, one solution may be to add more coaches; another may be to increase rail fares, which would reduce demand, shift some of the traffic to buses, and thus lead to the need for more buses and perhaps also road improvements. In this example, at least four alternatives may have to be considered before an intelligent decision can be made: doing nothing, adding more coaches, increasing fares only, or increasing fares and adding more buses. Similarly, if an urban road is congested, the relevant alternatives may be to widen it, to prohibit bullock carts and other slow-moving traffic, to improve traffic signals and controls, to prohibit parking, to impose charges on the traffic, or some combination of these. In the case of widening the pavement of a rural road, the alternatives might include constructing a twenty-four-foot pavement immediately or building only an eighteen-foot pavement now and widening it further later. To determine the desirability of providing extra railway capacity for transporting coal for thermal production of electricity, it may be necessary to compare locating the thermal plant near the coal mines with transmitting electricity to the markets via high-tension power lines. Since it is too expensive and time-consuming to consider all feasible alternatives, considerable imagination and good judgment are required to select those which deserve thorough investigation.

The most important benefits from transport include any or all of the following:

- Reduced operating expenses, initially for the users of the new or improved facility and sometimes also for those who continue to use the existing facilities, which may become less congested
- Stimulation of economic development
- Savings in time for both passengers and freight shipments
- Fewer accidents and reduced property damage
- Increased comfort and convenience.

Not all of these benefits exist in all projects, and their respective importance differs from project to project. At the present state of the art of project evaluation, the reduction in operating expenses can be measured in monetary terms more readily than the other benefits. This manual does not attempt to deal with the measurement of greater comfort and convenience; they would seem to have a relatively low social value in many developing countries, even though they may have considerable private value as reflected in the willingness of people to pay significantly higher fares for first- and second-class services.

It is sometimes stated that the value of a project should be measured by its contribution to the growth of national income. This approach is not inconsistent with the methods suggested in this manual, but in many cases it is not practical. One drawback is that it would exclude certain benefits altogether; in the case of the improvement of a highway, for example, neither the increase in driver and passenger comfort nor the increase in leisure time as a result of travel time saved would be reflected in national income. More important, the national income approach is simply too complicated and indirect to use in many developing countries. For example, to determine the increase in national income if transport costs are reduced, an analysis would have to be made of how the freed resources would be used in the future in other sectors of the economy. The approach is useful, however, in focusing on costs and benefits from the point of view of the economy as a whole rather than merely the parties directly involved. In this way it helps in selecting the benefits to be included and those to be omitted. It also reduces the likelihood of counting the same benefit twice in different forms, such as when an improved highway reduces transport costs and increases land values. In short, the national income approach is helpful in identifying economic costs and benefits, but not in measuring them.

The Distribution of Benefits

Before discussing the problems of measuring particular benefits, it may be useful to refer to a matter which is frequently neglected in the appraisal process: the distribution of benefits or losses among the beneficiaries or losers. For example, where improvement of a port reduces the turnaround time of ships, many of the benefits might go initially to foreign shipowners; the degree to which the benefits are passed on to the country making the investment will depend on the degree of competition in shipping and on the pricing policy adopted by the port authority (see case study 12, "Construction of an Ocean Port"). Instead of making investments to reduce the time foreign ships spend in port, it may be more advantageous for a developing country to improve storage facilities at the port, since storage charges are generally paid by shippers and consignees directly. Similarly, the improvement of a scenic highway may initially benefit foreign tourists primarily or people from other areas of the country. A government could, of course, recoup some or most of these benefits by imposing appropriate user charges. The matter of the distribution of benefits is therefore important in the selection of a policy of user charges which will channel the benefits to the desired recipients.

Perhaps even more important is the fact that the distribution of benefits affects their overall size. For example, if a railway maintains previously existing freight rates even though a transport improvement, such as dieselization, has lowered costs, the consumers would not benefit directly, but the railway might have higher profits. To determine the net benefits to the economy, it would be necessary to compare the benefits from whatever the railway would do with its higher profits (or the government with its "savings" from reduced railway losses) with the benefits consumers would get from lower freight rates. An important consideration is that if the rates are not lowered, the transport improvement will not stimulate new traffic. Where there is reason to believe that the likely distribution of benefits either reduces their overall size or is inconsistent with other public policies, the problem deserves greater attention than it now usually receives. (The distribution of benefits is discussed further in "Secondary Benefits.")

Reduced Operating Expenses

The most direct benefit from a new or improved transport facility, and frequently the most important one and the one most readily measurable in monetary terms, is the reduction of transport costs. While this benefit accrues initially to the users or the owners of the facility, competition, the desire to maximize profits, or government pricing policies lead them to share it in various degrees with other groups, such as producers, shippers, and consumers. The cost reduction therefore benefits the nation as a whole and not merely the immediate users of the facility.

As illustrated in the case studies, the types of reduction in transport costs vary widely. Road and rail improvements usually lead to lower operating costs for vehicles and rolling stock. Better maintenance of roads and railway lines not only can reduce vehicle operating costs, passenger and freight delays, accident costs, and the level of future maintenance and rehabilitation expenditures, but also can help to prevent road and line closures and the losses they could entail (see case study 6, "A Highway Maintenance Program"). Port improvements frequently lead to savings in the costs of ship delay and cargo handling; by making possible the use of larger ships, they often reduce shipping costs as well. The case studies also illustrate the fact that the improvement of one transport mode frequently affects the costs of other modes, as when a new port changes inland transport costs or a new road affects competitive rail service.

Normal Traffic

The basic criterion for measuring the economic benefits of a transport investment is the "with and without" test: what will the costs be with the investment, and what would they have been without it? In numerous project appraisals, however, a quite different standard is mistakenly applied—the "before and after" test: what were the costs before the new facility was constructed, and what will they be afterward? While in some cases the difference between the two standards might be small, the "before and after" test usually leads to a serious underestimate of economic benefits.

This point is illustrated in case study 1, "Paving a Gravel Road." On the gravel road the operating costs for a truck are 2.21 rupees (Rs) per mile, excluding taxes, whereas the costs on the new road are estimated at Rs1.41—a savings of Rs0.80 per truck-mile. If the new road is not built, however, the increasing congestion on the gravel road would raise operating expenses considerably over time, whereas costs on the new road are likely to remain relatively stable. For these reasons, it is estimated that costs per truck-mile would increase gradually from Rs2.21 to Rs2.68 on the old road. In other words, with the "before and after" test, the unit benefits would mistakenly be put at Rs0.80 for the life of the project; under the "with and without" test, it is recognized that they would grow gradually from Rs0.80 to Rs.1.27 because of increased congestion. Similar adjustments must be made for buses and passenger cars. With the "before and after" test the net worth of the project would be negative, and the project would appear unjustified; in fact, however, it is justified.

Using the "before and after" test can lead to curious results. In connection with a proposed highway improvement, investigation showed vehicle operating costs to be quite reasonable on the existing highway, whose surface and width were both satisfactory. Unfortunately, the highway had not been constructed to carry the prevailing heavy loads, and engineers advised that it would break up in about two years and that a complete reconstruction would be necessary (even if costly maintenance work were performed). After the reconstruction, however, the vehicle operating costs would not be significantly lower. Thus, the "before and after" test indicated that the reconstruction would bring only modest benefits and would not be justified, at least not at the time. The "with and without" test, however, indicated that without the new investment, vehicle operating costs would go up sharply, to say nothing of future maintenance costs; the avoidance of such increases would have been the proper basis for the economic evaluation of the benefits in this case.

The above examples deal only with highways, but the analysis is in principle identical for railways or ports. For example, in the case of a port improvement to reduce the waiting time of ships, the proper comparison is between the waiting time if the project is undertaken and the waiting time if no improvement is made; without the improvement, the waiting time may grow rapidly if traffic is increasing. In case study 11, "Construction of Additional Berths," for example, the annual waiting time with two berths would have increased from 105 to 1,250 days within seven years; with three berths it would have increased from four-teen to ninety days during the same period. With the "before and after" test, a third berth would not have been justified; the "with and without" test showed that it was.

Diverted Traffic

For traffic which is diverted to a new or improved facility from other modes of transport or from other routes, the benefits are measured by the difference between transport costs on the old route or mode of transport and those on the new facility.[1] The relevant costs, however, are not the average costs of transport on both facilities, but the avoid-able costs, that is, the amounts that would be saved. If, for example, traf-fic is diverted from a railway to a new highway, the benefits cannot be measured by comparing the transport costs on the new road with railway prices or even average railway costs; the appropriate com-parison is with the marginal costs of carrying the diverted traffic by rail. If the diverted traffic is only a small part of the railway's total traffic and if the railway has excess capacity, the marginal savings will be substan-tially less than would be indicated by a comparison of average costs; this is probably the usual case (see case study 9, on "Discontinuing Ser-vice on a Railway Line"). The data available in most countries do not permit precise estimates of such marginal costs, and a clear un-derstanding of the concepts involved is needed to make the best use of whatever data are available.

To complicate matters further, the services provided by each trans-port mode usually differ substantially and must therefore be brought to a common denominator. Total distribution costs are the primary con-cern, not just the line haul cost of shipment. For example, when coastal shipping traffic is diverted to a highway, the comparison of costs must take into account not merely shipping costs, but also such additional costs as those of loading and unloading, storage, insurance, breakage, delays, and so on. These additional costs could easily increase the basic shipping costs 50 percent or more. Similarly, in comparing the costs of railway and highway transport, adequate allowance must be made for the fact that while trucking is a door-to-door service, railway service will often require two loadings and unloadings. The extra handling not only adds to the direct costs but also tends to involve delays, breakage, and opportunities for theft (see case study 9, "Discontinuing Service on a Railway Line").

Another type of diverted traffic consists of a change from one type of conveyance to another on the same route—for example, passenger trips previously made by bus but now made by private car. Here, the higher relative operating costs of a private car are evidently outweighed by its qualitative advantages, especially the greater convenience and comfort; it is usually not possible to measure this difference in monetary terms.

Generated Traffic

In measuring the benefits of traffic generated by the lowering of transport costs, it is not appropriate to apply the total reduction in unit operating costs to this traffic since it would not have materialized without the reduction. If there is a reason to believe that in a particular situation the traffic would have been generated with a reduction in transport costs of only one-half the actual reduction, it would be appropriate to apply one-half of the unit cost reduction to the generated traffic. How much new traffic is created as a result of a reduction in transport costs depends on the elasticity of final demand for transport services, which in turn depends on the elasticity of demand for the individual commodities involved. In many situations, however, the available data are inadequate, and therefore the relation between the degree of transport cost reduction and the volume of generated traffic cannot be determined. As an operational matter it may be reasonable to assume that the traffic would have developed in proportion to the reduction in transport costs; if so, it would be appropriate to apply approximately one-half of the unit cost reductions to this traffic (see case studies 1 and 3).

To the extent that the main purpose of a new transport facility is to open up new lands for cultivation or otherwise to make possible new economic development, reductions in transport costs for generated traffic are not an adequate measure of the economic benefits of the project. In this situation the benefit consists of the expanded production; the problems of measuring this benefit are discussed in the next section.[2]

Economic Development

It is frequently assumed that all transport improvements stimulate economic development. The sad truth is that some do, some do not, and even some of those that do may not be economically justified because there may be better investment opportunities. This is so not only in the case of roads, which are discussed more fully below, but also for other transport modes. For example, Jansson and Shneerson (1982, p. 3) have found that "too great expectations that port investments could act as catalysts in regional development projects have resulted in deplorable overcapacity." Each project must therefore be investigated separately. Until such time as more reasearch can show that certain definite correlations between transport improvements and economic development do exist, generalizations are not helpful.

Before any transport improvement can be said to have stimulated economic development, a number of conditions must be met. The most important one is that the economic development would not have taken place without the transport improvement. It must also be true that the resources used in the new development would otherwise have remained unused or been used less productively. Moreover, it is essential that the economic activity stimulated does not replace activity which otherwise would have taken place.

These conditions may be obvious, but it is surprising how often they are forgotten in practice. In certain otherwise sophisticated studies, extensive research was undertaken to measure the growth in industrial output in the area of influence of a new highway; the studies concluded that the highway and the output were indeed causally related. While this finding was useful from a local point of view, it had much less significance for the economy as a whole. Further inquiry indicated that most of the resources used for the new production would have been employed in other ways and that the firms responsible for the new output had planned to expand in any case and had picked a location near the new highway because of its advantages. From a national point of view, therefore, the highway could not be regarded as having contributed significantly to the stimulation of new economic development. This is not to say that the locational shifts caused by the highway involved no economic benefits other than lower transport costs; they may have facilitated more efficient production, but this benefit can only be a fraction of the value of total net output.

Where a transport facility does lead to increased output and the aforementioned conditions are met, the net value of this additional output is the proper measure of the economic benefit. (The net value of output and the savings in vehicle operating costs for generated traffic are, of course, not additive.) In many situations, however, the transport improvement is not the only new investment needed to achieve the increased production. This raises the problem of allocating the benefit—the increased production—among the transport and other investments. There is no theoretically correct solution to this problem, and the proper approach is not to make an allocation at all, but to relate total benefits to total investments. An alternative approach allocates the benefits according to the ratio of the transport investment to the other investments, but this leads to essentially the same result as making no allocation and relating total benefits to total investments. A third approach consists of annualizing the other investment costs and deducting them from the benefits. This practice is dangerous since it may lead to ascribing all the benefits arbitrarily to the transport investment; the error is likely to be small, however, if the nontransport investments are only a small part of the project.

Each of these solutions is appropriate in different situations. For example, in a case involving the start-up of a coal mining operation, it was necessary to build a road to transport the coal from the mine to a port. The estimates indicated that the coal would account for more than 90 percent of the traffic using the new road. The road was an integral part of the coal mining scheme—just as integral a part as the mining equipment—and had virtually no other use. In this case an allocation of benefits between the road and the investments in the mine would be meaningless. An allocation of benefits might be useful, however, in the situation where a road is being built to facilitate new agricultural as well as industrial development, and other major investments will be required to achieve the increase in production. The important issue is to ensure that the design standards of the transport project and the costs involved are appropriate to the expected traffic.

Where the transport facility enlarges the market for commodities previously produced, the economic benefit consists of the difference between the value of the commodity in the old market and its value in the new market, minus the new costs of transport. For example, suppose that the price of a commodity is Rs10 in the old market and Rs20 in a second market, but because transport costs are Rs12, shipment to the second market is uneconomic. If a transport improvement cuts transport costs in half, to Rs6, the commodity can be delivered to the second market for Rs16 and be sold there for Rs20. The benefit from the new investment (assuming resources are fully employed both before and after the change) would be Rs4. To take account of the fact that the increased supply may affect prices in both markets, the benefit should be valued at an average of the prices prevailing before and after the transport improvement is completed, although this depends on the price elasticity of demand for the particular commodity. For passenger traffic, this benefit—that is, the difference between staying at home and traveling—minus the transport costs, cannot usually be measured in monetary terms, but could be indicated in other ways, such as the number of trips.

What can be done in practice to measure the net value of increased production or of wider markets will differ from case to case. In the coal mining operation mentioned above, for example, various experts made detailed studies of the supply of coal, the costs of production and transport, and probable market prices. The problem is usually much more difficult in the case of agricultural development because its success depends on the cooperation and ability of a large number of people and the development potential of large areas. In case study 4, "Construction of a Development Road," the likely increase in agricultural output could be estimated within a satisfactory margin of error because only a few commodities were involved and experience from similar projects involving transport improvements on land of comparable agricultural potential could be used as a guide in estimating probable future output and the other investments needed to achieve it.

With regard to transport improvements that are intended to open up new land for development, three situations might usefully be distinguished. In the first, the transport facility is an integral part of an agricultural, industrial, or mining project. Two examples are the coal mining operation described earlier and the limestone production project in case study 4. In cases like these the focus of the evaluation must be the entire project, and the objective the least-cost transport solution. In the second type of situation, transport is clearly the only significant bottleneck to development, all other requirements having already been met. An example would be a road to connect an existing town and a nearby fruit-growing area, whose products are now being transported by animal or cart and whose increased production has been prevented by high transport costs alone. Case study 4 also illustrates this situation. In the third situation, which occurs frequently, a transport facility is built in a new area, which, though promising, will not develop unless other investments and improvements are also made. Transport investments in this last group are rarely justified unless accompanied by the other improvements.

The link between transport and agricultural development arises most often in the case of rural roads. For new rural roads or for improvements of existing rural roads with little traffic (no more than 20–50 vehicles per day) as well as for all road projects which are predicated on large increases in economic activity and traffic, the appraisal must focus directly on the developmental impact, rather than merely on the savings to road users. Specifically, the analysis needs to address three critical issues:[3] First, how are the savings in transport cost distributed among producers, truckers, traders, and consumers? Second, how will the beneficiaries respond to the lower transport costs; for example, will lower input costs, higher farmgate prices, and better transport service encourage producers to increase production, and if so, by how much? And third, what nontransport constraints exist which may prevent the beneficiaries from responding to the transport improvement? Unless these constraints are addressed—by complementary investments, services, or changes in policies, such as extension services to farmers, land reform, marketing arrangements, and so on—the potential benefits are not likely to materialize. As Carnemark, Biderman, and Bovet (1976, p. 13) point out: "One should be wary of high estimates of 'generated traffic' or developmental impact in road project analyses unless the transport cost savings that are passed on to producers constitute a significantly large proportion of total production costs, or unless there are strong reasons to believe that the elasticity of supply is very high." The latter can occur, for example, where even a small reduction in transport costs makes the difference between profitability and unprofitability of a commodity. In most cases, however, transport costs tend to be less than 10 percent of the selling costs of agricultural commodities, so that even a significant reduction in transport costs has only marginal impact on farmer incentives (Bovill 1978, p. 8).[4]

Because the appraisal of rural roads frequently involves a large number of relatively short road sections which require only small investments, the application of cost-benefit analysis to each separate project decision could be excessively costly. To narrow the choice to the most promising sections and thus permit a fuller appraisal of each, a number of shortcuts have been developed. Several sufficiency rating systems have been established in which weights are given to various criteria, such as population density, percentage of fertile land cultivated, potential for intensification of agricultural activities, and so on. One problem with these systems is that the weighting is entirely subjective, and some systems neglect important criteria, such as costs. Recently, however, more sophisticated screening systems have been developed which allow more adequately for major criteria and which base weights on past experience with rural roads.[5]

Time Savings

Many transport improvements reduce travel time and increase the reliability of transport services. For passengers, time may be money, but it need not be. It depends primarily on how the opportunities made possible by the increased availability of time are used—whether for increased production or voluntary leisure on the one hand or for involuntary idleness on the other. Unfortunately, there is extensive underemploymcnt in many developing countries, and time savings may merely make the situation worse.

Studies of the value of time savings generally distinguish between travel for business and working purposes on the one hand and for non-working purposes (including leisure travel and travel to and from work) on the other.[6] In the industrialized countries the value of savings in working time is generally measured by the wage rate (including fringe benefits); this is what employers pay for the time, and the savings can be diverted to other productive uses, provided the time saved is reasonably certain and not too short. Empirical studies confirm that such time savings are directly related to income. The implication is that if income is expected to increase during the life of the project, benefits would increase in the same proportion. In many developing countries, however, wages do not properly reflect the economic costs of labor because there is so much unemployment or underemployment. The suggestions made in chapter 2 on shadow pricing labor are equally applicable here; savings of working time should be measured by the opportunity cost of the labor involved.

As for nonworking time, including travel time to and from work, there is no general agreement among economists as to the best measure of the value of time saved. Because there is no market for time which provides a price to indicate its value, values have had to be inferred from the choices people make which involve differences in time. For example, the choice of transport mode between two cities—highway or air transport—may indicate what individuals are prepared to pay for time savings. Another approach is based on choice of speed: it is assumed that drivers will choose a speed which minimizes total travel cost, including both operating and time costs, and since operating costs are known, the value of time can be inferred.[7] Unfortunately, theoretical models "have not been notably successful in providing a satisfactory framework for empirical measurement of the value of non-working travel time-savings" (Yucel 1975, p. v).

Various studies do, however, indicate that it is inappropriate to think in terms of a single value of travel time since many factors are involved, including the purpose of the trip, its length, the amount of time saved, the mode of travel, the characteristics of the traveler (income level and age, for example), whether time is saved in vehicle or in waiting, the certainty of time saving, the time of day, and so on.[8]

What can be done to measure the value of time may be illustrated by a study made in Japan of a new expressway that was expected to bring about substantial savings in travel time. Travelers were divided into two classes: the relatively few who could afford to travel in private cars and the many who traveled in buses. First, the average value of time was related to the per capita income of the two classes. The calculations showed that in one hour, the travelers in cars could earn the equivalent of at least $3.00 while those in buses could earn at least $0.60. Since there are ample employment opportunities in Japan, this approach was not unreasonable.

Next, to check their validity, these average values were compared with the amounts people were acutally willing to pay for time. For this purpose a study was made of surcharges imposed by the railway for different types of trains running between the same cities. On the Tokaido line, for example, travelers could choose among a wide selection of trains, ranging from slow local trains to very fast expresses. While speed was not the only difference between some of these trains—convenience and comfort being others—it was the most important one, and between at least two of the trains it was probably the only difference. The analysis of the surcharges indicated that travelers were willing to pay the equivalent of at least $6 in first class and $3 in second class for every hour saved. These findings and those based on the earnings method gave a clear indication of the range of values that might be given to time savings of passengers in Japan. The findings also suggested that in Japan for this type of trip many travelers prefer to take time savings in the form of leisure, even if they could devote them to income-producing activities. This is probably not true in most developing countries.[9]

Individuals do value nonworking time, and studies in industrialized countries have generally valued such time at 20–35 percent of the wage rates of travelers.[10] In developing countries, however, governments may well decide that the social value of leisure to society is less than its value to the individuals; it has therefore been suggested that such time savings be valued at 0–25 percent of wage rates for urban projects, but not be valued at all in rural transport projects.[11] According to Howe (1976, p. 118), the consensus among rural analysts is that the maximization of production is the correct basis for the evaluation of time savings, that only working time saved should be valued, and that increased leisure time, though of personal, social, and political importance, is not of economic significance in a developing country.

Time saved on the shipment of freight may well be more valuable in the developing countries than in the more advanced ones. Freight tied up during transit is in fact capital and is therefore of particular importance where capital is in short supply. This saving can be measured by the price of capital, that is, the rate of interest. In addition, faster delivery, which is usually accompanied by more reliable delivery, reduces spoilage and makes it possible to keep smaller inventories, which is another form of capital saving. Beyond this, where larger inventories are not possible, a delay may immobilize other resources. For example, the absence of a spare part may prevent the efficient utilization of expensive equipment. This is a frequent occurence in developing countries.

The Japanese also did a study of the prices shippers were willing to pay for various types of transport services which differed mainly, if not solely, in the amount of time they took. The study covered a dozen important commodities and indicated, for example, that the following prices were paid for a saving of one ton-hour: dairy products, $1.05; fresh fish, $0.64; vegetables, $0.60; fruit, $0.42; and minerals, $0.03. In the case of a project for exports of citrus fruit from Swaziland, the reduction in damage primarily attributable to faster transport was estimated to be between 46 and 61 percent of user benefits, depending on the particular alternative considered. Improved roads in St. Lucia were estimated to reduce damage in transit for bananas by 3 percent, which amounted to 9–15 percent of all benefits, depending on the particular improvement selected.[12]

The relative importance of time savings as against other benefits depends, of course, on the nature of the project. That it can be very significant is illustrated by the highway project for which the Japanese studies mentioned above were made. In that case the value of time savings was nearly half as great as the benefits from lower vehicle operating costs. Studies of intercity road improvments in the United Kingdom indicated that, on the average, time savings account for about 80 percent of total benefits, of which savings in working time account for nearly two-thirds. In contrast, as illustrated in case studies 3 and 5, the value of time tends to be very low in developing countries and tends not to be a significant benefit for most projects (see Mayworm and Lago 1982, pp. 16–17). A review of World Bank–financed projects indicates that time savings have not been a crucial factor for most transport projects (Yucel 1975, p. 54). Given the uncertainties in measuring the value of time savings, it is suggested that if they are included in project appraisal, they should be clearly identified and shown separately (see case studies 3 and 5). Important exceptions are aviation and urban projects. A major purpose of aviation is to save time, and the time of entrepreneurs and other persons relying on air transport may be very valuable (see case study 15, "Construction of an Airport"). In urban projects, time savings are particularly important in the case of expressways and public transit systems. Because the value of time is uncertain, it is important to test the sensitivity of the ultimate decision to differences in time values; this is discussed further under

"Risk and Uncertainty" in chapter 5. Moreover, if time savings are related to the income of the beneficiaries, it would be important to indicate to the decisionmakers what these benefits are at various income levels (such as the users of private cars and buses), so that they can take into account the income distribution implications of the project.

Accident Reduction

Road accident rates are high in many developing countries.[13] Annual injury rates are about two to four times higher than in Great Britain (where there were about 200 injuries per 10,000 vehicles in recent years), and fatality rates are about five to fifteen times higher than in Great Britain. In general, the lower the level of vehicle ownership in a country, the higher the accident rate. The losses involved in developing countries from road accidents "are believed, on average, to have reached one percent of gross national product per annum" (Hills and Jones-Lee, no date, p. i).

Road accident rates are high in developing countries for a number of reasons: pavements are narrow, and the shoulders are often dusty; geometric alignments tend to be poor; roads through towns are congested; a large number of slow-moving animal-driven vehicles are on the roads; law enforcement is not sufficently effective; road users receive limited training and education; drivers—especially bus and truck drivers—are often inexperienced and reckless; many vehicles are in poor mechanical condition; and trucks tend to be overloaded. Thus, accidents are the result of a complex interaction of vehicle, road, environment, and human factors. For purposes of accident reduction, the education of drivers and the enforcement of safety regulations may be more important than the engineering of safe roads.

This conclusion applies not only to developing countries. In the United Kingdom, for example, human factors such as drivers' skill and health, excessive speed, carelessness, and improper passing were involved in 74 percent of accidents; the road environment, design and visibility of junctions, effectiveness of hazard warning signs, and conditions of road surface were involved in 28 percent; and vehicle design and condition in 25 percent. Thus, human factors were by far the most important causes of accidents (Sharp and Jennings 1976, p. 127).

While accident reduction is clearly an economic benefit, there are many transport improvements that do not reduce accidents; each case must be investigated separately. For example, when a highway is improved the number of accidents and, more important, the accident rate per vehicle-mile and the severity of each accident may all increase at first. This could happen if the increased speed made possible by the improvement is not offset by additional safety factors—especially in a country where automobile driving is still in its early stages and drivers have not developed the discipline required for safe driving. Highway accidents are apparently most significantly reduced by building expressways with divided lanes and controlled access, but this cannot often be justified in developing countries. Other worthwhile investments are those to control speed and traffic—and thus reduce road accidents at intersections and along curvy sections—and to increase aviation safety.

Measuring the economic benefits of accident reduction involves two main steps. The first is to estimate the probable reduction in accidents. Unfortunately, because of the lack of documentation on the results of road safety measures in developing countries, such estimation will entail, for example, comparing the accident rate on the existing highway (without the improvement) with the rate on higher-standard highways elsewhere within the country or, if necessary, in other countries (but making adequate allowance for national differences). For example, a study in one country indicates that on a range of roads with 200–2,000 vehicles a day, an increase in width from five meters to seven meters might reduce the accident rate by 40 percent (Great Britain 1986).

The second step is to estimate the value of the accident reduction. For this purpose, it is useful to consider three types of damage: property damage, personal injuries, and fatalities. Of these, property damage— usually to the vehicles involved in the accident—is the most readily measurable in monetary terms; its value is often reflected in claims under vehicle insurance policies. Reduced breakage of cargo can also be a significant benefit, especially in port and railway operations. A study of road accident costs in six developing countries indicates that damage to property generally accounted for about 60–80 percent of total accident costs. Average costs per accident differ widely. A study of property damage in India placed the costs per accident at $300 (in 1979 price; Hills and Jones-Lee, no date, pp. 82, 85).

The cost of injuries is more difficult to measure. In principle, it includes the cost of lost output, medical services, and pain and suffering. A study of accidents by the Department of Transportation in the United Kingdom indicated the following average costs for an injury (in 1979 prices; Hills and Jones-Lee, pp. 75, 85):

Loss of output	$ 3,100
Medical services	470
Pain and suffering	3,770
Total cost	$ 7,340

Pain and suffering accounted for about one-half of total injury costs. While these are certainly private costs to the individuals involved, governments in developing countries may not be prepared to regard them as social costs. The costs of output would, of course, be much lower in developing countries, reflecting lower average earnings. In the Japanese studies cited earlier, the cost of injuries was estimated at about $300 per accident, which included an allowance for loss of earnings and the cost of medical treatment. In India estimated costs ranged from $200 for slight injuries to $1,900 for serious injuries (Hills and Jones-Lee, p. 85).

Measuring the benefit from fatality reduction requires putting a value on life, a task with philosophical as well as economic implications. Even apart from the philosophical questions, there is substantial disagreement on the appropriate methods of valuation. Among the most common ones are:

- The gross output approach, which uses the discounted value of the victim's future output, with or without allowance for the pain and suffering of the victim and his or her relatives
- The net output approach, which differs from the gross output approach in that it deducts from the gross output the present value of the victim's future consumption on the premise that it is needed to produce the output
- The insurance approach, which relates the value of life or of accident risk reduction to the amounts individuals are prepared to pay for such insurance
- An approach based on amounts awarded by the courts to surviving dependents.[14]

Depending on the method used, the value of a fatality in a developed country could range from $25,000 to more than $2 million; a review of studies in eleven developed countries indicates an actual range of about $35,000–$400,000 per fatality. Taking three developing countries, the value of a fatality ranges from about $1,550 in Thailand and $2,250 in India to $12,300 in Kenya (Hills and Jones-Lee, table 5, p. 85).

A review by the World Bank of the state-of-the-art of measuring the effectiveness of accident prevention programs concluded that the quantification of benefits is problematic and in many cases simply cannot be done (Willoughby 1983). In only very few Bank-financed projects involving safety components were reduced accidents included as a quantified benefit.[15] On balance, it would seem prudent in project analysis to limit the value of accident reduction in developing countries to estimates of vehicle and other property damage, medical costs, and losses of output. An indication of the number of lives saved and the orders of magnitude for other costs, such as pain and suffering, may be helpful, but they can rarely serve as a meaningful basis for investment decisions.

Secondary Benefits

Transport projects may have secondary benefits which are not fully allowed for in the analysis suggested above. For this purpose, it is useful to distinguish two types of secondary benefits. The first relates to the contribution of projects to objectives other than increases in national income and efficiency; they are sometimes referred to as intangible benefits. Projects may contribute, for example, to more effective national integration, to greater self-sufficiency, to a more equal distribution of income, or to the country's prestige. Reductions in the costs of transporting wheat to feed the poor may be valued more highly than identical cost reductions for the wealthier passengers who can afford air transport. Or a government may accord higher priority to a project in a less developed area of the country than to a project using the same resources in a more advanced area.

It has been suggested that in addition to calculating economic rates of return which are limited to efficiency considerations and take the existing income distribution as given, social rates of return be calculated which take explicit account of the impact of the project on the distribution of income both between investment and consumption and between different income levels (Squire and van der Tak 1975). This involves assigning weights to costs and benefits of the project that accrue in different forms (consumption or investment) or to different beneficiaries (rich or poor). For example, a benefit of $10 might be treated as worth $30 if it accrues to persons with an annual income of $300 but only $8 if to beneficiaries with an income of $1,000. The weights should reflect the socioeconomic objectives of the country. Social rates of return could be higher or lower than economic rates of return, depending on the income status of the beneficiaries.

In practice, social rates of return have not been used on any significant scale in the appraisal of transport projects because of a number of political, economic, and technical considerations. First, it could be argued that a country's income distribution is essentially politically determined and can hardly be influenced by such technical devices as applying social rates of return. Second, there may be more effective tools, such as monetary and fiscal policies, to achieve income distribution goals. In the transport sector, governments might give priority to investments in the poorer sections of the country, to feeder roads, or to public transport and impose heavy taxes on private cars. Third, the determination of the specific values for weights raises a host of issues. Since governments are rarely monolithic, who in the government provides the weights? Marginal income tax rates are sometimes suggested as an objective guide, but once exemptions and loopholes are allowed for, the result may be quite different. Fourth, determining the beneficiaries and their income level is particularly difficult in many transport projects. For example, if the transport costs of wheat are reduced, it would be extremely difficult to determine—over the life of the project—to what extent the benefits accrue to farmers, wholesalers, transporters, retailers, or consumers, and, for each of these groups, how they differ by income level. The benefits of an urban transport improvement may be shared among the transporters, travelers, landowners, and the affected businesses. To collect and analyze all the necessary data would be difficult and expensive.[16]

Nevertheless, national objectives other than greater efficiency are clearly important, and where a project makes a significant contribution to achieving them, or to hindering their achievement, this should be pointed out. And if assistance to certain income, ethnic, or other groups is an important social goal, priority may well be given to transport investments that benefit these groups or to specific transport modes (such as public bus service) that serve their needs.[17]

Another type of secondary benefit relates to changes in prices or competitive conditions, to external economies, or to the inducement of further investments which a project may cause. These benefits, to the extent to which they are relevant, are, however, fully allowed for in the analysis and are not additional benefits. For example, it is sometimes pointed out that a developmental road will increase the income of the people in the area and that this will increase their consumption, which, in turn, will give rise to additional employment, income and consumption. This multiplier effect of the original project is not, however, an additional benefit unless the obstacle to expansion is inadequate demand, and this is rarely the case in developing countries; moreover, other investments could also have a multiplier effect. It is also pointed out that a project may give employment, which is regarded as an additional benefit. If, however, the labor involved would have been employed on other work, its employment on the project is a cost, not a benefit; if it would otherwise have remained unemployed, this is fully allowed for in the use of shadow wages, and no additional benefit is involved. These types of secondary benefits can therefore be disregarded if the direct benefits have been estimated properly.

Notes

1. As mentioned above, while the benefits to the economy are measured by the reduction of economic costs, the financial costs to users are relevant in estimating the amount of traffic diversion.

2. In theory, the benefits of generated traffic are the same whether they are measured by the value of the expanded production or by the reduction in transport costs. In practice, the former approach tends to focus directly on increases in output while the latter tends to assume a certain volume of traffic generation without making an explicit analysis of the increases in production (See Carnemark, Biderman, and Bovet 1976, pp. 6–7).

3. They are spelled out in greater detail in Carnemark, Biderman, and Bovet (1976).

4. A study of the impact of road improvements on agricultural production in a province in Argentina found "a surprising lack of benefits." The study noted that the cost reductions made possible by the paving of a major highway would not have lowered total production and distribution costs significantly and that the cost reductions would not have been passed on to the farmers because of the lack of competition between traders and the absence of feeder roads (Miller 1973, p. 106). A study of new railway lines in Africa found that the impact "on the bulk of the farming population in the areas through which they pass has been disappointing" (O'Connor 1973, p. 146). Kresge and Roberts (1971, p. 155) found that in the case of Colombia, transport modifications by themselves do not have a significant impact on national income. Edmonds (1982, pp. 58–59) cites a number of studies in Jamaica, Nepal, and Tanzania which indicate that rural roads did not stimulate new economic development because of adverse social and economic policies. A review of numerous case studies by Devres (1980, p. 123) concludes that road projects almost invariably lead to at least some increases in agricultural production, particularly if (1) complementary inputs and services are provided, (2) most of the population did not previously live close to roads, (3) there is extensive competition in the transport sector, and (4) the cost of transport of agricultural produce is high as a percentage of price. The larger, wealthier farmers generally benefit the most. Hine (1975) finds that the major benefit of rural roads is not increased agricultural production but improved personal mobility, which facilitates improvements in social life, health, and education. For a review of the literature, see Howe (1981).

5. See Bovill (1978), Carnemark, Biderman, and Bovet (1976), and Beenhakker and Lago (1982).

6. For an excellent review of the subject, see Yucel (1975).

7. For a discussion of these and other approaches, see Mayworm and Lago (1982, pp. 2–8).

8. See Harrison (1974), chaps. 4 and 6. In Great Britain, the Department of Transport (1981, appendix 8.1) suggests that the value of nonworking time while waiting (or walking) is two times that of in-vehicle time.

9. For a study of the value of passenger time in Japan based on a comparison of air and railway fares, see Okano (1983).

10. The U.S. Department of Transportation (1981) recommends that in evaluating aviation investments, savings in business and nonbusiness time be valued at the same

rate on the basis of income, since "consumers will allocate their time between work, travel and other activities in such a way that the marginal value of time is equal in all activities."

11. Mayworm and Lago (1982, pp. 29–32) suggest that for the appraisal of World Bank-financed projects, 25 percent of the shadow wage rate be used in valuing nonworking time. Yucel (1975, pp. vii–viii) regards 20–25 percent of hourly earnings a prudent value for nonworking time savings.

12. Both cases are from Howe (1976, p. 119). According to Sharp (1983), the value of speeding up freight deliveries is ignored in British studies because estimates are not reliable and the size of the benefit is relatively insignificant. Sharp doubts the validity of the second reason. He points out that shippers are prepared to pay higher rates for speedy deliveries and that "the interest savings on a consignment valued at £10,000 could amount to as much as 17 p per hour" (p. 192).

13. This section draws heavily on a report to the World Bank by Hills and Jones-Lee (no date).

14. For a discussion of these and other methods, see Hills and Jones-Lee (chap. 4, pp. 30–58).

15. Accident savings, however, account on the average for about 20 percent of benefits from road improvements in the United Kingdom (Great Britain, Department of Transport, 1978). The few studies in developing countries incorporating the benefits from reduced accident rates indicate that these levels are not insignificant. For example, widening a poorly aligned five-meter highway conveying 6,000–9,000 vehicles a day to seven meters increased the net present value by about 15 percent (Great Britain 1986).

16. Even strong advocates of the use of social rates of return recognize that their application to transport projects is generally not possible (Ray 1984, pp. 126–27). A study of a highway project in Malaysia concluded that it was very difficult to trace the ultimate beneficiaries and that it was not possible to calculate a social rate of return (Anand 1975). Dickey and Miller (1984, p. 135), in a review of several World Bank-financed projects involving rural roads, found that "no attempt is made to identify the exact relationship between the project and the likely beneficiaries. To do so is felt to be too complicated and uncertain." See also Howe and Richardson (1984).

17. See Williams (1977), MacArthur and Amin (1978), Hylland and Zeckhauser (1981), and Harberger (1984). While rural roads may help the rural population generally, a review of numerous case studies indicates that "it seems usual that those in better position to take advantage of road improvements (landowners near the road, middlemen, retailers, bankers, urban dwellers, upper and middle income levels) will profit most in the absence of specific programs to counteract this" (Devres 1980, p. 93).

5

Comparing Costs and Benefits

ONCE THE COSTS AND BENEFITS have been measured for each year of the useful life of the project, they must be compared to determine whether the project is justified. The major difficulty in making this comparison is that merely adding up the costs, adding up the benefits, and comparing the two sums would neglect the time element. For example, costs may be incurred early and benefits received only later. An expenditure incurred this year has a higher economic cost than the same expenditure incurred five years from now, since the resources involved could be used in the meantime for other productive purposes; similarly, a benefit received this year has a higher value than the same benefit received twenty years from now. It, therefore, becomes necessary to bring the project's streams of future costs and benefits to a common denominator. This is done by discounting the two streams by an appropriate rate.

Discounting Costs and Benefits

The process of discounting is simply the reverse of the better known process of compounding interest. If the rate of discount is 12 percent, for example, the present value of a cost of Rs100 which will not be incurred until next year or a benefit of Rs100 which will not be received until next year is Rs89.3—Rs100 multiplied by 0.893 (see the discount table in the appendix at the end of this manual). Similarly, a cost or benefit of Rs100 two years from now would have a present value of Rs79.7. By the process of discounting, costs and benefits occurring at different times are revalued to make them comparable to present values. The discounted costs can be added up to give a single figure which expresses the present value of the costs of the project, and the discounted benefits can be added up to give the present value of the benefits. This point is illustrated in all of the case studies.

Economists are not in full agreement on what rate of discount to use, since the rate should reflect not merely what the resources used in the proposed project could have earned in other projects—that is, their opportunity costs—but also the value of time, which may differ between individuals and society as a whole and also between generations. The choice of the appropriate rate can, however, be very important. As indicated in the discount table (see Appendix), the present value of Rs1.00 fifteen years from now at a 6 percent discount is Rs0.42; at 12 percent, it would be only Rs0.18. One suggested discount rate is the consumption rate of interest, which indicates the rate at which the value of future consumption falls over time. Another rate is the opportunity cost of capital, which indicates the return to investment at the margin. These two rates are the same if there is no significant imbalance between the value attached to current consumption and the value attached to current savings. As was mentioned in chapter 2, the opportunity cost of capital in developing countries may frequently be 12 percent or even higher.[1] The World Bank generally does not accept projects for financing with an internal rate of return of less than 10 percent.

Methods of Comparison

There are four common methods of comparing costs and benefits. The comparison can measure the net worth of a project, that is, the difference between its discounted costs and benefits; the internal rate of return, that is, the rate at which discounted costs and benefits are equal; the ratio between costs and benefits; or the payback period—the number of years needed for annual net benefits to equal investment costs.

The advantages and disadvantages of these formulas are discussed below. It should be kept in mind, however, that there is unfortunately no uniformity of practice in the application of these formulas. In some cost-benefit ratios, for example, gross costs are compared with gross benefits, while in others some costs are first deducted from the benefits; the effect on the ratio can be substantial. Sometimes—and more correctly—it is the difference between benefits and costs which is used. In the case of rate of return calculations, the benefits are sometimes measured against the investment costs (with or without an allowance for depreciation) and are sometimes measured against the investment costs (with or without an allowance for depreciation) and are sometimes measured by the internal rate of return. It is essential to know exactly which formula is used if the final result is to be correctly interpreted.

While the basic ingredients—the value of the costs and benefits—are the same regardless of the final form in which they are expressed, one form may be more useful than another, depending on the purpose. A short payback period is important in cases where the future is unusually uncertain, where better investment opportunities are likely to arise soon, or where funds are not available on a long-term basis. These considerations are much more important for private businesses than for governments. And the fact that the benefits of an investment are large in the beginning may give no indication of their size over the life of the investment; therefore, comparing payback periods is a particularly poor method for choosing between investments with different time streams of benefits. Furthermore, there are better ways to account for uncertainty in investment analysis. The payback period is therefore not an appropriate formula for judging public investments.

Discounting benefits and costs by the opportunity cost of capital or the consumption rate of interest is generally the best method for comparing projects. The most important disadvantage of this approach is that a particular rate must be chosen. In practice, the one frequently—and mistakenly—selected is the interest rate being paid, which may or may not have any relation to the appropriate discount rate. Unfortunately, the latter is frequently not known or cannot be estimated without a considerable margin of error. Since the discount rate is one of the major determinants of the cost-benefit comparison, the particular rate chosen is of crucial importance. It may be necessary to use a range of discount rates to ascertain the extent to which a final decision on the project is sensitive to different rates. If it is highly sensitive, further work may be needed to narrow the range (see the discussion in the following section on the handling of risk and uncertainty).

This disadvantage can be minimized somewhat if the benefits and costs are expressed in terms of the internal rate of return on the investment, the rate which equalizes discounted costs and benefits. In this case the "correct" discount rate, such as the opportunity cost of capital, becomes important only in the marginal cases where the internal rate of return is not clearly above or below the area within which the opportunity cost of capital may be estimated to be. For example, in many developing countries an investment with a rate of return of 16 percent would almost certainly be justified, since the opportunity cost of capital in these countries is usually less. The rate of return formula also has a practical advantage: economists, financial experts, and many businessmen have some concept of what an interest rate is, so that for many audiences a rate of return is probably more meaningful than a cost-benefit ratio or a statement of the net present worth of the project.

Nevertheless, the internal rate of return formula has its disadvantages. While as a practical matter it usually leads to the correct choice among projects, it can be misleading when projects having different lives or different time streams of benefits are compared.[2] This situation, as well as the deficiencies of the cost-benefit ratio, is illustrated in the following comparison of three mutually exclusive projects.[3] Project A would construct a completely new highway, project B would improve the alignment of the existing highway at various points and rebuild the roadway, and project C would repair and maintain the existing roadway. The stream of net costs and net benefits for each project is shown in table 5-1. Table 5-2 shows the costs and benefits of each project discounted at 10 percent. Project C has the highest internal rate of return (18 percent) and the highest benefit-cost ratio (1.43) but the lowest net present worth (Rs22 million). Project B has the highest net present worth (Rs29 million) but stands in the middle position as far as the other criteria are concerned. The different methods of comparing costs and benefits thus lead to quite different results. Project C gives the highest return per rupee invested and the highest rate of benefits to costs, but the objective is to choose the project with the largest net benefit to the country. While project B costs Rs40 million more than project C, the additional benefits amount to Rs47 million (Rs119 million minus Rs72 million) at a 10 percent discount rate; the additional investment is therefore justified. In comparison, project A costs 10 million more than project B but provides additional benefits of only Rs7 million; thus, project A is not justified.[4]

In this example, then, selection of the project on the basis of the highest internal rate of return would lead to the wrong decision. But

Table 5-1. Stream of Net Costs and Net Benefits

(millions of rupees)

	Year										
Project	1	2	3	4	5	6	7	8	9	10	11
A	−100	2	10	15	20	30	35	38	35	25	15
B	−90	5	15	25	30	34	30	22	15	10	5
C	−50	2	8	12	15	20	22	18	10	8	5

Note: Negative amounts indicate net costs.

Table 5-2. Costs and Benefits Discounted at 10 Percent
(millions of rupees)

Project	Costs	Benefits	Net present worth	Benefit-cost ratio	Internal rate of return (percent)
A	100	126	26	1.26	15
B	90	119	29	1.32	17
C	50	72	22	1.43	18

selection of the project on the basis of the highest net present worth can also be erroneous if the wrong discount rate is used. In these projects, A has the highest net present worth at interest rates from 0 to about 8 percent; between 8 and 15 percent, B has the highest net worth; and between 15 and 18 percent, C has the highest. If the correct discount rate is not known and cannot be estimated within an acceptable range, the margin of error may be no greater when using an internal rate of return than when using a highly uncertain discount rate. Also where a project is compared not with a direct alternative but with investment opportunities in general, the internal rate formula is generally perfectly satisfactory.[5]

The internal rate formula has another disadvantage: there may be more than one rate that equalizes the costs and benefits of a project.[6] In practice this happens rarely with transport projects; since the costs are incurred predominantly in the early stages and the benefits arise later, there would be no ambiguity about the rate.

On balance, the choice of method for comparing costs and benefits depends somewhat on one's position. The World Bank, for example, has found it satisfactory to use the internal rate of return in the evaluation of transport projects which are submitted to it for financing. There are two major reasons for this: First, it has not been practical for the Bank to estimate appropriate discount rates for the more than a hundred developing countries who are members of the Bank. Second, the Bank must assure itself only that the project is justified; it need not be the highest priority project in the country. The Bank thus does not use the internal rate for deciding between mutually exclusive projects, a decision which is made during project preparation and which should generally be based on comparisons of net present worth.

However, since the preparation of a development plan and the concomitant determination of relative priorities do require the discounting of costs and benefits by an appropriate rate, this is the best method for countries planning their investments. These countries cannot, in any case, avoid selecting a rate for the opportunity cost of capital since it provides the cutoff point below which projects should not be included in the development program. Because this rate cannot be determined with precision, the following guidelines, which have been used by the Pakistan Planning Commission, may be appropriate for many developing countries:

- If the benefits of the investment are less than the costs at an 8 percent discount rate, it is almost certain that the investment is not justified.
- If benefits are equal to costs at a discount rate between 8 and 12 percent, the investment is probably not justified unless there are major benefits which could not be quantified and which are clearly larger than unquantified costs.
- If benefits are equal to costs at discount rates of 12 percent or higher, the investment is probably justified. If the projects are mutually exclusive, the one with the highest net present worth at 12 percent should be selected.

In the case studies, the costs and benefits have been compared on the basis of the present worth of the project at 12 percent. Most of the case studies also include the cost-benefit ratio and the internal rate of return.

Risk and Uncertainty

Since project appraisal requires forecasting, the factors entering into the calculation of costs and benefits are inevitably subject to various degrees of uncertainty. Construction costs may be affected by weather conditions, the useful life of equipment may be reduced by new inventions, the demand for transport may be altered by unforeseen changes in the pattern of economic development, and numerous other factors can influence the forecasts. Making conservative forecasts of traffic or of the life of the project and expecting higher rates of return for risky projects are ways of dealing with this problem, but they do not really bring out the uncertainties of a particular project. Moreover, a conservative bias throughout the analysis may have a cumulative effect and lead to very pessimistic final results. It may also prevent the identification of the best among mutually exclusive design options.

There are two basic methods of spelling out the uncertainties in a project decision: sensitivity analysis and risk analysis. Sensitivity analysis, the simpler method, tests the effects on the project's rate of return (or net present value) of variations in values of selected cost and benefit variables. It is a method of identifying key variables which most influence the net benefits of the project and of judging their relative importance. Sensitivity analysis may help to identify design options that need to be considered in detail and additional information which should by sought on key variables to narrow the range of uncertainty. It may also help to convey some idea of project risk.

The results of sensitivity analysis can be presented in different ways. Under one method, various values are given to some of the key factors, and rates of return are then calculated for the different values. For example, if the foreign exchange costs of a project are high but the standard conversion factor for foreign exchange is not know with certainty, the rate of return could be calculated at a higher or a lower conversion factor than the one posited; the resulting range of outcomes would give an indication of the sensitivity of the outcome to changes in the assumed conversion factor. The same procedure might be applied to traffic forecasts, cost estimates, unit benefits, and so on.

An alternative approach to sensitivity analysis focuses on "switching," or "crossover," values: the percentage change in the value of a variable at which the rate of return of the project equals the opportunity cost of capital or the net present value becomes zero. Switching values are particularly useful in judging which variables are of critical importance to the project. For example, if the switching values of a project are −20 percent for future traffic, +35 percent for construction costs, and +50 percent for the standard conversion factor, the most critical variable is the estimate of future traffic, since a decrease of more than 20 percent would make the project no longer acceptable. If increases in construction costs of more than 35 percent are a clear possibility, it may be desirable to review the estimates or to obtain firm construction bids before making a final decision. Since the project is not particularly sensitive to the standard conversion factor, rough estimates of this variable would be sufficient.

In the above examples it has been assumed that the variables being tested are independent of one another. If the variables are interdependent, however, they cannot be varied one at a time but must be varied jointly. For example, in some road projects, future traffic growth and savings in vehicle operating costs and in passenger time are all related; less traffic may reduce congestion and thus lower vehicle operating costs and increase time savings. In such a situation, one must examine the sensitivity of the outcome to changes in combinations of these variables since they are expected to vary together.

Although sensitivity analysis, which is illustrated in all the case studies, indicates the sensitivity of the conclusion to various factors and the range of possible conclusions, it does not throw any light on the probability of the results happening. The second and more difficult method of dealing with the uncertainties in a project decision does. Risk analysis relies on probability analyses of the various forecasts of costs and benefits and gives an indication of the probabilities of achieving specific rates of return.

The first step in risk analysis is to identify the most important variables. This is done through sensitivity analysis, as described above. In determining probabilities, it is useful to distinguish between risk and uncertainty. For risky events the probability distribution of outcomes is known; for uncertain ones it is not. For example, while it is not possible to know the amount of rainfall in a given month, the records of the past usually permit a determination of the probabilities of various amounts of rainfall. If a certain level of rainfall would prevent construction of a project, the probability of this happening can be determined. Unfortunately, similar determinations are not possible for uncertain events, such as changes in taste or technology; uncertain events cannot be analyzed so satisfactorily in terms of probability distributions because the relevant information is not available. In such cases, however, it is possible to determine subjective probabilities—the probabilities as judged by the persons making the various forecasts—and then treat uncertainty like risk (see Pouliquen 1970).

As in the case of sensitivity analysis, it is important that the variables being tested are truly independent. In a study of a port the risk of project failure was estimated at about 15 percent when two important variables, labor productivity and port capacity, were treated as independent and at about 40 percent when their positive correlation was allowed for in the analysis (see Pouliquen 1970, pp. 46–47). The reverse result is also possible. If, for example, the benefits of a project vary directly with traffic and inversely with vehicle operating costs, and traffic and savings in vehicle operating costs are negatively correlated but this correlation is neglected in the analysis, the risk of failure will be overstated since a lower volume of traffic will be partly compensated for by greater savings in vehicle operating costs.

Risk analysis requires special skills and experience, and usually the use of computer programs. The degree of refinement in the analysis of risks and uncertainties should depend on how important they are likely to be. If the benefits of a transport project depend on many independent variables, the expected outcome is more likely to be realized than if the project is highly specialized. For example, future road traffic may consist of a large number of commodities, but a pipeline may depend exclusively on one product; thus, the uncertainty involved in a pipeline project is inherently greater. The determination of probabilities may be justified for large projects, especially if the projects are mutually exclusive and involve different degrees of risk and uncertainty. Where the rate of return is close to the opportunity cost of capital, it may also be useful to apply risk analysis. In most other situations the simpler procedure of sensitivity analysis would be adequate.

Economic versus Financial Appraisal

In general, a project should be undertaken only if it is both economically and financially justified. When there are wide discrepancies between prices and economic costs, however, the financial and economic analyses may not lead to the same investment decision; such discrepancies may also affect the setting of rates and fares as well as operational decisions.

This conflict is illustrated in case study 7, where the costs of electrification and dieselization of a railway line are compared. The financial rate of return to the railway from electrification is estimated at 14 percent, which would justify electrification. There are, however, significant discrepancies between the financial and economic costs; the capital costs of the fixed installations involve a large foreign exchange component which must be shadow priced for the economic calculations, while a heavy tax on diesel fuel makes that source of power relatively more expensive for the railway than electricity, which is not taxed. Primarily as a result of these two adjustments, the economic rate of return on electrification is only 5 percent, which, from the country's point of view, makes dieselization the less costly alternative.

The resolution of such a conflict involves a difficult balancing of two conflicting values. On the one hand it would be undersirable for the government to approve investments whose economic benefits to the country are less than their costs. On the other hand it is highly desirable to have government organization, including the railway, bus companies, and airlines, operate as much as possible along commercial lines because this generally leads to greater efficiency and better investment decisions. To bridge these conflicting values, these agencies should undertake both economic and financial appraisals of new investments. If the two analyses lead to different conclusions because government policies result in wide differences between actual prices to the agencies and economic costs to the country, the government should review the desirability of altering its policies on foreign exchange, taxes, subsidies, transport charges, and so on, to bring prices and costs closer together. If such changes are not adopted and these agencies are permitted to operate along commercial lines in most other respects, it would appear preferable to have them operate in the same way in regard to their investment decisions and thus base their decisions on the financial analysis.[7]

Optimum Timing of Projects

While the fact that discounted benefits are larger than discounted costs indicates that a project is justified, it does not necessarily indicate that the project should be started at once. The proper timing of a project requires that the difference between discounted benefits and discounted costs be kept to a minimum. Ideally, the loss of benefits from postponement should be equal to the reduction in costs at the acceptable discount rate. If the cost savings are larger than the loss of benefits, the project should be postponed further.

To estimate the optimum time for starting a project, let us examine the effect of a one-year postponement in three situations that differ only in what happens at the end of the project life. In the first situation, the project has a life of, say, twenty-five years and is not expected to be replaced after that. A postponement of one year would reduce discounted costs, but the benefits of the first year would be lost and replaced (in whole or in part) by one year of additional benefits at the end of the period. In the second situation, the project will not be extended beyond its initial cutoff date (because of technological obsolescence, for example) and there will be no replacement; a postponement of one year would therefore shorten the life of the project to twenty-four years. In this case the reduction in discounted costs from the one-year postponement and from the shorter life should be compared with the loss of benefits during the same year; unlike the circumstances in the first situation, there would be no additional benefits at the end of the period. In the third situation, the project is expected to be replaced each time it reaches the end of its economic life. In this case the reduction in discounted costs in the first year will be repeated twenty-five years later and every twenty-five years thereafter, since the replacements can also be postponed by one year. The only benefits lost would be those in the first year.

The problem of determining the optimum time for starting a project is illustrated in case study 11, "Construction of Additional Berths." In that project the discounted benefits of a third berth amount to Rs140 million; since discounted costs are only about Rs54 million, the berth would appear to be well justified. Although the benefits in the early years are quite small, they rise rapidly thereafter, even when discounted at 12 percent. If the project were to be postponed by one year, the savings in discounted capital and maintenance costs would be Rs5.8 million. In the three situations described, the net result would be as follows:

- Situation 1. *Twenty-five year life, no replacement.* The benefits of the first year, which amount to a present value of Rs2.3 million would be lost, but benefits amounting to Rs1.7 million would accrue in the additional year at the end of the project life, making the net loss in benefits Rs0.6 million, compared with a saving in cost of Rs5.8 million. It would therefore be better to postpone the project for at least one year than to start it now.
- Situation 2. *Reduction in life to twenty-four years, no replacement.* The benefits of the first year, which amount to Rs2.3 million, would be lost. This loss would be offset by a reduction amounting to Rs0.03 million in the discounted costs in the last year. In other words, costs would be Rs5.8 million lower, while benefits would be cut by 2.3 million. A one-year postponement would therefore be justified.
- Situation 3. *Twenty-five year life, repeated replacement.* The benefits of the first year—Rs2.3 million—would be lost. The postponement of replacement by one year at the end of the project life has a discounted value of Rs0.3 million. The reduction in costs would therefore be Rs6.1 million, while the reduction in benefits would be Rs2.3 million. Under this assumption, too, a postponement of one year would be justified. It should be noted that the postponement of replacement after twenty-five years has a very low present value when discounted at relatively high rates, such as the 12 percent rate used here; the further benefit of the postponement fifty years hence would be too small to be considered.

The results of a one-year postponement for the three situations are given in Table 5-3. While a one-year postponement would be justified in all three situations, the net benefits of the delay are not the same.

To determine the optimum year for starting a project, a separate analysis has to be made for each year. For example, with situation 3 (twenty-five-year life, repeated replacement), postponing the project an additional year (a two-year delay) would reduce costs by a further Rs5.4

Table 5-3. Benefits of a One-Year Postponement

(millions of rupees)

Situation	Reduction in discounted costs	Reduction in discounted benefits	Net benefit
1	5.8	0.6	5.2
2	5.8	2.3	3.5
3	6.1	2.3	3.8

million, while the additional gross benefits lost would be Rs2.7 million; the result is a net benefit of Rs2.7 million. The reduction in discounted costs and benefits for annual postponements for each of the first seven years is summarized in table 5-4. This year-by-year analysis indicates that the project should be started in about four years; a postponement of five years would be too long, since the loss of benefits in that year exceeds the reduction in costs. When a similar analysis is made for situation 1 (twenty-five-year life, no replacement), it is seen that a delay of five years would be justified (see "Comparison of Costs and Benefits" in case study 11).

An approximate indication of the optimum starting time for a project can be obtained by comparing the net benefits in the first year, for example, with one year of capital savings as measured by the appropriate interest rate. In case study 11, the capital cost of a new berth is Rs53.4 million. At an interest rate of 12 percent, the annual capital cost would be about Rs6.4 million. The net benefits in the third year after completion of the project are only about Rs5.0 million (gross benefits of Rs5.6 million minus maintenance costs of Rs0.6 million), so that a postpone-

Table 5-4. Benefits of Postponement, by Number of Years of Delay

(millions of rupees)

Delay (year)	Reduction in costs	Reduction in benefits	Net benefit (+) or cost (−)
1	6.1	2.3	3.8
2	5.4	2.7	2.7
3	4.8	3.3	1.5
4	4.2	3.9	0.3
5	3.9	4.8	−0.9
6	3.3	5.4	−2.1
7	3.0	8.4	−5.4

ment of at least three years would appear justified. This is, however, only a rough guide, since it does not allow for some of the other relevant factors discussed above.

The Highway Design Model

In designing and evaluating a new highway or a highway improvement, the responsible agency must consider a wide range of options involving the initial standards of road pavement and alignment; pavement strengthening and geometric improvements; and the frequency and standards of subsequent routine and periodic maintenance. Public policies that affect the use of the highway, such as limitations on vehicle size and weights, must also be taken into account. All these choices affect the costs and benefits of road transport, including the cost of vehicle operating, and thereby the cost of freight and passenger transport, and the benefits of time savings and accident reduction.

The Highway Design and Maintenance Standards Model (HDM) was developed to predict total costs—including construction, maintenance, and road user costs—over the life of the project as a function of road design, maintenance standards, and other policy options.[8] The HDM makes it possible to calculate and compare rapidly the differing cost streams of alternative strategies so that the most economic solution can be identified.

The broad concept of the HDM is relatively simple. Three interacting sets of cost relationships are added together over time in discounted present values, with costs determined by multiplying physical quantities of required resources by unit costs or prices:

- Construction costs are a function of terrain, soils, and rainfall, as well as geometric design, pavement design, and unit costs.
- Maintenance costs are a function of road deterioration (pavement design, climate, time, traffic), maintenance standards, and unit costs.
- Road user costs are a function of geometric design, road surface condition, vehicle speed, vehicle type, and unit costs.

The HDM can compare the costs and benefits of different policies, including different timing and staging options, both for a given road project on a specific alignment and for groups of road links within an entire network. It can quickly estimate the total costs for many alternative project designs and policies, give a year-by-year breakdown for the life of each project, discount future costs at different interest rates, and indicate rates of return, net present values, or first-year benefits. It can also indicate the sensitivity of the results to changes in assumptions about key variables such as unit cost, traffic growth, the value of passenger time, and the discount rate.

To ensure that the theoretic models conform reasonably well to real world conditions, the HDM is based on extensive field studies in Brazil, the Caribbean, India, and Kenya, for which large quantities of data on the physical and economic relationships were collected. Among the important results of these studies are better measurements of the relationship of vehicle operating costs to road characteristics and of the impact of traffic and climate on road deterioration. The HDM has been applied in more than thirty countries, and the results indicate that the economic returns of expenditures on road maintenance are typically far higher than the returns to new construction.

While the HDM and the extensive research underlying it provide a major step forward in data-based decisionmaking in the highway sector, much research remains to be done. In three important areas—accidents, environmental impacts such as air and noise pollution, and user costs under congested traffic conditions—limitations in the current state of the art do not permit the establishment of generalized quantitative relationships. In these areas the HDM simply provides a facility for the user to input an exogenously determined estimate of the benefits and costs where available. Similarly, while the effects of alternative maintenance policies have been well quantified for unpaved roads, for paved roads only the initial effects on road deterioration, and not the longer term ones, have been well quantified. Nor can the pavement performance models yet be used for rigid concrete pavements or pavements subjected to freezing temperatures. Further research is needed to extend basic knowledge in these areas before quantitative models such as the HDM can be made more comprehensive.

Notes

1. A study of several Latin American countries suggests 12 percent as a first approximation (Powers 1981, p. 134). McDiarmid (1977, p. 128) suggests a discount rate of 12 percent for Taiwan and 10 percent for the Philippines. Bell, Hazell, and Slade (1982, p. 209) cite evidence that it may be 10 percent for Malaysia, but they suggest doing sensitivity analyses at 5, 10, and 20 percent. For Egypt, the opportunity cost of capital has been estimated at 10 percent, but the consumption rate of interest at only 5.5 percent (Page 1982). Page recommends 6 percent for project evaluation but suggests doing sensitivity analyses at 4 ,6, and 8 percent. A study of Turkey (Mashayekhi 1980, p. 43) suggests an accounting rate of interest of 5–6 percent, a marginal productivity of capital of 12 percent, and a con-

sumption rate of interest of 4.5 percent. For India, Lal (1980, p. 201) suggests a social rate of interest of 11 percent, and a consumption rate of interest of 7 percent. A review of the literature by Ray (1984, pp. 92–93) indicates that marginal returns to investments tend to be in the 8–12 percent range, while consumption rates of interest range between 2 and 5 percent.

2. See, for example, case study 13, "Cargo-Handling Equipment for a Port," where the cost-benefit ratio is only 1 : 1.2 but the internal rate of return is 30 percent.

3. The illustration is from Harral (1968), p. 89.

4. If a fourth alternative were introduced which included two projects C, with the second project C having the same costs and benefits as the first, this combination would become the most desirable alternative. Its costs would be Rs100 million and its benefits Rs144 million, which would give a net present worth of Rs44 million. The costs of this alternative would be Rs10 million more than those of project B, but the benefits would be Rs25 million more than those of B.

5. While a positive net present worth is a necessary condition for project approval, it is not a sufficient condition if the budget is inadequate to cover all projects whose benefits exceed costs (Pearce 1983, pp. 51–52).

6. For example, a project with annual net benefits of −1.0, +5.5, and −6.0 has internal rates of return of both 100 and 200 percent. Multiple internal rates of return are possible if there are periodic negative net benefits during the life of the project.

7. Heggie examines several methods of bridging the application of accounting prices to investment decisions with the pricing and financial management of the assets but finds that all have serious disadvantages. He concludes that particularly in the case of revenue-earning entities, such as ports and railways, "although accounting prices are desirable in principle, they are extremely difficult to apply in practice. What is quite clear is that accounting prices cannot simply be used for investment decisions, leaving the questions of pricing and financial management to look after themselves" (Heggie 1976, p. 24).

8. This section is based on Watanatada and others (forthcoming).

Part II

Case Studies

Introduction

PART II PRESENTS fifteen case studies of transport investments involving road, railway, pipeline, port and shipping, and airport projects. The major purpose of these case studies is to illustrate the methodology described in Part I. Although many of the cases are related to actual projects, the data have been modified and have no necessary relation to these projects; nor can the figures be used directly in analyzing other projects. Since each project has unique features, even the application of the methodology to other projects must be done with great care.

None of the case studies are intended to present a complete analysis of the various alternatives which should be examined in each case. For example, case study 4, "Construction of a Development Road," compares existing shipping via waterways only with shipping via paved road; a separate study should be made to determine whether the road should be gravel or paved. Case study 10, "Construction of an Oil Pipeline," compares pipeline with railway costs; separate studies are needed to determine the optimum size and locations of the pipeline. In the analysis of actual projects, a number of alternatives must be examined, not merely the ones illustrated in these case studies.

Since many of the data used, such as the forecasts of traffic and the measurements of some benefits, inherently involve substantial margins of errors, the figures have generally been rounded and totals may therefore not add. Tables comparing costs and benefits are included for each case study. Rupees (Rs) and paisas refer to local expenditures and are not intended to have any relation to the currency of any particular country. The equivalent of US$1 at the official exchange rate is assumed to be 4.75 rupees.

Case Study 1

Paving a Gravel Road

Proposed Project and Costs

TWO TOWNS ARE CONNECTED by a twenty-mile gravel road. The road is in reasonably good condition but is only twenty-four feet wide; it has several grades above 8 percent and three sharp curves. The traffic in the year before construction averages 350 vehicles per day. There is no congestion, but dust in the summer occasionally forces vehicles to keep a substantial distance apart and passing is then difficult. Nevertheless, trucks and buses can usually travel at an average speed of thirty miles an hour and cars at thirty-five miles an hour. There is no railway alternative.

The highway department proposes to pave the road to a width of twenty-four feet, widen the roadbed to thirty-two feet, and make minor improvements in the alignment. (See case study 2 for an appraisal of the appropriate pavement width.) The work is expected to start early in year 1 and to be completed by the end of that year. The cost is estimated at Rs1.65 million per mile (net of taxes) and the foreign exchange component at Rs600,000; with a shadow rate for foreign exchange of 1.75 times the official rate, the economic cost per mile, therefore, is Rs2.1 million. The capital costs of the twenty-mile project thus amount to Rs42.0 million (see column 1 of table 1-1).

The annual maintenance costs of the paved road are estimated at Rs12,600 per mile; with a foreign exchange component of 25 percent, the economic cost is Rs15,000 per mile, or Rs300,000 for the entire twenty-mile road (see column 2 of table 1-1). Every five years major repaving is needed; that economic cost is estimated at Rs1.5 million. The economic life of the project is estimated at twenty years, with no salvage value.

The economic appraisal consists of comparing the capital and maintenance costs of the paved road with the reduction in vehicle operating costs for future traffic, plus the avoidance of maintenance costs of the gravel road.

Table 1-1. Comparison of Costs and Benefits of Paving a Gravel Road
(millions of rupees)

Year	Costs			Benefits			Present worth (discounted at 12 percent)		Internal rate of return (discounted at 14 percent)	
	Capital costs (1)	Maintenance costs (2)	Total costs (3)	Reduced vehicle operating costs (4)	Eliminated maintenance costs (5)	Total benefits (6)	Costs (7)	Benefits (8)	Costs (9)	Benefits (10)
1	42.0	0	42.0	0	0	0	42.0	0	42.0	0
2	0	0.3	0.3	2.3	0.2	2.5	0.3	2.2	0.3	2.2
3	0	0.3	0.3	2.6	0.2	2.8	0.2	2.2	0.2	2.1
4	0	0.3	0.3	3.0	0.2	3.2	0.2	2.3	0.2	2.2
5	0	0.3	0.3	3.3	0.3	3.6	0.2	2.3	0.2	2.1
6	0	1.5	1.5	3.8	0.3	4.1	0.9	2.3	0.8	2.1
7	0	0.3	0.3	4.1	0.4	4.5	0.2	2.3	0.1	2.0
8	0	0.3	0.3	5.8	0.4	6.2	0.1	2.8	0.1	2.5
9	0	0.3	0.3	6.5	0.4	6.9	0.1	2.8	0.1	2.4
10	0	0.3	0.3	7.1	0.4	7.5	0.1	2.7	0.1	2.3

11	0	1.5	1.5	7.9	0.4	8.3	0.5	2.7	0.4	2.2
12	0	0.3	0.3	8.7	0.4	9.1	0.1	2.6	0.1	2.2
13	0	0.3	0.3	12.1	0.4	12.5	0.1	3.2	0.1	2.6
14	0	0.3	0.3	13.1	0.4	13.5	0.1	3.1	0.1	2.5
15	0	0.3	0.3	14.2	0.4	14.6	0.1	3.0	0.1	2.3
16	0	1.5	1.5	15.3	0.4	15.7	0.3	2.9	0.2	2.2
17	0	0.3	0.3	16.5	0.5	17.0	a	2.8	a	2.1
18	0	0.3	0.3	17.8	0.5	18.3	a	2.7	a	2.0
19	0	0.3	0.3	19.3	0.5	19.8	0.1	2.6	0.1	1.9
20	0	0.3	0.3	20.8	0.5	21.3	a	2.5	a	1.8
21	0	0.3	0.3	22.5	0.5	23.0	0.1	2.4	a	1.7
Total							45.7	52.4	45.2	43.4

Note: Net present worth equals Rs6.7 million; this is the difference between columns 7 and 8.

a. For these years the discounted costs are substantially less than 0.1; an allowance of 0.1 has therefore been made for these years only.

Traffic

The average daily traffic on the road in the year before construction amounts to 350 vehicles: 220 trucks, 40 buses, and 90 passenger cars. Traffic has been increasing in recent years by 12 percent annually for trucks and buses and by 15 percent for cars. Taking into account past traffic growth, probable agricultural and industrial development in the area, and the present capability of the road transport industry, truck and bus traffic is estimated to increase by 12 percent annually in the first five years after completion of the project, by 10 percent annually in the second five years, and by 8 percent annually during the last ten years of the project. The annual growth rates for cars are estimated to be 15, 12, and 9 percent, respectively.

In addition to this growth in normal traffic, paving the road is expected to generate traffic. Better transport allows, for example, expansion of the market for dairy products and fruits in the area. A review of such opportunities and of the traffic developments in nearby areas when gravel roads were paved indicates that the generated traffic is likely to be about 10, 15, and 20 percent of the normal traffic during the first three years after completion of the project. No traffic is anticipated to be diverted to the road from other roads or other modes of transportation.

Based on these assumptions, estimates of average daily traffic in selected years are shown in table 1-2. Until the traffic level in year 21 reaches about 3,300 vehicles a day, no significant congestion is expected on the paved road, although new improvements may be justified thereafter.

Project Benefits

The benefits of the paving project consist primarily of reduction of vehicle operating costs and the elimination of the maintenance costs of a gravel road.

Reduced Vehicle Operating Costs

Studies of vehicle operations on gravel and paved surfaces indicate costs per vehicle-mile as shown in table 1-3. The costs are net of taxes, and the foreign exchange costs have been shadow priced. The costs also take into account that paving and minor improvements in the alignment increase the average speed of trucks and buses from about thirty

Table 1-2. Estimates of Average Daily Traffic by Vehicle
(number of vehicles)

	Trucks		Buses		Cars		
Year	Normal	Generated	Normal	Generated	Normal	Generated	Total
Preconstruction	220	0	40	0	90	0	350
2	275	30	50	5	110	10	480
3	310	45	55	10	125	20	565
4	345	70	65	15	145	30	670
7	485	100	90	20	220	45	960
12	780	160	140	30	385	80	1,575
21	1,660	320	280	60	840	175	3,335

to forty miles an hour and the average speed of cars from about thirty-five to forty-five miles an hour.

The unit benefits for the normal traffic are thus about 80 paisas per truck-mile, 98 paisas per bus-mile, and 24 paisas per car-mile. For generated traffic, the unit benefits are one-half of these. (For an explanation of this assumption, see "Economic Development" in chapter 4.) The total benefits from reduced vehicle operating costs (in millions of rupees) in the first year after completion of the project (year 2) are shown in table 1-4.

Although the paved road can carry the future traffic without significant congestion, congestion on the gravel road would have become increasingly important. Such congestion would increase vehicle operat-

Table 1-3. Comparison of Costs per Vehicle-Mile by Vehicle and Road Surface
(paisas)

	Truck		Bus		Car	
Cost item	Paved	Gravel	Paved	Gravel	Paved	Gravel
Fuel and oil	21.3	27.3	21.6	27.3	17.7	19.5
Tire wear	21.9	48.6	21.9	48.6	4.5	10.2
Depreciation	36.3	54.0	52.2	78.0	28.5	36.6
Interest	21.0	30.0	30.0	42.0	21.0	27.0
Maintenance	28.2	44.7	39.9	63.3	7.8	10.5
Wages	12.0	16.2	12.0	16.2	—	—
Total	140.7	220.8	177.6	275.4	79.5	103.8
Benefit		80.1		97.8		24.3

— Not applicable.

Table 1-4. Reduced Vehicle Operating Costs for the First Year
(millions of rupees)

Traffic and Vehicle	Calculation	Costs
Normal traffic		
Truck	275 trucks × 20 miles × 365 × 80 paisas	1.61
Bus	50 buses × 20 miles × 365 × 98 paisas	0.36
Car	110 cars × 20 miles × 365 × 24 paisas	0.19
Subtotal		2.16
Generated traffic		
Truck	30 trucks × 20 miles × 365 × 40 paisas	0.09
Bus	5 buses × 20 miles × 365 × 49 paisas	0.02
Car	10 cars × 20 miles × 365 × 12 paisas	0.01
Subtotal		0.12
Total		2.28

ing costs by an estimated 8 percent after year 7, when the average daily traffic will exceed 1,000 vehicles, and by an additional 12 percent after year 12, when the average daily traffic will be about 1,700 vehicles. For trucks, this implies increases in vehicle operating costs from 221 paisas a mile to 239 paisas and later to 268 paisas; the unit benefits increase from 80 paisas to 98 paisas and then to 127 paisas. For buses the unit benefits would rise from 98 paisas to 119 paisas and later to 155 paisas; for cars, they rise from 24 paisas to 33 paisas and later to 46 paisas.

The growth in benefits in line with the growth in traffic and in unit benefits is shown in column 4 of table 1-1.

Maintenance Costs of Gravel Road

Although the maintenance costs of the paved road are not expected to increase significantly with the increase in traffic, the costs of maintaining the gravel road are estimated to increase sharply. Maintenance expenditures on the gravel road, with a shadow rate for foreign exchange costs, have been about Rs9,000 per mile in recent years, but experience from other roads indicates that this will rise sharply with growing traffic. Taking into consideration such factors as the condition of the soil and the climate, annual maintenance costs are estimated to increase from Rs10,500 per mile in year 2 to Rs18,000 in year 7 and

Rs21,000 in year 12. These costs for the twenty-mile road are shown in column 5 of table 1-1.

Although in the early years maintenance costs of the paved road exceed those of the gravel road, the situation reverses in year 7. In any case, the benefits from lower maintenance expenditures are slight and for all practical purposes could be omitted from the appraisal of this particular project.

Other Benefits

This analysis takes into account the time savings for vehicles (including truck and bus drivers) but not for passengers and freight. This amounts to ten minutes a bus and truck trip and seven minutes a car trip. Consideration of passenger time depends on whether passengers can use the extra time for work or voluntary leisure or whether such time merely increases unemployment. In view of the prevalent unemployment and underemployment in the area, it is doubtful that most passengers are willing to pay anything for the extra time. On the assumption that the value of time for all passengers per bus is Rs12 an hour and Rs7.50 a car (for details, see case study 5, "Construction of a Bridge") and one-half of these for generated traffic, the value of the time benefits in year 7 is about Rs87,000 for the bus passengers and Rs144,000 for car passengers or a total of Rs231,000. This is only about 5 percent of the benefits in that year. The benefits to freight (on the assumption also explained in case study 5) are Rs165,000, or about 3 percent of total benefits. The inclusion of these highly speculative benefits does not affect the justification of the project.

Paving also increases the comfort of the trip for drivers and passengers by providing a smoother ride, eliminating dust in dry seasons, facilitating passing, and so forth. Separate studies of accidents indicate that the effect of paving is minor, with a slight reduction in the number of accidents offset by greater damage per accident because of higher speeds (see "Accident Reduction" in chapter 4).

A further benefit might arise during construction; as sections of the road are paved, those portions can be used. This, however, is more or less offset by the fact that the paving to some extent interferes with existing traffic.

The generated traffic benefits may be over- or understated since the net value of the generated output may be smaller or larger than one-half the unit benefits of normal traffic. The margin of error is likely to be small; even if the benefits are half or double those used here, this change does not significantly affect the basic conclusion.

Comparison of Costs and Benefits

As shown in columns 7 and 8 of table 1-1, the benefits of the proposed paving project exceed the costs—both discounted at 12 percent—by Rs6.7 million during the project's economic life. The cost-benefit ratio is about 1 : 1.15 and the internal rate of return is somewhat less than 14 percent (see columns 9 and 10). The project is therefore justified. In fact, the project should have been undertaken earlier since the benefits would have exceeded costs at a 12 percent discount rate at a traffic level of 400 vehicles a day; completion of the project is thus about one to two years late.

The conclusion of the analysis is particularly sensitive to the capital costs of the project. If, for example, the costs are 20 percent higher than estimated, the net worth is reduced from Rs6.7 million to a negative Rs1.5 million, and it is necessary either to delay the project until traffic has increased further or to reduce the design standards. The switching value for the capital costs, that is, the costs which equalize discounted costs and benefits at 12 percent and thus bring the net present value to zero, is Rs48.9 million, or about 16 percent above the project cost estimate. The conclusion to proceed with the project should therefore be reviewed after the costs have been confirmed.

Estimates of reductions in vehicle-operating costs can be based on physical measurements and experience on other roads, so that the margin of error need not be large. Traffic forecasts are inherently more speculative, however. If the rate of traffic increase is 25 percent lower than estimated, the net worth of the project becomes negative, and the project might have to be postponed. The appraisal is not particularly sensitive to the assumption about generated traffic since it accounts for less than one-tenth of total discounted benefits. Similarly, as indicated in "Project Benefits," the appraisal is not sensitive to assumptions about maintenance costs.

Case Study 2

Widening the Pavement of a Road

Proposed Project and Costs

IN MANY DEVELOPING COUNTRIES, a considerable part of the intercity road network has pavement less than eighteen feet wide and much of it may be only twelve feet wide. A highway department wants to instruct the district offices regarding the optimum timing for widening the pavement to twenty feet. Although in developed countries the standard pavement width of a two-lane road is usually twenty-four feet, twenty feet is quite adequate to allow trucks and buses to pass each other comfortably and remain on the pavement. Although the capacity of a twenty-four-foot pavement is greater than that of a twenty-foot pavement, this difference is not relevant for the traffic volumes that are typical in developing countries and are used in this case study.

Many of the existing roads in the country have a twelve-foot-wide bituminous pavement on a thirty-two-foot-wide formation. The project consists, therefore, of widening the pavement to twenty feet. In addition, it is necessary to widen or replace some drainage structures and to make other minor improvements. The economic cost of a typical widening project is estimated at Rs750,000 a mile, including Rs600,000 for widening the pavement and Rs150,000 for structures and miscellaneous items. This is net of taxes and reflects a shadow rate for the foreign exchange component (primarily for bitumen) of 1.75 times the official rate. The estimated economic life of the investment is ten years.

Traffic

To determine the optimum timing for widening the pavement on typical roads, the estimates of costs and benefits are presented in table 2-1 for daily traffic volumes ranging from 244 to 1,000 vehicles. Much of the traffic prevailing on roads with a twelve-foot pavement, and for

Table 2-1. Comparison of Project Costs and Benefits of Widening Road Pavement, at Different Traffic Levels

(thousands of rupees)

| Average daily vehicles | Annual benefits | | | Present worth of benefits | | | |
| | Reduced vehicle operating costs (1) | Change in mainten- ance costs (2) | Total benefits (3) | Discounted at 12 percent | | | Discounted at 8 percent (7)[d] |
				(4)[a]	(5)[b]	(6)[c]	
244	15.9	−2.7	13.2	—	—	—	—
264	20.1	−2.4	17.7	—	—	—	—
286	21.9	−2.4	19.5	—	—	—	—
314	27.6	−2.4	25.2	—	—	22.5	—
340	37.2	−2.4	34.8	—	—	27.7	32.2
369	46.5	−2.1	44.4	—	39.6	31.6	38.1
400	57.0	−2.1	54.9	49.0	43.8	34.9	43.6
432	71.1	−2.1	69.0	55.0	49.1	39.1	50.7
466	91.8	−1.8	90.0	64.1	57.2	45.6	61.3
504	110.4	−1.8	108.6	69.1	61.6	49.1	68.4
544	136.8	−1.8	135.0	76.5	68.4	54.5	78.7
588	167.4	−1.5	165.9	84.1	75.0	59.9	89.6
636	201.9	−1.2	200.7	90.7	81.1	64.6	100.4
686	255.3	−0.9	254.4	102.8	91.8	0	117.8
740	315.9	−0.6	315.3	113.8	101.5	0	0
800	385.5	−0.3	385.2	124.0	0	0	0
860	470.7	0	470.7	0	0	0	0
927	578.7	0	578.7	0	0	0	0
1,000	711.9	0.3	712.2	0	0	0	0
Total				829.1	669.1	429.5	680.8

— Not applicable.
a. Stream of benefits beginning at 400 vehicles.
b. Stream of benefits beginning at 369 vehicles.
c. Stream of benefits beginning at 314 vehicles.
d. Stream of benefits beginning at 340 vehicles.

which widening might well be considered, falls within this range. Composition of traffic by vehicle type is estimated to be trucks, 50 percent; buses, 30 percent; and cars, 20 percent.

Traffic is projected to grow by about 7.5 percent annually for the ten-year life of the project; this means approximately a doubling of traffic in ten years. The estimate of traffic is shown by type of vehicle in table 2-2 for daily traffic volumes from 400 to 800 vehicles and for the total of all vehicles for the entire range from 244 to 1,000 vehicles in table 2-1.

Project Benefits

The benefits of widening the pavement consist of reductions in vehicle operating costs and in road maintenance costs. Maintenance costs on the wider pavement, however, are lower only at traffic levels above 900 vehicles a day; they are treated as negative benefits below that level (this is discussed later in this section).

Reduction in Vehicle Operating Costs

On a pavement width of twelve feet, vehicles passing each other must generally leave the pavement and run on the earth shoulder until the pavement is clear again. The amount of time that a vehicle spends on the shoulder is a function of the volume of traffic. At a volume of 100 vehicles a day, vehicles rarely leave the pavement, so that the operating costs are more or less the same as on a paved road. As traffic increases,

Table 2-2. Composition of Projected Daily Traffic by Type of Vehicle
(number of vehicles)

Daily traffic volume	Trucks	Buses	Cars
400	200	120	80
432	216	130	86
466	234	140	92
504	252	152	100
544	272	164	108
588	296	176	116
636	320	190	126
686	344	206	136
740	370	222	148
800	400	240	160

Table 2-3. Vehicle Operating Costs by Vehicles a Day
(paisas a vehicle-mile)

	Trucks		Buses		Cars		Weighted average of benefits
Vehicles a day	Costs (1)	Benefits (2)	Costs (3)	Benefits (4)	Costs (5)	Benefits (6)	benefits (7)
100	141	0	177	0	81	0	0
200	153	12	189	12	84	3	10
300	168	27	204	27	87	6	23
400	186	45	225	48	93	12	39
500	207	66	252	75	99	18	59
600	231	90	282	105	105	24	81
700	258	117	315	138	111	30	106
800	288	147	351	174	117	36	133
900	321	180	390	213	123	42	162
1,000	360	219	432	255	132	51	196

however, the time spent on the shoulders increases; studies have shown that vehicle operating costs on a twelve-foot pavement at a traffic level of 1,000 vehicles a day are almost the same as on an earth road. With the increase in traffic, vehicle operating costs increase gradually from costs on a paved road to those on an earth road. The relation between vehicle operating costs and the traffic level is shown in columns 2, 4, and 6 of table 2-3.

Since the vehicle operating costs on a twenty-foot pavement remain about the same within the traffic range of 100 to 1,000 vehicles a day, the unit benefits from widening equal the difference between the costs at 100 vehicles and the higher trafic level. For example, the operating costs of a truck are 141 paisas on a twenty-foot pavement; this increases to 153 paisas at 200 vehicles a day on a twelve-foot pavement, so that the benefits of widening are 12 paisas per truck-mile. The unit benefits for each vehicle-mile are shown in columns 2, 4, and 6 of table 2-3; column 7 gives the average unit benefit for each vehicle weighted by the traffic composition in table 2-2.

To calculate the benefits of the project, these unit benefits must then be multiplied by the traffic. For example, the following calculations are for the first four years of a project involving 400 vehicles a day in the opening year; the unit benefits for traffic levels between those shown in table 2-3 have been interpolated.

Year 1   400 vehicles × 365 days × 39 paisas =   Rs57,000
Year 2   432 vehicles × 365 days × 45 paisas =   Rs71,100

Year 3   466 vehicles × 365 days × 54 paisas =   Rs91,800
Year 4   504 vehicles × 365 days × 60 paisas = Rs110,400

The benefits from reduced vehicle operating costs at different traffic levels are shown in column 1 of table 2-1.

Changes in Maintenance Costs

The annual maintenance costs of a twenty-foot paved road average Rs9,300 a mile; these costs are net of taxes, with an appropriate adjustment for the foreign exchange costs. Maintenance costs are estimated to be almost the same regardless of traffic level up to 800 vehicles a day and thereafter rise only gradually, as shown in table 2-4.

The annual maintenance costs of a twelve-foot paved road vary more directly with the traffic level. For example, these estimated costs average Rs6,600 a mile at a daily traffic of 200 vehicles, but rise to Rs7,200 when the traffic increases to 400 vehicles and to Rs10,200 at 1,000 vehicles a day. The differences in annual maintenance costs per mile between a twelve- and a twenty-foot pavement are shown in table 2-4.

The costs and benefits from the differences in maintenance costs are shown in column 2 of table 2-1; costs and benefits for traffic levels between those shown in table 2-4 have been interpolated. The total benefits, including reduced vehicle operating costs and differences in maintenance costs, are shown in column 3 of table 2-1.

Table 2-4. Comparison of Maintenance Costs of Twenty-Foot and Twelve-Foot Pavement

Average daily vehicles	*Maintenance cost on twenty-foot pavement*	*Maintenance cost on twelve-foot pavement*	*Benefit (+) or cost (−) of twenty-foot pavement*
200	9.3	6.6	−2.7
300	9.3	6.9	−2.4
400	9.3	7.2	−2.1
500	9.3	7.5	−1.8
600	9.3	7.8	−1.5
700	9.3	8.4	−0.9
800	9.3	9.0	−0.3
900	9.6	9.6	0
1,000	9.9	10.2	+0.3

Comparison of Costs and Benefits

As shown in column 4 of table 2-1, the net present worth of the benefits of paving beginning at a level of 400 vehicles a day amounts to Rs829,000 a mile when discounted at 12 percent. Column 5 indicates that the benefits amount to Rs669,000 if the traffic level in the base year is 369 vehicles. Since paving costs are estimated at Rs750,000, paving becomes justified when the traffic level reaches 380–390 vehicles a day in the base year. In other words, at that traffic level the internal rate of return is 12 percent.

The purpose of this case study is to show how a general standard for widening road pavements can be established. The particular standard is sensitive to a number of factors.

An important consideration is the paving costs. As shown in column 5 of table 2-1, if paving can be undertaken at about Rs670,000 a mile, it can be initiated when the traffic is only 369 vehicles a day in the base year. Column 6 indicates that if the costs are as low as Rs430,000, paving is justified when the traffic is only 310 vehicles a day.

The conclusion of the analysis is affected by the discount rate used. As shown in column 7, if the paving costs are about Rs681,000 and if 8 percent is regarded as a satisfactory rate of return, paving is justified at 340 vehicles a day. In other words, the difference between 8 and 12 percent is approximately an initial traffic level of 30 vehicles a day. Since the annual traffic growth at this level is 25 to 30 vehicles a day, paving will have to be delayed slightly more than one year to satisfy a 12 percent rate rather than an 8 percent rate.

The conclusion is also affected by the composition of traffic and the projected growth of traffic. Since the unit benefits for cars are only about one-quarter of those for trucks and buses, a larger proportion of cars delays the time when paving becomes justified. No allowance, however, has been made for nonmotorized traffic, which in many developing countries tends to be significant. Such slow-moving traffic interferes seriously with the flow of motorized traffic and may justify separate handling or a twenty-four-foot pavement even at the traffic level suggested for a twenty-foot pavement.

The decision depends also on the condition of the shoulders. In the case study, they are assumed to be the equivalent of earth roads. The quality of earth roads can vary widely, depending on weather, the condition of the soil, and so forth. These factors must be taken into account in the application of the suggested standard to a particular road.

The case study makes no allowance for the value of time for passengers and freight. Since the average speed of vehicles on the twenty-foot pavement might be about five miles an hour greater than on the twelve-foot pavement, this makes some difference—although at almost any reasonable allowance for the value of time in developing countries, the difference would be small. The case study also neglects the impact of a wider pavement on accident reduction, which might be significant in some situations (see "Accident Reduction" in chapter 4).

Finally, the calculation makes no allowance for the greater comfort and convenience of travel on a wider pavement, especially at higher traffic levels. Depending on the condition of the shoulders, traveling on a twelve-foot pavement can be a nerve-racking experience.

Case Study 3

Construction
of a Major Highway

Proposed Project

A PORT CITY with a population of more than 2 million is connected
with an inland city with a population of about 500,000 by a 110-mile
railway line and a 120-mile bituminous road. The road has a twelve-
foot-wide, single-lane pavement which is in poor condition, and there
are frequent pavement failures. Maintenance is expensive because the
road was not designed for the existing traffic level and because some of
the embankment is waterlogged.

The highway department is proposing the construction of a new
highway between the two cities. The highway would have a bituminous
pavement, with two twelve-foot-wide lanes and stabilized gravel shoulders that are ten feet wide. The right-of-way width is about 220 feet in
order to permit construction of two additional lanes when traffic
warrants it. The highway would have limited access and a design speed
of seventy miles an hour. Slow-moving, animal-drawn vehicles would
not be permitted to use the highway but would use either the existing
road or the contractor's construction road outside the drainage ditches.
Modern geometric standards and design criteria would be utilized
throughout. Consideration has been given to improving the existing
road rather than constructing a new highway, but the new highway
would be only ninety miles long, a saving of thirty miles, and the
waterlogging conditions of the old road would require expensive
countermeasures.

Project Costs

The financial costs of the project are estimated at Rs3.6 million per
mile, or Rs324 million for the entire ninety miles. To calculate economic costs, three adjustments must be considered. First, the foreign
exchange costs of the project are estimated at Rs162 million. At a

shadow rate of 1.75 times the official exchange rate, the economic costs are Rs120 million more than the financial costs, or Rs444 million. Second, customs duties and sales taxes account for about Rs36 million; these must be deducted, making total economic costs Rs408 million. Third, some of the labor involved in the construction is unskilled and might otherwise be unemployed. No adjustment is made for this, however, because the amount is estimated to be very small and more or less offset by the fact that some of the labor is skilled. Construction of the project is expected to take three years (see column 1 of table 3-1).

The annual maintenance costs of the highway are estimated at Rs18,000 per mile, or Rs1.62 million for the entire project. The foreign exchange component is estimated at Rs315,000; with a shadow rate for foreign costs, the economic cost of annual maintenance is Rs1,855,000. At least 30 percent of the maintenance costs, however, are accounted for by unskilled labor which would otherwise remain largely unemployed; applying a shadow price of 50 percent of actual wages paid reduces the economic cost of annual maintenance by about Rs240,000 to about Rs1,615,000. This cost is assumed to increase gradually with the growth of traffic (until year 22) and an increase in the economic cost of labor as employment opportunities in the area expand. In addition, major repaving would be needed every sixth year, at an economic cost of Rs9 million. Maintenance costs are estimated for thirty years, the economic life of the project; no allowance is made for any salvage value thereafter (see column 2 of table 3-1).

Traffic

The average daily traffic on the old road amounts to about 600 vehicles: 350 trucks, 220 cars, and 30 buses. In the six years before completion of the new highway, truck and passenger car traffic is estimated to increase by 12 percent annually and bus traffic by 10 percent annually, that is, to 615 trucks, 385 cars, and 50 buses—a total of 1,050 vehicles. This forecast takes into account traffic growth in recent years, the probable agricultural and industrial development of the region, and the present stage of the road transport industry. Traffic on the new highway would come from three sources: traffic diverted from the existing road, traffic diverted from the parallel railway, and traffic generated by the reduced transport costs.

Origin and destination studies reveal that about 92 percent of the existing traffic is through traffic which would divert to the new highway, while 8 percent is local traffic which would remain on the existing road.

Table 3-1. Comparison of Costs and Benefits of Construction of a Major Highway
(millions of rupees)

| Year | Costs | | | Benefits (reduction in vehicle operating costs only) | | | | | | Net worth (discounted at 12 percent) | | Internal rate of return (discounted at 17 percent) | |
	Capital costs (1)	Maintenance costs (2)	Total costs (3)	Traffic diverted from old road (4)	Generated traffic (5)	Traffic diverted from railway (6)	Subtotal traffic on new highway (7)	Traffic on old road (8)	Total benefits (9)	Costs (10)	Benefits (11)	Costs (12)	Benefits (13)
1	120.00	0	120.00	0	0	0	0	0	0	120.00	0	120.00	0
2	150.00	0	150.00	0	0	0	0	0	0	133.95	0	128.25	0
3	138.00	0	138.00	0	0	0	0	0	0	109.99	0	100.88	0
4	0	1.62	1.62	41.55	1.04	0.17	42.76	0.43	43.19	1.15	30.75	1.01	26.95
5	0	1.65	1.65	46.47	1.80	0.18	48.45	0.45	48.90	1.05	31.10	0.88	26.11
6	0	1.68	1.68	52.02	2.55	0.21	54.78	0.45	55.23	0.95	31.32	0.77	25.18
7	0	1.71	1.71	58.23	2.85	0.21	61.29	0.48	61.77	0.87	31.32	0.67	24.09
8	0	1.74	1.74	65.19	3.18	0.24	68.61	0.51	69.12	0.79	31.24	0.58	23.02
9	0	10.77	10.77	76.50	3.66	0.24	80.40	0.54	80.94	4.35	32.70	3.07	23.07
10	0	1.80	1.80	82.80	3.96	0.24	87.00	0.57	87.57	0.65	31.61	0.44	21.28
11	0	1.83	1.83	89.40	4.26	0.24	93.90	0.60	94.50	0.59	30.43	0.38	19.66
12	0	1.86	1.86	96.90	4.59	0.27	101.46	0.63	102.09	0.53	29.30	0.33	18.17
13	0	1.89	1.89	104.31	4.95	0.27	109.53	0.66	110.19	0.49	28.32	0.29	16.75
14	0	1.92	1.92	109.65	5.34	0.30	115.29	0.69	115.98	0.44	26.56	0.25	15.08
15	0	10.95	10.95	118.50	5.76	0.30	124.56	0.72	125.28	2.24	25.68	1.22	13.91

16	0	1.98	1.98	127.98	6.21	0.30	134.49	0.75	135.24	0.36	24.75	0.19	12.85
17	0	2.01	2.01	138.21	6.69	0.33	145.23	0.78	146.01	0.33	23.80	0.16	11.83
18	0	2.04	2.04	171.00	8.25	0.33	179.58	0.81	180.39	0.30	26.34	0.14	12.45
19	0	2.07	2.07	180.90	8.70	0.36	189.96	0.87	190.83	0.27	24.81	0.12	11.26
20	0	2.10	2.10	191.40	9.00	0.36	200.76	0.90	201.66	0.24	23.39	0.11	10.28
21	0	11.13	11.13	202.80	9.54	0.39	212.73	0.96	213.69	1.16	22.22	0.48	9.19
22	0	2.16	2.16	214.95	10.11	0.39	225.45	0.99	226.44	0.20	21.06	0.08	8.38
23	0	2.16	2.16	214.95	10.11	0.39	225.45	0.99	226.44	0.18	18.79	0.07	7.25
24	0	2.16	2.16	214.95	10.11	0.39	225.45	0.99	226.44	0.16	16.75	0.06	6.11
25	0	2.16	2.16	214.95	10.11	0.39	225.45	0.99	226.44	0.14	14.95	0.05	5.21
26	0	2.16	2.16	214.95	10.11	0.39	225.45	0.99	226.44	0.13	13.36	0.04	4.53
27	0	11.16	11.16	214.95	10.11	0.39	225.45	0.99	226.44	0.59	12.00	0.19	3.85
28	0	2.16	2.16	214.95	10.11	0.39	225.45	0.99	226.44	0.10	10.64	0.03	3.17
29	0	2.16	2.16	214.95	10.11	0.39	225.45	0.99	226.44	0.09	9.51	0.03	2.72
30	0	2.16	2.16	214.95	10.11	0.39	225.45	0.99	226.44	0.08	8.38	0.02	2.49
31	0	2.16	2.16	214.95	10.11	0.39	225.45	0.99	226.44	0.07	7.47	0.02	2.04
32	0	2.16	2.16	214.95	10.11	0.39	225.45	0.99	226.44	0.06	6.79	0.02	1.81
Total										382.50	645.35	360.83	368.69

Note: Net present worth equals Rs262.85 million; this is the difference between columns 10 and 11.

87

Table 3-2. Estimates of Daily Traffic on Project Road in Selected Years

Year	Trucks				Buses				Cars			Total Vehicles
	Diverted from existing road	Diverted from railway	Generated	Total	Diverted from existing road	Diverted from railway	Generated	Total	Diverted from existing road	Generated	Total	
4	565	30	55	650	45	5	5	55	355	35	390	1,095
5	635	30	95	760	50	5	5	60	395	60	455	1,275
6	710	35	140	885	55	5	10	70	440	90	530	1,485
7	795	35	155	985	60	5	10	75	485	100	585	1,645
8	875	35	170	1,080	65	5	10	80	535	110	645	1,805
17	1,750	50	340	2,140	130	10	20	160	1,260	260	1,520	3,820
22	2,205	55	430	2,690	165	10	25	200	1,715	350	2,065	4,955
32	2,205	55	430	2,690	165	10	25	200	1,715	350	2,065	4,955

Of the daily traffic of 1,050 vehicles in year 4, about 965 would divert to the new highway (see table 3-2). On the basis of these factors, and taking into account the greater uncertainty of the more distant future, the following percentage increases in annual traffic have been estimated:

Years	Trucks	Buses	Cars
4–7	12	10	11
8–17	8	8	10
18–22	6	6	8

No increase in traffic is allowed for after year 22 because in that year the highway's capacity of about 5,000 vehicles would have been reached and further investments would be justified (see table 3-2).

In addition to the traffic diverted from the existing road, studies of the volume of passenger and high-value freight traffic on the railway indicate that some of this traffic would be diverted to the highway. Major difficulties in estimating this volume arise because comparative transport costs do not measure properly the full distribution costs and because the railway can meet the increased competition to some extent by lowering its rates, since the railway tariffs for high-value commodities exceed costs. Allowing for such factors, daily traffic diverted from the railway in year 4 is estimated at forty trucks and five buses. No diversion of cars is anticipated since bus transport is the only practical alternative for the type of passengers using the railway on this section. The traffic diverted from the railway is estimated to increase at half the rates forecast for traffic diverted from the existing road, in line with the slower growth in railway traffic (see table 3-2).

Finally, the reduced transport costs on the new highway are expected to generate new traffic. On the basis of industrial and agricultural studies and experience with similar improvements in other areas, generated traffic is estimated to be 10 percent of the traffic diverted from the existing road in the first year after construction, 15 percent in the second year, and 20 percent in the third year. Thereafter, the generated traffic is estimated to increase at the same rate as the traffic diverted from the existing road. The traffic forecast for selected years is shown in table 3-2.

Project Benefits

The benefits of the project consist of (1) reduced vehicle operating costs on the new highway for traffic diverted from the old road, generated traffic, and traffic diverted from the railway; (2) reduced vehicle operating costs for the traffic remaining on the old road; and (3) time savings for passengers and freight. Maintenance costs on the old road might be slightly reduced, but this benefit would be minimal and has not been included in this appraisal.

Reduced Vehicle Operating Costs on the Highway

TRAFFIC DIVERTED FROM THE OLD ROAD. As indicated, average daily traffic on the existing road will reach about 1,050 vehicles in year 4, in addition to numerous animal-drawn carts, bicycles, pedestrians, and animals, and cause considerable congestion. Already, when a vehicle meets an oncoming vehicle on the two-way, one-lane roadway, the two must reduce speed and one or both must partially use the shoulders to permit passing. Similarly, passing another vehicle requires driving on the shoulder. As a result, the present travel time between the two cities is almost four hours for cars (at thirty-two miles an hour) and about five hours for trucks and buses (at twenty-four miles an hour). On the new and shorter highway this would be reduced to less than two hours for cars (at fifty miles an hour) and about two and one-quarter hours for trucks and buses (at forty miles an hour).

Studies of vehicle operations on the existing road and the new highway indicate costs per vehicle-mile as shown in table 3-3 (in paisas). The costs are net of taxes and the foreign exchange costs have been shadow priced.

Table 3-3. Vehicle Operating Costs on Old Road and New Highway
(paisas)

Cost item	Truck and bus		Car	
	Old road	New highway	Old road	New highway
Fuel and oil	60	51	21	18
Tire wear	36	24	9	6
Depreciation	81	66	36	30
Interest	39	33	24	18
Maintenance	75	51	9	6
Wages	21	15	—	—
Total	312	240	99	78
Benefit		72		21

— Not applicable.

**Table 3-4. Benefits for Traffic Diverted
from Old Road, Year 4**
(millions of rupees)

Traffic variable and vehicle	Calculation	Benefits
Shorter distance		
Truck	565 trucks × 30 miles × 365 days × 312 paisas	19.30
Bus	45 buses × 30 miles × 365 days × 312 paisas	1.53
Car	355 cars × 30 miles × 365 days × 99 paisas	3.85
Subtotal		24.68
Higher design standards		
Truck	565 trucks × 90 miles × 365 days × 72 paisas	13.36
Bus	45 buses × 90 miles × 365 days × 72 paisas	1.06
Car	355 cars × 90 miles × 365 days × 21 paisas	2.45
Subtotal		16.87
Total		41.55

The unit benefits for the traffic diverted from the existing road are thus 72 paisas per truck- and bus-mile and 21 paisas per car-mile. The traffic would also benefit from the fact that the distance on the new highway would be thirty miles shorter. The benefits for this diverted traffic in year 4 are shown in table 3-4. Of the total benefit of Rs41.6 million for this traffic, Rs24.7 million, or about 60 percent, is thus accounted for by the shorter distance and Rs16.9 million by the higher design standards of the new highway.

Although the new highway would be able to carry the future traffic without significant congestion, congestion will become increasingly serious on the existing road. Vehicle operating costs on the old road will therefore increase by an estimated 5 percent after year 4, when the average daily traffic reaches about 2,000 vehicles, and by an additional 5 percent after year 17, when the average daily traffic reaches about 4,000 vehicles. For trucks and buses this implies increases in vehicle operating costs from 312 paisas to 328 paisas and later to 344 paisas; the unit benefits increase from 72 to 88 paisas and then to 104 paisas. For cars, the unit benefits rise from 21 paisas to 26 and later to 31 paisas. The growth in benefits for traffic diverted from the old road, in line with the growth in traffic and in unit benefits, is shown in column 4 of table 3-1.

GENERATED TRAFFIC.   For generated traffic, the unit benefits are estimated to be one-half of those used for traffic diverted from the old road. (For an explanation of this assumption, see "Reduced Operating Expenses" in chapter 4). Furthermore, it is assumed that somewhat more than half of the traffic generation arises from the shorter distance and the remainder from the higher design standards; this is more or less in line with the relative benefits of these improvements. The benefits in year 4 are shown in table 3-5. The growth in these benefits in line with the growth in traffic is shown in column 5 of table 3-1.

TRAFFIC DIVERTED FROM THE RAILWAY.   The unit benefits for traffic diverted from the parallel railway are difficult to estimate because the proper comparison of the road transport costs is with the marginal railway costs and because most of the diversion is not the result of lower transport costs, but lower overall distribution costs, especially speedier and more reliable service. When allowance is made for these factors, the benefits are estimated at 15 paisas per truck- and bus-mile, or about Rs150,000 for trucks and Rs24,000 for buses in year 4. These benefits are shown in column 6 of table 3-1.

SUMMARY.   The total benefits of 42.76 million rupees in year 4 for traffic on the new highway from lower vehicle operating costs, by type of vehicle, can be summarized as follows (in millions of rupees): trucks, 33.62; buses, 2.68; and cars, 6.46. In year 4, almost 80 percent of the benefits of traffic on the new highway is thus accounted for by trucks.

Table 3-5. Benefits for Generated Traffic, Year 4

(millions of rupees)

Traffic variable and vehicle	Calculation	Benefits
Shorter distance		
Truck	30 trucks × 30 miles × 365 days × 156 paisas	0.51
Bus	3 buses × 30 miles × 365 days × 156 paisas	0.05
Car	20 cars × 30 miles × 365 days × 49.5 paisas	0.11
Subtotal		0.67
Higher design standards		
Truck	25 trucks × 90 miles × 365 days × 36 paisas	0.30
Bus	2 buses × 90 miles × 365 days × 36 paisas	0.02
Car	15 cars × 90 miles × 365 days × 10.5 paisas	0.05
Subtotal		0.37
Total		1.04

According to the source of traffic, the benefits arise as follows (in millions of rupees): diverted from the old road, 41.55; generated, 1.04; and diverted from the railway, 0.17, for a total of 42.76. The traffic diverted from the old road thus accounts for 97 percent of total benefits. Although during the life of the project the relative benefits from generated traffic increase somewhat more rapidly, the benefits for the traffic diverted from the railway decline somewhat because of the slower traffic growth, so that the traffic diverted from the old road always accounts for the overwhelming proportion of the benefits. The total benefits for the traffic on the new highway are shown in column 7 of table 3-1.

Reduced Vehicle Operating Costs on the Old Road

As indicated early in this section, the existing road is now congested. The diversion of 92 percent of the traffic to the new highway would reduce congestion on the existing road and thus benefit the remaining local traffic, which in year 4 is estimated at fifty trucks, five buses, and thirty passenger cars, or a total of eighty-five motor vehicles daily (see "Traffic"). The reduction in congestion would, however, be relatively modest because much of the congestion is caused by numerous animal-drawn carts, bicycles, pedestrians, and animals, which would remain on the old road. Nevertheless, a reduction in vehicle operating costs of 5 percent can reasonably be expected. The benefits in year 4 are calculated as follows (in millions of rupees):

$$50 \text{ trucks} \times 120 \text{ miles} \times 365 \text{ days} \times 15 \text{ paisas} = 0.33$$
$$5 \text{ buses} \times 120 \text{ miles} \times 365 \text{ days} \times 15 \text{ paisas} = 0.03$$
$$30 \text{ cars} \times 120 \text{ miles} \times 365 \text{ days} \times 5 \text{ paisas} = 0.07$$
$$\text{Total} \qquad\qquad\qquad\qquad\qquad\qquad\qquad 0.43$$

This benefit is shown in column 8 of table 3-1; it is expected to increase by 5 percent annually in line with the more modest increase of traffic on this road. The total benefits from reduced vehicle operating costs are shown in column 9.

Time Savings for Passengers and Freight

The time savings for vehicles (including truck and bus drivers) have been taken into account, but not those for passengers and freight. As indicated in "Reduced Vehicle Operating Costs on the Highway," these amount to about two and three-quarter hours for trucks and buses and two hours for passenger cars; the time savings for traffic diverted from the railway are similar. Whether the time for passengers should be allowed for depends on whether they can use the extra time for work or voluntary leisure or whether the time merely increases unemployment. In view of prevalent unemployment and underemployment, it is doubtful whether most passengers are willing to pay anything for the extra time. On the assumption that the value of time for all passengers per bus is Rs12 an hour and Rs7.5 per car (for details see case study 5, "Construction of a Bridge") and one-half of these values for generated traffic, the value of the time benefits in year 4 is about Rs600,000 for the bus passengers and Rs2,025,000 for car passengers, or a total of Rs 2,625,000. This is only about 6 percent of the benefits in that year. The benefits to freight (on assumptions also explained in case study 5) are about Rs2.7 million, or about 6 percent of total benefits. The inclusion of these highly speculative benefits thus does not affect the basic justification of the project.

The total benefits of the project for year 4 are shown in table 3-6.

Comparison of Costs and Benefits

As shown in columns 10 and 11 of table 3-1, the benefits of the proposed highway project exceed its costs—both discounted at 12 percent—by about Rs263 million during its economic life. The cost-benefit ratio is almost 1 : 1.7 and the internal rate of return is slightly more than 17 percent (see columns 12 and 13). This indicates that the project is well justified.

Because the project has a high net worth, the conclusion is not particularly sensitive to changes in any single factor. If, for example, the capital costs of the project are 25 percent higher than estimated, the net present worth of the project is still Rs171 million. The switching value for capital costs, that is, the extent to which these costs can rise so that

Table 3-6. Project Benefits in Year 4
(millions of rupees)

Cost item	Benefits
Reduction in vehicle operating costs	
For traffic on new highway	42.76
For traffic on old road	0.43
Subtotal	43.19
Time savings of passengers and freight	5.33
Total	48.52

the net present worth of the project becomes zero, is about 70 percent.

In the calculation of benefits, estimates of reductions in vehicle operating costs can be based on physical measurements and experience on other roads, so that the margin of error need not be large. Traffic forecasts, however, are inherently more speculative. In the present case, about 90 percent of the beneftis arise from traffic diverted from the old road. If the initial traffic diversion to the new road or the rate of traffic growth is less than estimated so that the benefits are 25 percent lower, the net present worth is reduced from Rs263 million to about Rs102 million, which is still substantial. The switching value for benefits is 40 percent.

If the project capital costs are 25 percent higher and the benefits 25 percent less than estimated, the project's net worth still is Rs11 million and the rate of return still exceeds 12 percent. Under these circumstances, it is highly likely that the project is justified.

If the life of the project is reduced from 30 to 20 years, and assuming no salvage value, the net present worth is still Rs146 million and the internal rate of return is 16 percent. The conclusion is therefore not sensitive to the assumption concerning the life of the project.

Construction
of a Development Road

Proposed Project

ACCESS TO A CERTAIN AREA is limited to river transport except during
the dry season, when access by foot is also possible. A few fair-weather
roads have been constructed between some market centers in the area,
but these are not motorable even in the dry season. The population
density of the area and the standard of living are low. The area has a
surplus of food, however, and is a major source of fish for the
country.

Industrial and commercial development is virtually nonexistent, but
significant potential exists for the production of limestone and other
minerals. A limestone quarry supplies the needs of a cement plant
which amount to about 400 tons a day. The cement plant is planning to
increase its output; this requires an additional 600 tons of limestone a
day. The limestone is carried about 100 miles by river to the plant. Since
transport on the inland waterways is costly, consideration is being
given to a road which will eliminate about two-thirds of the inland
water transport between the quarry and the cement plant (see figure
4-1). This part of the river is navigable for only six months of the year,
while the river from the waterhead to the cement plant is navigable the
entire year.

The project involves, therefore, the construction of a twenty-one-mile
all-weather road. The road and its bridges and culverts would have a
pavement width of eighteen feet and embankment width of thirty-two
feet and would be able to accommodate heavy truck traffic. (It is
assumed that other alternatives, such as a gravel road to be paved in
later years, are examined in other studies.)

The economic appraisal of the project consists of comparing the
costs of the road, of road transport, and of shipping limestone from
the waterhead to the cement plant with the benefits, consisting of
the savings in the costs of river transport from the limestone quarry to
the cement plant if the road is built, plus the agricultural and fishing

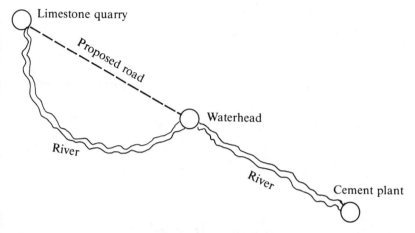

Figure 4-1. Proposed Road to River Area

benefits which the road is likely to generate. The costs and benefits are compared over the estimated twenty-year economic life of the road.

Costs of Road and Road Transport

Capital Costs

The capital costs of constructing the road and carrying the limestone from the quarry to the cement plant consist of the costs of the road, the trucks to carry the limestone from the quarry to the waterhead, a jetty at the waterhead, a grab to transfer the limestone from the trucks to the barges, and tugs and barges to carry the limestone from the waterhead to the cement plant. The costs of a jetty at the cement plant and of equipment to unload the barges are not included because they are the same whether or not the road is built.

The financial costs of the road are estimated at Rs108 million. To calculate economic cost, three adjustments are necessary. First, taxes of Rs9.0 million must be deducted. Second, a shadow rate of 1.75 times the official exchange rate should be applied to the Rs30 million foreign exchange component of the project. This adjustment increases these costs from Rs30 million to Rs52.5 million, or by Rs22.5 million. Since the area suffers from widespread unemployment and underemployment, however, it is appropriate to apply a shadow rate of 50 percent to the wages of unskilled labor used in the project. This reduces the costs for

Table 4-1. Comparison of Costs and Benefits of a Development Road

(millions of rupees)

Year	Costs					Benefits		
							Avoided inland waterway costs	
	Road (1)	Equipment (2)	Road maintenance (3)	Operating costs (4)	Total costs (5)	Capital expansion (6)	Replacement (7)	Operating (8)
1	36.00	0	0	0	36.00	0	0	0
2	45.00	0	0	0	45.00	0	0	0
3	29.40	21.78	0	0	51.18	48.00	0	0
4	0	0	0.33	5.15	5.48	0	0	7.80
5	0	0	0.36	5.15	5.51	0	0	7.80
6	0	0	0.39	5.15	5.54	0	0	7.80
7	0	0	0.42	5.15	5.57	0	0	7.80
8	0	1.08	0.45	5.15	6.68	0	0	7.80
9	0	0	0.48	5.15	5.63	0	0	7.80
10	0	0	0.51	5.15	5.66	0	33.60	7.80
11	0	0	0.54	5.15	5.69	0	0	7.50
12	0	0	0.57	5.15	5.72	0	0	7.50
13	0	10.38	0.60	5.15	16.13	26.10	0	7.50
14	0	0	0.63	5.15	5.78	0	0	7.50
15	0	0	0.66	5.15	5.81	0	0	7.50
16	0	0	0.69	5.15	5.84	0	0	7.50
17	0	0	0.72	5.15	5.87	0	0	7.50
18	0	11.88	0.75	5.15	17.78	21.00	0	7.50
19	0	0	0.78	5.15	5.93	0	0	7.50
20	0	0	0.81	5.15	5.96	0	18.60	7.50
21	0	0	0.84	5.15	5.99	0	0	7.50
22	0	0	0.87	5.15	6.02	0	0	7.50
23	0	0	0.90	5.15	6.05	0	0	7.50
24	0	−5.40	0	0	−5.40	−10.50	−9.30	0
Total								

Note: Net present worth equals −Rs13.91 million; this is the difference between columns 13 and 14.

Benefits				Present worth (discounted at 12 percent)		Internal rate of return (discounted at 10 percent)	
Agriculture benefits		Fishing benefits (11)	Total benefits (12)	Costs (13)	Benefits (14)	Costs (15)	Benefits (16)
Paddy (9)	Fruits (10)						
0	0	0	0	36.00	0	36.00	0
0	0	0	0	40.19	0	40.91	0
0	0	0	48.00	40.79	38.26	42.27	39.65
2.40	0.30	0.39	10.89	3.90	7.75	4.12	8.18
3.30	0.60	0.42	12.12	3.50	7.71	3.76	8.28
4.00	0.96	0.45	13.11	3.14	7.43	3.44	8.14
4.02	0.99	0.48	13.29	2.82	6.74	3.14	7.50
4.14	1.02	0.51	13.47	3.02	6.09	3.43	6.91
4.26	1.05	0.54	13.65	2.27	5.51	2.63	6.37
4.38	1.08	0.57	47.43	2.04	17.12	2.40	20.11
4.53	1.11	0.60	13.74	1.83	4.42	2.20	5.30
4.68	1.14	0.63	13.95	1.64	4.00	2.00	4.88
4.83	1.17	0.66	40.26	4.15	10.35	5.15	12.84
4.98	1.20	0.69	14.37	1.32	3.29	1.68	4.17
5.16	1.23	0.72	14.61	1.19	3.00	1.53	3.84
5.34	1.26	0.75	14.85	1.07	2.72	1.40	3.55
5.52	1.29	0.78	15.09	0.96	2.46	1.28	3.29
5.70	1.32	0.81	36.33	2.60	5.30	3.52	7.19
5.88	1.35	0.84	15.57	0.77	2.02	1.07	2.80
6.06	1.38	0.87	34.41	0.69	3.99	0.98	5.64
6.27	1.41	0.90	16.08	0.62	1.67	0.89	2.40
6.48	1.44	0.93	16.35	0.56	1.52	0.81	2.21
6.69	1.47	0.96	16.62	0.50	1.38	0.74	2.04
0	0	0	−19.80	−0.40	−1.47	−0.60	−2.22
				155.17	141.26	164.75	163.07

such labor from Rs22.2 million to Rs11.1 million. The net result of these three adjustments is that the economic cost of the road is Rs110.4 million, (Rs108 million − Rs9 million + Rs22.5 million − Rs11.1 million). These costs are incurred during a three-year period (see column 1 of table 4-1).

To carry the 1,000 tons of limestone daily a distance of twenty-one miles requires about eleven 15-ton dump trucks. With eight return trips each sixteen-hour day, one 15-ton truck could carry 120 tons a day, so that eight to nine trucks are required, plus a reserve of two to three trucks. Their cost, shadow priced to allow for the fact that the entire cost is in foreign exchange but net of all taxes, is about Rs99,000 a truck, or Rs1.09 million for the fleet of eleven trucks. They are estimated to have an economic life of only five years because of their intensive utilization.

The economic cost of the jetty at the waterhead, with a capacity for three barges, is estimated at Rs0.6 million, with an economic life of twenty years. The economic cost of a mechanical grab (with a capacity of eighty tons per hour) to load the limestone on the barges is estimated at Rs1.8 million, with an economic life of ten years.

The economic cost of two tugs is estimated at Rs7.5 million and of six 500-ton barges at Rs10.8 million. The useful life of a tug is about ten years and of a barge, fifteen years; a salvage value of one-half of their original cost has been put on those barges which are procured at the end of the fifteenth year.

The initial capital costs (in millions of rupees), excluding the road, are trucks, 1.08; jetty, 0.60; grab, 1.80; tugs and barges, 18.30, for a total of 21.78. These costs, as well as the periodic replacement costs and the salvage value of the barges, are shown in column 2 of table 4-1.

Operating Costs

The operating costs of transporting the limestone by road (with the waterway), net of taxes and shadow priced for their foreign exchange and unskilled labor components, follow: the annual maintenance costs of the road are about Rs18,000 a mile, or Rs378,000 for the twenty-one-mile road. Of this, about 15 percent (or about Rs57,000) is in foreign exchange, so that at a foreign exchange shadow rate of 1.75 times the official rate, the economic costs are an additional Rs43,000. About one-half of the maintenance costs is accounted for by unskilled labor, whose economic cost is only one-half of the wages paid. This reduces annual economic maintenance costs by about Rs90,000. The annual maintenance costs are therefore Rs331,000 (Rs378,000 − Rs90,000 + Rs

43,000). These costs are estimated to rise gradually because of the growth of traffic and because the shadow price for labor is likely to increase in time and approach actual wages as employment opportunities in the area become more ample (see column 3 of table 4-1).

The estimated operating costs for the equipment and the jetty are shown in table 4-2. These costs are shown in column 4 of table 4-1, and the total costs of the road and road transport alternative in column 5.

Costs of Water Transport

The alternative to the road (with the waterway) is to continue the present inland water transport but to enlarge its capacity from 400 tons of limestone a day to the required 1,000 tons. The following analysis deals with the capital costs of this expansion, the capital replacement costs for the existing equipment, and the operating costs for both.

Capital Costs for Expansion

The investments required to expand the daily output by 600 tons consist of barges, tugs, grabs, and a jetty. Under the weather conditions prevailing in the area, reasonably reliable transport between the limestone quarry and the waterhead is possible for only six months of the year. This requires daily shipments of about 1,200 tons during this period. Since the most suitable barge has a capacity of 350 tons, there are about three and one-half barge loads a day. The round trip is estimated to take four days, so that fourteen barges are required. Of these, about ten are traveling and four berthed at any time. Since a tug can pull two

Table 4-2. Estimated Operating Costs of Equipment and Jetty
(millions of rupees)

Item	Expenditures	Costs
Trucks	9 trucks × 340 miles a day × 300 days × Rs3.48 a mile	3.20
Jetty	Maintenance	0.06
Grab	Fuel, lubricants, maintenance, and labor	0.33
Tugs and barges	Fuel, lubricants, maintenance, and labor	1.56
Total		5.15

barges, five tugs are required for continuous operation, with a sixth required for standby. The economic cost of fourteen barges is estimated at Rs21.0 million and of six tugs at Rs22.5 million. Two grabs, estimated to cost Rs3.6 million, are required to load the barges, and a jetty adequate to handle four barges costs 0.9 million. The total initial capital costs are thus Rs48 million. These, the periodic replacements for them, and the salvage value of the barges at the end of the project life are shown in column 6 of table 4-1.

Capital Replacement Costs for Existing Equipment

The equipment currently in use to transport the daily requirements of 400 tons could not be used for other purposes and must be replaced in about nine years. It is assumed that it will be replaced by the identical equipment used for the expansion already discussed. The costs, estimated in the same manner as described, consist of ten barges (Rs15 million), four tugs (Rs15 million), and two grabs (Rs3.6 million), or a total of Rs33.6 million. These costs, the replacements required in future years, and the salvage value are shown in column 7 of table 4-1.

Operating Costs

The annual operating costs of Rs7.5 million for the inland water transport alternative are estimated as follows (in millions of rupees):

Item	Expenditures	Costs
Tugs and barges	Fuel, lubricants, maintenance, labor	6.60
Grab	Fuel, lubricants, maintenance, labor	0.75
Jetty	Maintenance	0.15

Because some of the shipments in the early years use older equipment, the costs in these years are estimated at Rs7.8 million (see column 8 of table 4-1).

Development Benefits

The construction of the road, in addition to eliminating part of the water transport of limestone, is expected to have three major developmental benefits. First, it will lead to an increase of paddy production. Second, it will result in greater output of fruits and vegetables. And third, it will permit the marketing of more valuable fresh fish instead of dried fish.

Increased Paddy Production

Production of paddy in the immediate vicinity of the proposed road is estimated at 24,000 tons a year. Increasing this production requires improved seeds, application of fertilizers, use of low-lift pumps for irrigation, agricultural extension service, and so forth. On the basis of experience in areas with similar conditions, agricultural experts estimate that without a road these measures would increase output 10 percent within three years; with the road output would be increased by 20 percent, or an additional 2,400 tons.

The average wholesale price of rice in the area is Rs3,300 per ton, so that the gross value of the additional output of 2,400 tons is Rs7.9 million. To determine the net benefit, the additional costs of production and distribution must be deducted. On the basis of studies conducted on agricultural improvement projects in the area, these costs are estimated at one-half of the additional output. The net benefit is therefore Rs4.0 million, which is expected to be reached in three years and to increase 3.5 percent annually (see column 9 of table 4-1).

Increased Output of Fruits and Vegetables

Although fruits and vegetables are grown in the area, they are not sold commercially because they are too perishable to be brought to the markets. Agricultural experts estimate that if the road is constructed, 500 acres near the road will be used for the production of fruits, especially bananas, and vegetables. The annual yield per acre is estimated at 200 maunds in the case of bananas (one maund equals eighty-two pounds) and 75 maunds for other fruits and vegetables; a weighted average is about 85 maunds. The weighted average wholesale price is Rs45 a maund, so that the gross value of the output is about Rs1,912,500 (500 acres × 85 maunds × Rs45). Production costs account for about one-half of this, so that the net value of the output is Rs956,250. This output should be reached in three years and thereafter increase gradually (column 10 of table 4-1).

Fishing Benefits

The area adjacent to the proposed road is a productive inland fishing region. The annual catch consists of about 25,000 maunds of carp and other large fish and 25,000 maunds of smaller fish. The wholesale price of fish during the fishing season (January–March) is approximately Rs120 a maund for carp and Rs60 a maund for small fish, or on the average Rs90 a maund. During the off-season months, the price is about twice as much, but little fish is then available. The price for dry fish is about Rs300 a maund all year round. One maund of dry fish, however, requires five maunds of fresh fish. Since five maunds of fresh fish sell for Rs450, it is more profitable to sell it fresh than to dry it.

The only acess from the fisheries to the urban market areas is by country boat through devious river routes to a rail or road head and from there to the market by train or truck. Because of the long time involved in river transport, a large amount of fish must be dried and then transported in this less perishable form to the markets.

The proportion of fish that is dried each year ranges from 25 to 40 percent. Since the proposed road will provide rapid access to markets, nearly all of this fish can be sold as fresh instead of being dried. The benefit to the fishing industry due to the construction of the road consists therefore of this conversion from dry fish to fresh fish marketing.

It is reasonable to assume that of the present annual catch of 50,000 maunds, at least 12,500 maunds will not be dried but will be sold as fresh fish if the road is constructed. The value of 12,500 maunds of fresh fish, at Rs90 per maund, is Rs1,125,000. Drying the fish reduces the weight from 12,500 to 2,500 maunds. The net income per maund of dried fish is Rs270 (allowing Rs30 a maund for the cost of drying), so that the net income from the sale of the 2,500 maunds of dried fish is only Rs675,000, compared with Rs1,125,000 for fresh fish. Thus the total annual benefit from shipping fresh fish rather than dried fish is Rs450,000.

In the calculations presented in column 11 of table 4-1, it is assumed that the changeover from the sale of dried to fresh fish will be gradual, that the annual benefit level of Rs450,000 will be reached in the third year, and that it will increase in line with past experience. The total benefits of the project are shown in column 12.

Comparison of Costs and Benefits

As shown in columns 13 and 14 of table 4-1, the costs of the proposed road project exceed the benefits—both discounted at 12 percent—by about Rs13.9 million during its economic life. The cost-benefit ratio is 1 : 0.9 and the internal rate of return is nearly 10 percent (see columns 15 and 16). The project therefore appears to be of doubtful justification, but for the following reasons deserves careful attention, nevertheless.

The conclusion of the analysis is particularly sensitive to the capital costs of the road project. If, for example, it is possible to reduce the design standard of the road and thus reduce its construction costs by 20 percent without significantly affecting benefits, the net present worth of the project will increase by about Rs20 million and become positive. The possibility of lower design standards for the road therefore deserves careful review.

The conclusion is less sensitive to changes in the costs of equipment because these costs would affect to some extent both costs and benefits; in any case, the price of equipment can usually be determined with a greater degree of accuracy than the cost of construction. If it is possible to operate on the inland waterways between the limestone quarry and the waterhead less than six months per year, however, more equipment will be needed to carry the same annual volume of limestone during a shorter period. If, for example, it is possible to operate only four to five months, capital costs will go up by about one-fifth and the road project will become justified. The conclusion is therefore sensitive to the number of months during which the waterways are navigable.

The forecast of agricultural and fishing benefits is inherently uncertain. If the output is 30 percent higher, the net present worth of the project becomes positive at 12 percent and the project becomes justified. In estimating these benefits, however, it has been assumed that the increased production does not lower prices; if it does, benefits also are less.

Finally, the project is sensitive to the discount rate selected since benefits would exceed costs at a rate slightly below 10 percent.

In view of these considerations, it may be entirely possible with certain modification in the project—especially somewhat lower design standards for the road—to turn it into a viable project.

Construction of a Bridge

Proposed Project and Costs

SERVICE ACROSS a 1,000-foot-wide river is provided by a small ferry. Construction of a 1,660-foot-long, two-lane bridge and elimination of the ferry service have been proposed. The bridge would be part of a larger project to improve the adjoining highway. There is no other ferry service or bridge in the area.

The construction costs of the bridge are estimated at Rs42 million, of which Rs6 million is accounted for by taxes. With a foreign exchange component of Rs24 million and a shadow rate for foreign exchange of 1.75 times the official rate, the economic cost of the bridge would be Rs54 million. Construction is estimated to take four years (see column 1 of table 5-1). The annual maintenance costs are estimated at Rs105,000; after allowance for some foreign exchange costs and taxes, the economic costs are about Rs120,000, rising in time to Rs150,000 with growing traffic (see column 2). The estimated economic life of the bridge is fifty years, with no salvage value. The total costs of the bridge are shown in column 3.

Traffic

Current daily ferry traffic of about 100 vehicles does not adequately indicate the level of traffic if a bridge were constructed since traffic on the adjoining roads is much higher and the ferry service imposes considerable delays. Traffic on the existing ferry has been increasing by about 15 percent annually in recent years. Taking into account traffic growth, traffic on adjoining roads, and probable industrial and commercial development on the riverbank which the bridge would encourage, average daily traffic in the opening year of the bridge (year 5) is estimated at 900 vehicles. Of the increase of 800, about 100 vehicles represent the normal traffic growth in any case and 700 vehicles the volume generated by the proposed bridge.

Table 5-1. Comparison of Costs and Benefits of Construction of a Bridge

(millions of rupees)

| | | Costs | | | Benefits | | Present worth (discounted at 12 percent) | |
| | | | | | Reduced cost of | | | |
Year	Capital costs (1)	Mainte-nance costs (2)	Total costs (3)	Elimi-nated ferry costs (4)	delay (vehicles and drivers) (5)	Total benefits (6)	Costs (7)	Benefits (8)
1	9.00	0	9.00	0	0	0	9.00	0
2	15.00	0	15.00	0	0	0	13.40	0
3	15.00	0	15.00	0	0	0	11.96	0
4	15.00	0	15.00	0	0	0	10.68	0
5	0	0.12	0.12	14.55	1.06	15.61	0.08	9.93
6	0	0.12	0.12	2.25	1.25	3.50	0.07	1.98
7	0	0.12	0.12	2.25	1.50	3.75	0.06	1.90
8	0	0.12	0.12	2.25	1.75	4.00	0.05	1.81
9	0	0.12	0.12	2.25	2.00	4.25	0.05	1.72
10	0	0.12	0.12	8.70	2.16	10.86	0.04	3.92
11	0	0.12	0.12	3.30	2.45	5.75	0.04	1.85
12	0	0.12	0.12	3.30	2.75	6.05	0.03	1.74
13	0	0.12	0.12	3.30	3.00	6.30	0.03	1.62
14	0	0.12	0.12	11.40	3.25	14.65	0.03	3.35
15	0	0.12	0.12	4.50	3.52	8.02		1.64
16	0	0.12	0.12	4.50	4.00	8.50		1.56
17	0	0.12	0.12	10.95	4.50	15.45		2.52
18	0	0.12	0.12	5.55	5.00	10.55		1.54
19	0	0.12	0.12	5.55	5.50	11.05	0.18	1.44
20	0	0.12	0.12	12.00	6.00	18.00		2.09
21	0	0.12	0.12	6.60	6.50	13.10		1.36
22	0	0.12	0.12	6.60	7.00	13.60		1.26
23	0	0.12	0.12	6.60	7.50	14.10		1.17

(Table continues on the following page.)

Table 5-1 *(continued)*

Year	Capital costs (1)	Maintenance costs (2)	Total costs (3)	Eliminated ferry costs (4)	Reduced cost of delay (vehicles and drivers) (5)	Total benefits (6)	Costs (7)	Benefits (8)
		Costs			Benefits		Present worth (discounted at 12 percent)	
24	0	0.15	0.15	6.60	7.95	14.55		1.08
25	0	0.15	0.15	18.90	7.95	26.85		1.77
26	0	0.15	0.15	6.60	7.95	14.55		0.86
27	0	0.15	0.15	6.60	7.95	14.55		0.77
28	0	0.15	0.15	6.60	7.95	14.55		0.68
29	0	0.15	0.15	6.60	7.95	14.55		0.61
30	0	0.15	0.15	12.00	7.95	19.95		0.74
31	0	0.15	0.15	6.60	7.95	14.55		0.48
32	0	0.15	0.15	6.60	7.95	14.55		0.44
33	0	0.15	0.15	6.60	7.95	14.55		0.39
34	0	0.15	0.15	13.50	7.95	21.45		0.51
35	0	0.15	0.15	6.60	7.95	14.55		0.31
36	0	0.15	0.15	6.60	7.95	14.55		0.28
37	0	0.15	0.15	12.00	7.95	19.95		0.34
38	0	0.15	0.15	6.60	7.95	14.55		0.22
39	0	0.15	0.15	6.60	7.95	14.55	0.06	0.19
40	0	0.15	0.15	12.00	7.95	19.95		0.24
41	0	0.15	0.15	6.60	7.95	14.55		0.16
42	0	0.15	0.15	6.60	7.95	14.55		0.15
43	0	0.15	0.15	6.60	7.95	14.55		0.13
44	0	0.15	0.15	6.60	7.95	14.55		0.12
45	0	0.15	0.15	15.90	7.95	23.85		0.17
46	0	0.15	0.15	6.60	7.95	14.55		0.09
47	0	0.15	0.15	6.60	7.95	14.55		0.07
48	0	0.15	0.15	6.60	7.95	14.55		0.06
49	0	0.15	0.15	6.60	7.95	14.55		0.06
50	0	0.15	0.15	12.00	7.95	19.95		0.06
51	0	0.15	0.15	6.60	7.95	14.55		0.04
52	0	0.15	0.15	6.60	7.95	14.55		0.04
53	0	0.15	0.15	6.60	7.95	14.55		0.03
54	0	0.15	0.15	6.60	7.95	14.55		0.03
55	0	0.15	0.15	−15.00	7.95	−15.00		−0.02
Total						45.76		55.50

Note: The net present worth equals Rs9.74 million; this is the difference between columns 7 and 8.

After year 5, the following annual rates of traffic increase are estimated (in percentages), taking into account the growth of population and of agricultural and industrial production in the area and assumed relationships between them and road transport:

Years	Trucks	Buses	Cars
5–10	20	10	15
10–15	10	7	10
15–24	10	7	10

These increases are more or less in line with past traffic growth and make no allowance for traffic generation beyond that estimated with the opening of the bridge. Traffic is assumed to remain at the year 24 level for the remaining thirty-year life of the bridge since the traffic would reach the bridge's capacity in that year and further investments would be required. The forecast of average daily traffic for selected years is shown in table 5-2.

Project Benefits

The economic appraisal consists primarily of determining the least-cost solution to the problem of moving traffic across the river. The two alternatives, bridge and ferry, differ not only in capital and operating costs, but also in the quality of service in that the ferry takes more time and is less convenient. As a result, the traffic levels would, in fact, differ substantially under the two alternatives. To allow for this difference, it is desirable to measure the net value of the traffic generated by the bridge. Because data to do so directly are not available, the approach

Table 5-2. Forecast of Average Daily Traffic for Selected Years

	Trucks		Buses		Cars		
Year	Normal traffic	Generated traffic	Normal traffic	Generated traffic	Normal traffic	Generated traffic	Total
0	35	—	15	—	50	—	100
5	70	180	30	90	100	430	900
10	170	430	50	150	200	800	1,800
15	280	720	70	210	340	1,360	2,980
24	640	1,660	130	400	800	3,200	6,830

— Not applicable.

here is based on comparing the costs of the estimated traffic on the bridge with the costs of ferry service, including the costs of delay.

The benefits of the bridge consist primarily of the avoidance of the ferry capital and operating costs and the elimination of delays for vehicles, drivers, passengers, and freight.

Ferry Costs

The appraisal assumes specifically designed tug and barge-type ferries, each with a capacity of twenty-two vehicles (assuming the vehicle composition presented in table 5-2). At four crossings an hour each ferry has an hourly capacity of eighty-eight vehicles. No standby ferries are assumed since all ferries would be fully employed only during peak hours. Taking into account the hourly distribution of traffic, the number of ferries needed increases gradually: 2, year 5; 3, year 10; 4, year 14; 5, year 17; and 6, year 20.

The capital costs of one ferry barge and tug are estimated at Rs3.6 million (net of taxes); with a 75 percent foreign exchange component and a shadow rate for foreign exchange of 1.75 times the official rate, the economic costs are Rs5.6 million. The economic life of a ferry is estimated to be twenty years. The annual operating costs of a ferry (net of taxes) are estimated as follows (in thousands of rupees): ferry maintenance, 360; fuel, 390; and wages, 150, for a total of 900. With a foreign exchange component of about 25 percent (especially for fuel and spare parts), total economic operating costs are about Rs1,050,000.

The cost of two terminals (including access) is estimated at Rs1.5 million and their annual maintenance at Rs150,000, with no significant foreign exchange component. The number of terminals would have to be increased from one on each riverbank initially to two in year 14. The estimated economic life of the terminals is twenty years.

The annual economic costs of ferry service in the first twenty-five years after construction of the bridge are shown in table 5-3.

The costs for the life of the project are shown in column 4 of table 5-1. The salvage value of the six ferries at the end of the project life is assumed to be somewhat less than half their cost, or about Rs15 million.

The operating costs for motor vehicles are about the same for the bridge and ferry alternatives. Although the bridge would involve driving an additional 1,000 feet, the ferry requires vehicles to slow twice to a stop and then accelerate to resume their previous speed; these two costs more or less offset each other.

Table 5-3. Annual Economic Costs of Ferry Service
(millions of rupees)

Years	Capital costs		Operating costs		Total costs
	Ferry	Terminal	Ferry	Terminal	
5	10.8	1.5	2.10	0.15	14.55
6–9	0	0	2.10	0.15	2.25
10	5.4	0	3.15	0.15	8.70
11–13	0	0	3.15	0.15	3.30
14	5.4	1.5	4.20	0.30	11.40
15–16	0	0	4.20	0.30	4.50
17	5.4	0	5.25	0.30	10.95
18–19	0	0	5.25	0.30	5.55
20	5.4	0	6.30	0.30	12.00
21–24	0	0	6.30	0.30	6.60
25	10.8	1.5	6.30	0.30	18.90
26–29	0	0	6.30	0.30	6.60
30	5.4	0	6.30	0.30	12.00

Elimination of Delay

Assuming reasonably efficient ferry service, the difference between it and the drive across the proposed bridge is about twenty minutes. This involves capital costs for vehicles, wages for bus and truck drivers, and time savings for passengers and freight.

VEHICLES.   At year 5 traffic levels, the annual time savings for the normal traffic are as follows:

$$70 \text{ trucks} \times 360 \text{ days} \times \tfrac{1}{3} \text{ hour} = 8{,}400 \text{ hours}$$
$$30 \text{ buses} \times 360 \text{ days} \times \tfrac{1}{3} \text{ hour} = 3{,}600 \text{ hours}$$
$$100 \text{ cars} \times 360 \text{ days} \times \tfrac{1}{3} \text{ hour} = 12{,}000 \text{ hours}$$

The effective utilization of either a bus or truck under the conditions prevailing in the country is about 7,000 hours during its economic life; this is the equivalent of a lifetime mileage of 210,000 miles, assuming an average speed in intercity traffic of thirty miles an hour. The delay calculated for year 5 involves the equivalent of 1.2 trucks or 0.5 buses. At about Rs105,000 per truck and Rs135,000 per bus—both net of taxes but with a shadow rate for foreign exchange—this involves a cost of Rs126,000 for trucks and Rs68,000 for buses. Assuming an effective utilization of 4,000 hours for cars during their economic life, the cost of the delay in year 5 is the equivalent of about three vehicles, with a value

Table 5-4. Benefits from Reduction in Delay

Traffic and vehicle	Calculation	Benefits
Generated		
Truck	180 trucks × 360 days × 1/3 hour ÷ 2 ÷ 7,000 hours × Rs104,700	Rs162,000
Bus	90 buses × 360 days × 1/3 hour ÷ 2 ÷ 7,000 hours × Rs135,500	Rs105,000
Car	430 cars × 360 days × 1/3 hour ÷ 2 ÷ 4,000 hours × Rs45,100	Rs291,000
Subtotal		Rs558,000
Normal		
Subtotal		Rs329,000
Total, all traffic		Rs887,000

of about Rs45,000 each (considering that some of these vehicles are auto-rickshaws and motorcycles). The total delay for normal traffic in year 5 therefore involves a capital cost for vehicles of Rs329,000.

Additional traffic is assumed to be generated in proportion to the reduction in transit time, so that the unit benefits for generated traffic are only one-half of those for normal traffic (table 5-4). The cost of delay increases after year 5 in proportion to the traffic growth.

DRIVERS. The wages of bus and truck drivers are a reasonable indication of the costs of delay for them. Since drivers are moderately skilled workers, no shadow wages are applied. Hourly wage costs per truck and bus are assumed to be Rs6; this includes the wages of the driver as well as an allowance for a conductor on buses and an assistant on trucks. The benefits for normal and generated traffic are given in table 5-5. The cost of delay for drivers and assistants is about Rs170,000 in year 5 and increases in line with the traffic growth.

PASSENGERS AND FREIGHT. Whether the time of passengers should be allowed for depends on whether they can use the extra time for work or voluntary leisure or whether the time merely increases unemployment. In view of the large-scale unemployment in the area, it is doubtful whether most passengers are willing to pay anything for the extra time. Their valuation of the time saving also depends on whether the twenty-minute saving is part of a long trip, in which case it might make little difference to them, or part of a short trip, in which case it might be valued more. The following calculations indicate the magnitude of benefits in year 5.

For buses, an average of twenty-five passengers is estimated, of which one-fourth earn an average of Rs380 a month, or about Rs1.96 an hour; the value of time for each bus load is then Rs12 an hour. For the delay of 3,600 hours for normal traffic, this involves a benefit of somewhat more than Rs43,000 in year 5; for the delay of 10,800 hours for generated traffic, and assuming one-half the unit benefits, the annual benefits are about Rs65,000.

For cars, it is estimated that every second vehicle carries one passenger with an income of Rs3,000 a month, or Rs15 an hour, making the value per average car-hour saved Rs7.5. For the 12,000 hours' delay for normal traffic, this involves a cost of Rs90,000; for the generated traffic, the delay of about 50,000 hours involves a cost of Rs187,500.

The total time savings for passengers in buses and cars thus amount to about Rs390,000 in year 5.

Finally, there are the time benefits to freight. Since no information is available on the nature of the commodities or the value of time to shippers, any estimate is essentially a guess. Nevertheless, to indicate possible magnitudes, it is assumed that each truck carries three tons and that shippers are willing to pay Rs1.50 per ton-hour saved (see "Time Savings" in chapter 4). For the 8,400 hours of delay of normal traffic, this implies a cost of somewhat less than Rs38,000; for the 21,600 hours of delay for generated traffic, it implies a cost of about Rs49,000. The total benefit to freight thus is about Rs90,000.

The total benefits from the elimination of delay in year 5 are summarized as follows (in rupees): vehicles, 887,000, and drivers, 170,000,

Table 5-5. Benefits for Drivers from Reduction in Delay

Traffic and vehicle	Calculation	Benefits
Normal		
Trucks	8,400 hours × Rs6	Rs50,400
Buses	3,600 hours × Rs6	Rs21,600
Subtotal		Rs72,000
Generated		
Trucks	21,600 hours ÷ 2 × Rs6	Rs64,800
Buses	10,800 hours ÷ 2 × Rs6	Rs32,400
Subtotal		Rs97,200
Total (rounded)		Rs170,000

for a subtotal of 1,057,000; passengers, 390,000, and freight, 90,000, for a subtotal of 480,000; the total is 1,537,000. Since the annual benefits from the elimination of ferry service in the first ten years after the bridge opens average Rs7.5 million (Rs.5.4 million for the cost of ferries and Rs2.1 million for the elimination of delay for vehicles and drivers), the inclusion of the highly speculative values for passenger and freight time does not significantly affect the justification for the project; they are, therefore, not considered in the appraisal (see column 5 of table 5-1).

Comparison of Costs and Benefits

As shown in columns 7 and 8 of table 5-1, the benefits of the proposed bridge exceed the costs—both discounted at 12 percent—by Rs9.7 million during its economic life of fifty years; the cost-benefit ratio is 1 : 1.21 and the internal rate of return is about 14 percent. Subject to the following reservations, the project appears justified.

Since the net present value of the project is relatively small, the justification for the project is sensitive to any important adverse factor. As usual, one of the primary considerations is the capital cost of the project. If, for example, the actual cost is 25 percent higher than estimated, the present worth is reduced from Rs9.7 million to a negative Rs1.5 million. Such an increase in costs equals one-fifth of the total discounted benefits during the fifty years. The justification for the bridge should therefore be reviewed after firm bids have been received.

The costs of a ferry can be determined with a reasonable degree of accuracy, especially if similar ferries have recently been procured. In any case, the conclusion is less sensitive to the ferry costs than to the bridge costs since ferries are a more divisible investment and can, therefore, be procured over time. If, for example, the cost of the ferries is 25 percent higher than estimated, their discounted cost during the fifty-year life of the project increases by Rs3.3 million, compared with an increase of Rs11.3 million if the bridge costs are 25 percent higher.

The traffic forecast presents a special problem in this case because an estimated three-quarters of the traffic is generated and it is difficult to make firm estimates of traffic generation. The seriousness of this problem is reduced only slightly by the fact that no traffic increase is assumed after year 24 and no allowance is made in the benefit estimates for time savings of passengers and freight. Unless daily traffic averages 800 vehicles, construction of the bridge is premature. At a cost of capital of 12 percent annually, this could be an expensive mistake.

With allowance for the time benefits of passengers and freight, however, the internal rate of return is 15 percent, which strengthens the justification somewhat.

In reference to the traffic forecast, the appraisal does not deal with the desirability of tolls despite the implicit assumption of neither bridge nor ferry tolls. Tolls reduce the volume of traffic to some extent. Since this increases the costs of the bridge somewhat (primarily for toll collection facilities) while reducing the costs of ferry service, the bridge then is no longer justified until the traffic level with tolls rises to somewhat more than 800 vehicles a day.

The case study assumes reasonably efficient ferry service. Whether this can be achieved deserves careful review. If the ferries cannot be operated properly because of inadequate maintenance and missing spare parts, for example, ferry service may be more costly than anticipated. The bridge would not involve similar managerial problems.

The case also illustrates the fact that at high discount rates, the life of the project beyond thirty—or even twenty—years is relatively unimportant. Of the discounted costs of the project of 45.76 million, Rs45.39 million would be incurred within the first ten years. The situation is somewhat less extreme on the benefit side. Nevertheless, assuming a life of thirty instead of fifty years reduces discounted benefits only from Rs55.50 million to Rs53.04 million, or by 4 percent; a life of twenty years reduces them to Rs47.25 million. Any salvage value at the end of the project life is, therefore, also unimportant.

A Highway Maintenance Program

Proposed Program

THE HIGHWAY DEPARTMENT wants to establish an overall ten-year maintenance program for the highway network based on economic costs and benefits. As a first step, three alternative maintenance policies are defined: a good, a fair, and a minimum policy. They represent varying levels of maintenance expenditure and result in different road surface conditions. The policies are based on a combination of routine and periodic maintenance activities for four different road surfaces: concrete asphalt, double surface treatment, gravel, and earth roads. The maintenance activities include cleaning ditches, cleaning drainage channels and structures, cutting grass and brush, repairing and grading the surface, replenishing materials, repairing and reshaping the shoulder, repairing pavement and sealing, and applying single surface treatment and overlay of concrete asphalt.

The difference between the policies is the frequency with which each activity is performed for a section of road. The frequency matrices are based on studies in other developing countries, the Highway Design and Maintenance Standards Model (developed by the Massachusetts Institute of Technology, the Transport and Road Research Laboratory, and the World Bank), the structural characteristics of the country's road network, climatic and soil conditions, and traffic characteristics. For example, the annual frequencies for cleaning ditches for the three maintenance policies are given in table 6-1.

The frequency matrices are related to the condition of the road surface so that, for a given maintenance level, the surface condition of the road section can be ascertained. The indicator of surface quality is road roughness, which is based on a recording of road distortions measured in millimeters per kilometer. Surface quality is a crucial factor in estimating vehicle operating costs; the reduction of such costs is the main benefit of better maintenance. The roughness factors which correspond to the three maintenance policies are shown in table 6-2.

Table 6-1. Annual Frequencies for Cleaning Ditches, by Maintenance Policy

	Maintenance policy		
Average daily traffic	*Good*	*Fair*	*Minimum*
0–24	3	1	0
25–50	4	2	1
51–100	5	3	1
More than 100	6	4	2

Road Network and Traffic

On the basis of a detailed inventory of the road network, roads are classified according to the four types of surface and three conditions of the surface: good, fair and minimum (see table 6-3). The existing network is further subdivided according to ranges of traffic volumes: three ranges for asphalt concrete roads, two ranges for double surface treatment roads, and four ranges each for gravel and earth roads. An average traffic volume (weighted by the number of vehicles of each type) is calculated to represent the typical level of average daily traffic within each range. For purposes of the economic evaluation, two typical distributions of vehicle types are applied: one for paved roads and one for unpaved roads; the main difference is that heavy trucks are limited to paved roads.

Table 6-2. Road Roughness by Type of Road Surface

Surface	*Maintenance policy*	*Road roughness (millimeters/kilometers)*
Concrete asphalt	Good	3,000
Double surface treatment	Fair	4,000
	Minimum	4,500
Gravel	Good	6,000
	Fair	9,000
	Minimum	12,000
Earth	Good	8,000
	Fair	10,000
	Minimum	13,000

Table 6-3. Inventory of Existing Road Network by Type of Road Surface, Traffic Level, and Surface Condition

Road surface	Average daily traffic	Condition (kilometers)			
		Good	Fair	Minimum	Total
Concrete asphalt	649	171	161	93	425
	1,757	523	176	59	758
	4,786	112	30	55	197
Subtotal		806	367	207	1,380
Double surface treatment	649	905	90	9	1,004
	1,757	221	141	19	381
Subtotal		1,126	231	28	1,385
Gravel	15	201	883	125	1,209
	36	409	726	27	1,162
	62	542	447	69	1,058
	230	519	779	114	1,412
Subtotal		1,671	2,835	335	4,841
Earth	13	46	830	1,228	2,104
	30	38	196	236	470
	67	38	69	20	127
	200	2	2	43	47
Subtotal		124	1,097	1,527	2,748
Total		3,727	4,530	2,097	10,354
Percent		36	44	20	100

Taking into account past traffic growth, as well as anticipated economic growth and changes in fuel prices, traffic is expected to increase by 7.5 percent annually: 9 percent in the earlier years and 6 percent thereafter. No generated traffic is projected. These forecasts are reflected in table 6-4.

Program Costs and Benefits

On the basis of the department's accounts, and with adjustments for the economic costs of labor and foreign exchange, unit costs are estimated for each maintenance activity. For example, for asphalt roads, the annual costs per kilometer of cleaning ditches are Rs111 for good maintenance, Rs74 for fair maintenance, and Rs37 for minimum maintenance. The costs of this particular maintenance activity are not affected by traffic levels. The costs of repairing pavement and sealing, however, increase substantially with higher traffic. The incremental costs of the maintenance program—above the minimum level currently prevailing—are shown in Table 6-5; they are broken down by capital and operating costs, including additional investments and replacements required during the ten-year period. Allowance is made for the residual value of the equipment in the last year.

The benefits from improved maintenance consist of savings in vehicle operating costs because of the improved riding surface. Operating costs are estimated for four vehicle types and three classes of highway, each with three levels of road surface conditions. The data are presented in table 6-6. The table indicates that for automobiles, for ex-

Table 6-4. Forecast of Road Conditions in Year 8 with and without the Maintenance Program

Type of road surface	Average daily traffic	Road condition (kilometers)					
		Good		Fair		Minimum	
		With	Without	With	Without	With	Without
Concrete							
asphalt	1,188	425	78	0	0	0	347
	3,219	758	194	0	0	0	564
	8,772	197	68	0	0	0	129
Subtotal		1,380	340	0	0	0	1,040
Double surface							
treatment	596	1,504	500	0	0	0	1,004
	3,219	381	0	0	0	0	381
Subtotal		1,885	500	0	0	0	1,385
Gravel	28	0	0	0	0	1,209	1,209
	66	0	0	0	0	1,162	1,162
	113	127	127	1,058	0	0	1,058
	209	959	47	0	0	0	912
Subtotal		1,086	174	1,058	0	2,371	4,341
Earth	23	0	0	0	0	2,104	2,104
	55	0	0	0	0	470	470
Subtotal		0	0	0	0	2,574	2,574
Total		4,351	1,014	1,058	0	4,945	9,340

Table 6-5. Comparison of Costs and Benefits

(thousands of rupees)

| Year | Incremental costs[a] | | | | Present worth (discounted at 12%) | |
	Capital	Operating	Total costs	Benefits	Costs	Benefits
1	8,098	0	8,098	0	8,098	0
2	1,369	1,500	2,869	4,340	2,562	3,876
3	4,971	3,100	8,071	22,353	6,433	17,815
4	135	4,400	4,535	26,780	3,229	19,067
5	0	5,800	5,800	32,813	3,689	20,869
6	0	7,500	7,500	41,012	4,253	23,254
7	0	9,300	9,300	52,135	4,715	26,432
8	1,200	9,300	10,500	55,263	4,746	24,979
9	1,200	9,300	10,500	58,579	4,242	23,666
10	−3,600[b]	9,300	5,700	62,094	2,058	22,416
Total					44,025	182,374

Note: Net present worth equals Rs138,349,000; this is the difference between columns 5 and 6.

a. Incremental is defined as the level above minimum maintenance, costing Rs7,700.

b. Includes Rs1,200 for capital costs minus Rs4,800 for residual value of equipment.

Table 6-6. Economic Vehicle Operating Costs on Varying Road Surfaces with Different Maintenance Policies

(rupees for each 1,000 kilometers)

| Road surface | Vehicle | Maintenance policy and resultant road condition | | |
		Good	Fair	Minimum
Paved	Automobile	115	124	128
	Bus	297	306	310
	Light truck	318	334	341
	Heavy truck	733	807	843
Gravel	Automobile	157	182	208
	Bus	347	378	409
	Light truck	382	432	512
	Heavy truck	926	1,072	1,182
Earth	Automobile	192	213	243
	Bus	393	420	457
	Light truck	502	524	556
	Heavy truck	1,104	1,190	1,317

ample, the operating costs on a paved road are about 10 percent higher with minimum than with good maintenance, but on gravel roads, the difference is about 33 percent.

The next step consists of translating the reduction in vehicle operating costs under alternative maintenance policies into net benefits per kilometer at different traffic levels. The results are shown in table 6-7. Good maintenace has higher net benefits in all cases except for gravel and earth roads with low traffic levels, where fair or even minimum maintenance has higher benefits.

The impact of the maintenance program on road conditions is shown in table 6-4. The table indicates that with the maintenance program, 4,351 kilometers of road would be in good condition, compared with 1,014 kilometers without the program; roads with minimum conditions would decrease from 9,340 kilometers to 4,945 kilometers.

Comparison of Costs and Benefits

As shown in table 6-5, the highway maintenance program is well justified, with a net present worth of about Rs138 million and with a cost-

Table 6-7. Annual Net Economic Benefits of Alternative Maintenance Policies
(rupees per kilometer)

| | | Net benefits | |
Road surface	Average daily traffic	Fair policy	Good policy
Concrete asphalt	500	762	2,010
	2,000	3,785	10,885
	4,000	7,817	22,717
Double surface treatment	500	789	2,633
	2,000	3,641	12,178
	4,000	7,444	24,905
Gravel	15	−1	−301
	35	262	138
	75	791	1,018
	230	2,839	4,424
Earth	15	47	−5
	35	259	346
	75	685	1,048
	200	2,013	3,304

benefit ratio of about 1 : 4.1; the internal rate of return exceeds 100 percent. The high return, typical of many highway maintenance projects, reflects the low cost to sustain the productive capacity of the initial investment in highway construction.

In view of the high return on maintenance, the conclusion of the analysis is not likely to be changed as a result of changes in any single factor. This is illustrated by the impact of the following changes in assumptions on the net present value (in millions of rupees):

Two-year delay in project	110
25 percent reduction in benefits	93
25 percent increase in costs	127
Excluded time savings of operators of commercial vehicles	102

If the program is delayed two years the net present worth drops from Rs138 million to Rs110 million, a loss of Rs28 million. The program should therefore be started at once.

Although the benefits make no allowance for accident reduction or for time savings for passengers and freight, they do include time savings for the drivers and helpers of buses and trucks. These benefits are based on increased speeds and hourly wage rates. They account for about one-fifth of total benefits during the ten-year period but are relatively greater in the early years because the speed changes by improving roads from minimum to fair condition are more pronounced than when a road is improved to a good condition. Most of these savings are accrued by truck operators traveling on gravel roads.

Although the cost of labor is not shadow priced, a test was made of costing unskilled labor at 60 percent of the normal wage rate. Such an adjustment does not affect the cost or benefit streams substantially or the selected policy for any of the typical road segments.

The benefits accrue directly to the personal automobile operators and the road transport industry. But for bus transport, it appears likely that the lower costs reduce the pressure for tariff increases somewhat so that the passengers benefit indirectly. Intense competition among truckers should result in lower freight tariffs for shippers.

Case Study 7

Electrification or Dieselization of a Railway Line

Proposed Project

A 177-MILE MAIN RAILWAY LINE connecting two cities is being operated with steam locomotives. A previous study indicates that is is economic to replace these locomotives with either diesel or electric locomotives. The present study, therefore, evaluates the alternatives of electrifcation and dieselization of the line. Electrification involves installing a 50-cycle single-phase alternating current system with 25-kilovolt contact wire voltage. An alternative of 2,400-horsepower diesel-electric locomotives is considered.

Most of the line section is flat; gradients are rare and do not exceed 0.5 percent. The track gauge is five feet, six inches (1,676 mm). The track has recently been strengthened by renewal with 100-pound rails, a sleeper density of 2,650 per mile, a ballast cushion of twelve inches, and welded rail joints.

The maximum speed on the line is seventy-five miles an hour for express trains, forty-five miles an hour for ordinary passenger trains, and forty miles an hour for freight trains. The basic operating requirements to haul trains at specified loads and at these speeds, when translated into tractive effort, stipulate a 3,000-horsepower electric locomotive, or a 2,400-horsepower diesel-electric locomotive.

Electrification necessitates costly, fixed installations for power supply (substations) and power transmission (contact wire system) as well as cabling of telecommunication lines alongside the railway line and reconstruction of some existing buildings. The capital requirements of electrification are thus substantially greater than those for dieselization. The current operating costs for electric power and maintenance, however, are lower for electric traction than for diesels. The economic analysis consists of comparing these two different patterns of costs. Since the railway is expected to operate as a commercial enterprise, the calculations are made in terms of both financial costs to the railway (table 7-1) and economic costs to the country (table 7-2).

Table 7-1. Financial Analysis of Costs for Electrification and Dieselization of a Railway Line
(millions of rupees)

Year	Capital cost of fixed installation (1)	Capital cost of locomotives (2)	Maintenance cost of fixed installation (3)	Maintenance cost of locomotives (4)	Cost of electricity (5)	Total electrification costs (6)
1	30.0	0	0	0	0	30.0
2	75.0	0	0	0	0	75.0
3	75.0	0	0	0	0	75.0
4	54.0	0	0	0	0	54.0
5	0	149.7	2.1	3.0	18.3	173.1
6	0	0	2.1	3.0	18.3	23.4
7	0	0	2.1	3.3	18.3	23.7
8	0	0	2.1	3.3	18.3	23.7
9	0	20.7	2.1	3.3	18.3	44.4
10	0	0	2.4	3.6	20.1	26.1
11	0	0	2.4	3.6	20.1	26.1
12	0	0	2.4	3.6	20.1	26.1
13	0	10.2	2.4	3.6	20.1	36.3
14	0	0	2.4	3.6	20.1	26.1
15	0	0	2.4	3.9	21.9	28.2
16	0	0	2.4	3.9	21.9	28.2
17	0	0	2.7	4.2	21.9	28.8
18	0	10.2	2.7	4.2	21.9	39.0
19	0	0	2.7	4.2	21.9	28.8
20	0	0	2.7	4.5	23.7	30.9
21	0	0	2.7	4.5	23.7	30.9
22	0	0	2.7	4.5	23.7	30.9
23	0	0	2.7	4.5	23.7	30.9
24	0	0	2.7	4.5	23.7	30.9
25	0	0	2.7	4.5	23.7	30.9
26	0	0	2.7	4.5	23.7	30.9
27	0	0	2.7	4.5	23.7	30.9
28	0	0	2.7	4.5	23.7	30.9
29	0	0	2.7	4.5	23.7	30.9
30	0	0	2.7	4.5	23.7	30.9
31	0	0	2.7	4.5	23.7	30.9
32	0	0	2.7	4.5	23.7	30.9
33	0	0	2.7	4.5	23.7	30.9
34	0	0	2.7	4.5	23.7	30.9
35	−6.0	−18.0	0	0	0	−24.0
Total						

Note: Net present worth equals Rs37.9 million; this is the difference between columns 11 and

Cost of dieselization				Present worth (discounted at 12 percent)		Internal rate of return (discounted at 14 percent)	
Capital cost of locomotives (7)	Maintenance costs of locomotives (8)	Fuel costs (9)	Total dieselization costs (10)	Electrification (11)	Dieselization (12)	Electrification (13)	Dieselization (14)
0	0	0	0	30.0	0	30.0	0
0	0	0	0	67.0	0	65.8	0
0	0	0	0	59.8	0	57.7	0
0	0	0	0	38.4	0	36.5	0
195.6	11.4	36.0	243.0	110.1	154.5	102.5	143.9
0	11.4	36.0	47.4	13.3	26.9	12.1	24.6
0	11.4	36.0	47.4	12.0	24.0	10.8	21.6
0	11.4	36.0	47.4	10.7	21.4	9.5	19.0
0	14.7	36.0	50.7	17.9	20.5	15.6	17.8
27.9	14.7	42.0	84.6	9.4	30.5	8.0	26.1
0	14.7	42.0	56.7	8.4	18.3	7.0	15.3
0	14.7	42.0	56.7	7.5	16.3	6.2	13.4
0	14.7	42.0	56.7	9.3	14.6	7.6	11.8
0	18.0	42.0	60.0	6.0	13.7	4.8	10.9
11.1	18.0	49.5	78.6	5.8	16.1	4.5	12.6
0	18.3	49.5	73.8	5.2	13.5	3.9	10.3
0	18.3	49.5	73.8	4.7	12.0	3.5	9.1
0	18.3	49.5	73.8	5.7	10.8	4.2	8.0
16.8	21.6	57.6	96.0	3.7	12.5	2.7	9.1
0	21.6	57.6	79.2	3.6	9.2	2.6	6.6
0	21.6	57.6	79.2	3.2	8.2	2.3	5.8
0	21.6	57.6	79.2	2.9	7.4	2.0	5.1
0	21.6	57.6	79.2	2.6	6.6	1.7	4.4
0	21.6	57.6	79.2	2.3	5.9	1.5	4.0
195.6	21.6	57.6	274.8	2.0	18.1	1.3	11.8
0	21.6	57.6	79.2	1.8	4.7	1.2	3.0
0	21.6	57.6	79.2	1.6	4.2	1.0	2.6
0	21.6	57.6	79.2	1.5	3.7	0.9	2.3
0	21.6	57.6	79.2	1.3	3.3	0.8	2.1
27.9	21.6	57.6	107.1	1.1	4.0	0.7	2.4
0	21.6	57.6	79.2	1.0	2.6	0.6	1.6
0	21.6	57.6	79.2	0.9	2.4	0.5	1.3
0	21.6	57.6	79.2	0.8	2.1	0.5	1.2
0	21.6	57.6	79.2	0.7	1.9	0.4	1.0
−14.1	0	0	−14.1	−0.5	−0.3	−0.3	−0.2
				451.7	489.6	410.6	408.5

Table 7-2. Economic Analysis of Costs for Electrification and Dieselization of a Railway Line
(millions of rupees)

	Cost of electrification					
Year	Capital cost of fixed installation (1)	Capital cost of locomotives (2)	Maintenance cost of fixed installation (3)	Maintenance cost of locomotives (4)	Cost of electricity (5)	Total electrification costs (6)
1	36.0	0	0	0	0	36.0
2	90.0	0	0	0	0	90.0
3	90.0	0	0	0	0	90.0
4	61.2	0	0	0	0	61.2
5	0	200.1	2.4	3.6	22.2	228.3
6	0	0	2.4	3.6	22.2	28.2
7	0	0	2.4	3.6	22.2	28.2
8	0	0	2.4	3.9	22.2	28.5
9	0	27.6	2.4	3.9	22.2	56.1
10	0	0	2.7	4.2	24.3	31.2
11	0	0	2.7	4.2	24.3	31.2
12	0	0	2.7	4.2	24.3	31.2
13	0	13.8	2.7	4.5	24.3	45.3
14	0	0	2.7	4.5	24.3	31.5
15	0	0	2.7	4.8	26.7	34.2
16	0	0	2.7	4.8	26.7	34.2
17	0	0	3.0	4.8	26.7	34.5
18	0	13.8	3.0	4.8	26.7	48.3
19	0	0	3.0	5.1	26.7	34.8
20	0	0	3.0	5.4	29.1	37.5
21	0	0	3.0	5.4	29.1	37.5
22	0	0	3.0	5.4	29.1	37.5
23	0	0	3.0	5.4	29.1	37.5
24	0	0	3.0	5.4	29.1	37.5
25	0	0	3.0	5.4	29.1	37.5
26	0	0	3.0	5.4	29.1	37.5
27	0	0	3.0	5.4	29.1	37.5
28	0	0	3.0	5.4	29.1	37.5
29	0	0	3.0	5.4	29.1	37.5
30	0	0	3.0	5.4	29.1	37.5
31	0	0	3.0	5.4	29.1	37.5
32	0	0	3.0	5.4	29.1	37.5
33	0	0	3.0	5.4	29.1	37.5
34	0	0	3.0	5.4	29.1	37.5
35	−6.0	−24.0	0	0	0	−30.0
Total						

Note: Net present worth equals Rs132 million; this is the difference between columns 11 and 12

Cost of dieselization				Present worth (discounted at 12 percent)		Internal rate of return (discounted at 14 percent)	
Capital cost of locomotives (7)	Maintenance costs of locomotives (8)	Fuel costs (9)	Total dieselization costs (10)	Electri-fication (11)	Diesel-ization (12)	Electri-fication (13)	Diesel-ization (14)
0	0	0	0	36.0	0	36.0	0
0	0	0	0	80.4	0	84.9	0
0	0	0	0	71.7	0	80.1	0
0	0	0	0	43.6	0	51.4	0
242.4	14.4	18.3	275.1	145.2	175.0	180.8	217.9
0	14.4	18.3	32.7	16.0	18.5	21.1	24.4
0	14.4	18.3	32.7	14.3	16.6	19.9	23.1
0	14.4	18.3	32.7	12.9	14.8	19.0	21.7
0	14.4	18.3	32.7	22.7	13.2	35.2	20.5
34.8	18.9	21.3	75.0	11.3	27.1	18.5	44.4
0	18.9	21.3	40.2	10.0	12.9	17.4	22.4
0	18.9	21.3	40.2	9.0	11.5	16.4	21.2
0	18.9	21.3	40.2	11.6	10.3	22.5	20.0
0	18.9	21.3	40.2	7.2	9.2	14.8	18.9
13.8	23.1	25.2	62.1	7.0	12.7	15.1	27.4
0	23.1	25.2	48.3	6.3	8.8	14.3	20.1
0	23.1	25.2	48.3	5.6	7.9	13.6	19.0
0	23.1	25.2	48.3	7.1	7.1	17.9	17.9
20.7	27.6	29.4	77.7	4.5	10.1	12.2	27.2
0	27.6	29.4	57.0	4.4	6.6	12.4	18.9
0	27.6	29.4	57.0	3.9	5.9	11.7	17.8
0	27.6	29.4	57.0	3.5	5.3	11.0	16.8
0	27.6	29.4	57.0	3.1	4.7	10.4	15.8
0	27.6	29.4	57.0	2.8	4.2	9.8	14.9
242.4	27.6	29.4	299.4	2.5	19.8	9.3	74.0
0	27.6	29.4	57.0	2.2	3.4	8.7	13.3
0	27.6	29.4	57.0	2.0	3.0	8.3	12.5
0	27.6	29.4	57.0	1.8	2.7	7.8	11.8
0	27.6	29.4	57.0	1.6	2.4	7.4	11.2
34.8	27.6	29.4	91.8	1.4	3.4	6.9	17.0
0	27.6	29.4	57.0	1.2	1.9	6.5	9.9
0	27.6	29.4	57.0	1.1	1.7	6.2	9.3
0	27.6	29.4	57.0	1.0	1.5	5.8	8.8
0	27.6	29.4	57.0	0.9	1.4	5.5	8.3
−17.4	0	0	−17.4	−0.6	−0.4	−4.1	−2.4
				555.2	423.2	814.7	804.0

Traffic

The railway has prepared detailed traffic forecasts for year 5, when electrification is estimated to be completed, and for fifteen years thereafter. The average number of trains, the gross ton-miles, and the locomotive-miles for these years are shown in table 7-3.

These estimates show an increase of about 28 percent in gross ton-miles and 24 percent in locomotive miles by year 20. No growth in traffic has been allowed for after year 20 because any increase thereafter is not likely and new investments would be required to expand capacity.

Costs of Electrification

The costs of electrification consist of the capital costs of installations and locomotives, their maintenance costs (including substation operating personnel), and the cost of electric energy. The wages of the train crews are the same for electric and diesel trains and have therefore been omitted.

Table 7-3. Railway Traffic Forecasts after Electrification, in Selected Years

	Year 5				Year 20			
Category	Express	Passenger	Freight	Total	Express	Passenger	Freight	Total
	Average daily no. of trains each way							
Section 1	8	10	10	28	9	12	14	35
Section 2	8	9	10	27	9	11	13	33
Section 3	8	9	8	25	9	11	11	31
	Average annual gross ton-miles (in millions)							
Electric-hauled trains	600	709	1,619	2,928	675	859	2,229	3,763
Diesel-hauled trains	623	736	1,645	3,004	701	892	2,264	3,857
	Average annual locomotive-miles (in millions)[a]							
All trains			3.44					4.28

a. Figures are the same for electric and diesel locomotives.

Capital Costs

FIXED INSTALLATIONS.   The capital costs of the fixed installations are estimated at Rs234 million. Installation is expected to take four years. The useful economic life of the items varies but on a weighted basis is estimated at thirty years. A scrap value of Rs6 million has been allowed for at the end of the project life (see column 1 of table 7-1).

To calculate economic costs, a shadow rate of 1.75 times the official rate is applied to the foreign exchange cost of Rs118.8 million, making total costs Rs323.1 million. The costs of about Rs45.9 million for customs duties and sales tax must be deducted. Thus the economic costs of the fixed installations amount to Rs277.2 million (see column 1 of table 7-1).

LOCOMOTIVES.   The number of electric locomotives required is estimated to increase from twenty-nine in year 5 to thirty-seven in year 20, more or less in line with the growth in gross ton-miles. The cost of a locomotive to the railway is about Rs5.16 million. Total costs are, therefore, Rs149.7 million in year 5, with an additional Rs41.1 million required by year 19 (see column 2 of table 7-1). The life of an electric locomotive is estimated at thirty-five years; no replacements would therefore be needed during the life of the project. A salvage value of Rs18 million has been allowed for at the end of the project life.

To calculate economic costs, two adjustments are necessary. First, customs duties and sales tax must be eliminated; they comprise about 30 percent of the imported cost. Second, a shadow rate must be applied to foreign exchange costs of Rs3.9 million per locomotive. These adjustments make the economic costs of a locomotive Rs6.9 million. The economic costs of twenty-nine locomotives required in year 5 are thus Rs200.1 million, with an additional Rs55.2 million required by year 19 (see column 2 of table 7-2).

Operating Costs

The maintenance costs of the fixed installations are estimated at Rs2.1 million in year 5, rising to Rs2.7 million in year 17. With a shadow price for foreign exchange, which is estimated at 13 percent of the maintenance costs, and deductions for customs duties, sales taxes, and so forth, on imported parts, the economic costs come to Rs2.4 million and Rs3 million, respectively (see columns 3 of tables 7-1 and 7-2, respectively).

The maintenance costs of the electric locomotives is Rs0.9 per locomotive-mile. For the 3.44 million locomotive-miles estimated for year 5, this amounts to Rs3 million; of this, Rs0.9 million is in foreign exchange and Rs2.1 million in local currency so that the economic costs amount to Rs3.6 million (after deducting taxes). Maintenance costs are expected to rise to Rs4.5 million by year 20, which is Rs5.4 million in economic costs (see column 4 of tables 7-1 and 7-2).

The cost of electricity to the railway is estimated at Rs0.2 a kilowatt-hour. At that rate, the total costs of electricity are Rs18.3 million in year 5, rising to Rs23.7 million by year 20. With a foreign exchange component of about 30 percent, the economic costs of electricity increase from year 5 to year 20 from Rs22.2 million to Rs29.1 million (see column 5 of tables 7-1 and 7-2).

The total costs of electrification are shown in column 6 of tables.

Costs of Dieselization

The costs of dieselization include the capital costs of the locomotives and their operating and maintenance costs. Wages are omitted from the discussion; they are the same for electric and diesel trains.

Capital Costs

The capital costs of dieselization are limited to the locomotives. The railway estimates that thirty-five diesel locomotives would be required in year 5 and another ten by year 19 to handle the increased volume in traffic. The costs per diesel locomotive to the railway are about Rs5.59 million, so that the cost of the fleet is Rs195.6 million in year 5, with an additional Rs55.9 million required by year 19. The economic life of the diesels is estimated at twenty years, so that replacements are needed periodically after that period. The salvage value of diesels remaining at the end of the thirty-year life of the project is limited to those newer than ten years old and is estimated at about one-half their cost (see column 7 of table 7-1).

To calculate economic costs, two adjustments are required in the preceding estimates of financial costs. First, a shadow rate of 1.75 times the official rate must be applied to the foreign exchange component of Rs3.63 million per locomotive. Second, payments for customs duties, sales taxes, and so forth must be eliminated; these amount to about Rs1.32 million per locomotive. Thus, the economic costs of the diesel locomotives are Rs242.4 million in year 5, with an additional Rs69.3 million required by year 19 as well as periodic replacements thereafter (see column 7 of table 7-2).

Operating Costs

The maintenance costs of diesels are about Rs3.3 per locomotive-mile; for the 3.44 million locomotive-miles estimated for 1983, total costs come to Rs11.4 million. With the expansion in the locomotive fleet and an increase in its average life, maintenance costs are estimated to rise to Rs21.6 million by year 19. Since one-half of these costs are in foreign exchange and since customs duties, taxes, and so forth are about 10 percent of total costs, the economic costs of maintenance are Rs14.4 million in year 5, rising to Rs27.6 million by year 19 (see column 8 of tables 7-1 and 7-2).

The fuel costs for running diesel locomotives are estimated at Rs6.75 a gallon. For traffic in year 5, 5.2 million gallons of diesel are required, making the total fuel cost about Rs36 million. In line with the traffic growth, this cost is expected to rise to Rs57.6 million in year 19 (see column 9 of table 7-1).

The price of Rs6.75 a gallon includes taxes of Rs4.11, so that the price net of taxes is Rs2.64. Of this, freight costs from the refinery and incidental charges account for Rs1.35, of which about 10 percent, or Rs0.13, is in foreign exchange. Of the remaining Rs1.29, about 75 percent, or Rs0.97, is in foreign exchange. The total foreign exchange component is thus Rs1.1. The economic cost of fuel is thus Rs3.5 per gallon, or Rs18.3 million in year 5 and Rs29.4 million in year 19 (see column 9 of table 7-1).

The total costs of dieselization are shown in column 10.

Comparison of Electrification and Dieselization Costs

As shown in columns 11 and 12 of table 7-2, the economic costs of electrification exceed those of dieselization—both discounted at 12 percent—by Rs132 million during the thirty-year life of the project. The ratio of electrification to dieselization costs is about 1 : 0.8. Even at a discount rate of 8 percent, the net present worth of electrification is a negative Rs71 million. As shown in columns 13 and 14, the internal rate of return is slightly less than 6 percent. The electrification project does not, therefore, appear to be economically justified.

The conclusion of the analysis is particularly sensitive to the capital costs of the fixed installations. At a 12 percent discount rate, these costs account for more than 40 percent of total costs during the life of the project. If they are reduced by 25 percent, the present worth of electrification of a negative Rs132 million is cut almost in half to about a negative Rs74 million.

Probably the second most sensitive factor is the relative cost of diesel fuel and electricity. An increase in fuel costs of 25 percent increases the present discounted cost of dieselization by almost Rs180 million and thus justifies electrification. Similarly, a reduction of 25 percent in electricity costs reduces the present discounted costs of electrification by about Rs195 million and thus also justifies electrification.

As pointed out, the railway is expected to operate as a commercial enterprise so that a comparison of financial costs is more relevant to it than relative economic costs. As shown in columns 11 and 12 of table 7-1, the financial costs of electrification are lower than those of dieselization—both discounted at 12 percent—by Rs37.9 million. The ratio of electrification to dieselization costs is 1 : 1.1 and the internal financial rate of return is about 14 percent (see columns 13 and 14). At a financial discount rate of 8 percent, the net present worth is about Rs179 million. From the point of view of the railway, electrification is therefore justified.

The case study illustrates the distortions which can be caused by government tax and foreign exchange policies. The availability of foreign exchange at the official rate makes the financial costs of the fixed installations much lower than the economic ones and this is not fully offset by taxes. The financial costs thus amount to about Rs234 million, while the economic costs are Rs277 million, or about 18 percent higher. The tax on diesel fuel, however, increases its costs to the railway about 150 percent, although there is no such tax on electricity.

Under the circumstances, there can be no definitive answer on whether the railway should electrify or dieselize. If the prevailing principle is that the railway is to operate as a commercial enterprise, the railway should electrify. If the government nevertheless insists on dieselization, it should either modify its foreign exchange and tax policies or grant the railway funds equal to the extra financial costs of dieselization (see "Economic versus Financial Appraisal," chapter 5, for a further discussion of this problem).

Modernization
of a Marshaling Yard

Proposed Project

THE PROPOSED PROJECT consists of the modernization and expansion of a marshaling yard which has become outdated and congested. The existing yard was constructed more than fifty years ago; it covers an area of about 110 acres and has twenty track-miles. It occupies a strategic position in the railway network since it is located in the middle of a main line and serves a number of other routes. The yard is a clearinghouse for less-than-trainload blocks of wagons, which are sorted out and then dispatched as through-train loads to further destinations. In addition, through trains running on the main line are serviced in the yard. Because of insufficient sorting lines, there are many shunting movements; the absence of a hump necessitates pull-and-push flat shunting movements which are time-consuming, cumbersome, and entail arduous manual effort. As a result, the average wagon moves through the yard slowly, taking about fifteen to twenty hours.

Modernization involves the construction of a mechanized hump marshaling yard, about twice the size of the present yard. It would have thirty-six track-miles, including thirty-two main sorting sidings, secondary sorting sidings, fifteen reception sidings, and six departure sidings. The sorting operation would be automated by electronic techniques for route-setting and wagon control, and the yard would be equipped with modern signaling and telecommunications. Construction of the project is estimated to take four years.

Traffic

An average of seventeen trains involving 1,200 wagons, were handled daily at the yard in the most recent year. During the peak consecutive ten days, twenty-two trains, involving 1,550 wagons, were handled daily; congestion occurs when the daily traffic exceeds this traffic volume. The railway's forecast indicates that the average daily traffic will grow to about twenty-one trains (1,500 wagons) in the opening year of the new yard (year 5) and reach thirty-three trains (2,300 wagons) fifteen years later and forty-two trains (3,000 wagons) after a further fifteen years, which would be the end of the project life.

Project Costs

Capital Costs

The capital costs of the project are estimated at Rs98.4 million. They consist primarily of permanent way (Rs41.7 million), equipment (Rs21 million), structural works (Rs12.6 million), and electrification (Rs7.2 million). However, certain materials from the existing yard, valued at Rs8.7 million, are usable in the new yard; net capital costs thus are Rs89.7 million.

To estimate the economic costs, two adjustments are necessary. First, taxes and customs duties estimated at Rs18.3 million must be deducted. Second, the foreign exchange component of Rs36.8 million must be shadow priced at 1.75 times the official rate, making these costs Rs64.4 million, or Rs27.6 million more than the financial costs. The economic costs of the project are thus Rs99 million (Rs89.7 − Rs18.3 million + Rs27.6 million). Some of the equipment would have to be replaced after fifteen years and some after twenty years. The costs of construction and of replacements are shown in column 1 of table 8-1. A salvage value of Rs15 million is allowed for at the end of the project life.

Operating Costs

The operation and maintenance costs of the new yard are expected to exceed the costs of the existing yard by about Rs1.5 million. When allowance is made for the foreign exchange component of these costs and for taxes and duties, the additional economic costs are estimated at Rs1.8 million (see column 2 of table 8-1). These costs do not include the operating costs of the shunting locomotives, which will be lower in the new yard; the reduction is considered a benefit. The total costs of the project are shown in column 3.

Project Benefits

The benefits of the new yard consist of lower shunting costs, reduced wagon detention in the yard and less waiting time outside the yard, and less damage to wagons and freight.

Lower Shunting Costs

At present, shunting is performed by five shunting engines as well as by train engines. By the time the new yard opens, an estimated 190 hours of shunting will be required daily; this will increase with the growth of traffic to 285 hours daily in year 19 and to 380 hours daily in year 34, the last year of the project's life.

The mechanized hump yard would reduce shunting engine-hours by about two-thirds, that is, by 130 hours daily in year 5, by 195 hours in year 19, and by 260 hours in year 34. The financial costs of a shunting engine-hour are estimated at Rs123; with deductions for taxes and shadow pricing of foreign exchange, the economic costs are estimated at Rs133. In year 5, the annual saving is thus Rs6.3 million (130 hours × 365 days × Rs133); it increases with the growth of traffic to Rs12.6 million by the end of the project's life (see column 4 of table 8-1).

Reduced Wagon Detention in Yard

Because of the slow and flat shunting operations in the existing yard, the average detention of wagons in the yard is eighteen hours. In the new yard, this would be reduced to eight hours, for a saving of ten hours. For the 1,500 wagons handled daily in year 5, this is a saving of 15,000 wagon-hours daily, or 5.5 million hours for the entire year, which is the equivalent of 625 wagon-years. Since the life of a wagon is about forty years, this is the equivalent of about sixteen wagons. With the economic cost of a wagon at about Rs150,000, the total saving is Rs2.4 million in year 5 and increases to Rs4.8 million by year 34 (see column 5 of table 8-1).

Less Waiting Time outside Yard

A study made for the most recent year indicates that because of congestion in the yard, about 3,300 trains were detained an average of one and one-half hours at roadside stations for a total waiting time of 5,000 train-hours. By the application of queuing theory, the railway estimates that with the increase in traffic, the waiting time at the old yard will increase to 6,000 hours in year 5 and 38,000 hours in year 34. Although there would be virtually no waiting time in the initial years at the new yard, the waiting time by year 34 would be about 8,000 hours, so that the net reduction is 30,000 hours. (For a detailed application of queuing theory in estimating waiting time, see case study 10.)

With about seventy wagons per-train, the waiting time in year 5 involves 420,000 wagon-hours, which is the equivalent of forty-seven

Table 8-1. Comparison of Costs and Benefits of Modernization of a Marshaling Yard
(millions of rupees)

Year	Costs of yard			Benefits					Present worth (discounted at 12 percent)		Internal rate of return (discounted at 8 percent)	
	Capital costs (1)	Operating costs (2)	Total costs (3)	Lower shunting costs (4)	Reduced wagon detention in yard (5)	Lower waiting time outside yard (6)	Less damage (7)	Total benefits (8)	Costs (9)	Benefits (10)	Costs (11)	Benefits (12)
1	12.0	0	12.0	0	0	0	0	0	12.0	0	12.0	0
2	45.0	0	45.0	0	0	0	0	0	40.2	0	41.7	0
3	30.0	0	30.0	0	0	0	0	0	23.9	0	25.7	0
4	11.4	0	11.4	0	0	0	0	0	8.1	0	9.1	0
5	0	1.8	1.8	6.3	2.4	0.6	0.3	9.6	1.1	6.1	1.3	7.1
6	0	1.8	1.8	6.3	2.4	0.6	0	9.3	1.0	5.3	1.2	6.3
7	0	1.8	1.8	6.6	2.4	0.6	0.3	9.9	0.9	5.0	1.1	6.2
8	0	1.8	1.8	6.9	2.4	0.6	0	9.9	0.8	4.5	1.0	5.8
9	0	1.8	1.8	7.2	2.7	0.6	0.3	10.8	0.7	4.4	1.0	5.8
10	0	1.8	1.8	7.2	2.7	0.6	0	10.5	0.6	3.8	0.9	5.3
11	0	1.8	1.8	7.5	2.7	0.6	0.3	11.1	0.6	3.6	0.8	5.1
12	0	1.8	1.8	7.8	3.0	0.9	0	11.7	0.5	3.4	0.8	5.0
13	0	1.8	1.8	8.1	3.0	0.9	0.3	12.3	0.5	3.2	0.7	4.9
14	0	1.8	1.8	8.4	3.0	0.9	0	12.3	0.4	2.8	0.7	4.5
15	0	1.8	1.8	8.7	3.3	0.9	0.3	13.2	0.4	2.7	0.6	4.5

16	0	1.8	1.8	8.7	3.3	0.9	0	12.9	0.3	2.4	0.6	4.1
17	0	1.8	1.8	9.0	3.3	0.9	0.3	13.5	0.3	2.2	0.5	3.9
18	0	1.8	1.8	9.3	3.3	1.2	0	13.8	0.3	2.0	0.5	3.7
19	9.0	1.8	10.8	9.6	3.6	1.2	0.3	14.7	1.4	1.9	2.7	3.7
20	0	1.8	1.8	9.6	3.6	1.2	0.3	14.7	0.2	1.7	0.4	3.4
21	0	1.8	1.8	9.9	3.6	1.2	0.3	15.0	0.2	1.6	0.4	3.2
22	0	1.8	1.8	10.2	3.9	1.2	0.3	15.6	0.2	1.5	0.4	3.1
23	0	1.8	1.8	10.2	3.9	1.5	0.3	15.9	0.1	1.3	0.3	2.9
24	33.0	1.8	34.8	10.5	3.9	1.5	0.3	16.2	2.6	1.2	5.9	2.8
25	0	1.8	1.8	10.8	4.2	1.5	0.3	16.8	0.1	1.1	0.3	2.7
26	0	1.8	1.8	11.1	4.2	1.5	0.3	17.1	0.1	1.0	0.3	2.5
27	0	1.8	1.8	11.1	4.2	1.8	0.3	17.4	0.1	0.9	0.2	2.3
28	0	1.8	1.8	11.4	4.5	1.8	0.3	18.0	0.1	0.8	0.2	2.3
29	0	1.8	1.8	11.4	4.5	1.8	0.3	18.0	0.1	0.8	0.2	2.1
30	0	1.8	1.8	11.7	4.5	2.1	0.3	18.6	0.1	0.7	0.2	2.0
31	0	1.8	1.8	12.0	4.5	2.1	0.3	18.9	0.1	0.6	0.2	1.9
32	0	1.8	1.8	12.0	4.8	2.4	0.3	19.5	0.1	0.6	0.2	1.8
33	0	1.8	1.8	12.3	4.8	2.7	0.3	20.1	0.1	0.5	0.2	1.7
34	0	1.8	1.8	12.6	4.8	3.0	0.3	20.7	0	0.5	0.1	1.6
35	-15.0	0	-15.0	0	0	0	0	0	-0.3	0	-1.1	0
Total									97.9	68.1	111.3	112.2

Note: Net present worth equals −Rs29.8 million; this is the difference between columns 9 and 10.

wagon-years. Since the life of a wagon is about forty years, this is the equivalent of nearly 1.2 wagons. With the economic cost of a wagon at Rs150,000, the reduction in waiting time for wagons would save about Rs180,000 in year 5; by year 34, this increases to Rs900,000.

The waiting time of locomotives is 6,000 hours in year 5, the equivalent of about two-thirds of a locomotive-year. With the economic cost of a locomotive at about Rs4.5 million and assuming a twenty-year life, the saving is Rs150,000 (Rs4.5 million ÷ 20 × 2/3). By year 34, this rises to Rs750,000. The savings for locomotives and wagons thus increase from Rs330,000 to Rs1.65 million during the life of the project. With allowance for wages and other operating costs, the total savings are estimated to rise from Rs0.6 million in year 5 to Rs3 million in year 34. The rise is gradual in the early years but becomes more rapid in later years (see column 6 of table 8-1).

Less Damage to Wagons and Freight

Automation eliminates rough shunting and thus reduces damage to both wagons and freight. The railway estimates the reduction in damage to rise from about Rs0.15 million to Rs0.3 million during the project life (see column 7, table 8-1; because of rounding, the benefit in the early years is shown as Rs0.3 million every second year). This estimate also makes some allowance for the lower time of freight shipments. The total benefits of the marshaling yard are shown in column 8.

Comparison of Costs and Benefits

As shown in columns 9 and 10 of table 8-1, the net present worth of the project is a negative Rs29.8 million with costs and benefits discounted at 12 percent. The cost-benefit ratio is 1 : 0.7 and the internal rate of return is 8 percent (see columns 11 and 12). The project is therefore of doubtful justification.

The conclusion is particularly sensitive to the capital costs of the project, the traffic forecast, and the estimate of improved efficiency at the new yard. Capital costs must be reduced by 34 percent for the project to be justified (at a 12 percent discount rate). If such a reduction is not feasible, consideration might be given to constructing a smaller yard initially and expanding it later with the growth of traffic. If this can be done by postponing investments of about Rs36 million from years 2 and 3 to year 20, allowing also for the fact that some of the replacements can be postponed, the discounted costs of the project decline by about Rs24 million and the net present worth declines from a negative Rs29.8 million to a negative Rs5.8 million. The project then becomes justified within a few years or immediately if a slightly lower discount rate is acceptable.

The project is sensitive to the traffic forecast because the benefits are more or less proportionate to the traffic except that congestion rises more rapidly than traffic. The traffic, however, must be about 40 percent higher than forecast in order to justify the project.

The estimate of improved efficiency deserves careful review because the introduction of modern equipment in developing countries frequently does not lead to cost reduction as quickly, or to the same extent, as in more developed countries. It may take some time to get the full benefits of the new equipment, and its operation may be more costly if spare parts are not readily available, if maintenance is inadequate, and so forth. These considerations should, of course, be allowed for in a realistic estimate of benefits.

Discontinuing Service on a Railway Line

ALTHOUGH THE OTHER CASE STUDIES deal primarily with the evaluation of new investments, this case study shows that the same methods of project appraisal are equally applicable for reaching decisions on whether existing investments should be continued or phased out.

Proposed Project

A railway operates a seventy-five-mile branch line connecting city X, located on the main line, with city Y (see figure 9-1). The gauges of the two lines are the same. When the branch line was built at the turn of the century, it provided the only transport link between X and Y, but a gravel road has subsequently been built and recently paved. As a result, the railway has been losing traffic on the line to competing trucks and buses. The area of influence of the line has not developed significantly and its economic potential is limited. Because of the light traffic on the line (see "Traffic"), abandonment of the railway line has been proposed; all traffic would be carried on the parallel road.

Because the government wants the railway to operate as a commercial enterprise which earns a reasonable return on its investments, the railway's criterion for continuing the line is its financial profitability: that is, will the revenue from operating the line cover its costs (see "Financial Analysis")? The government, however, must know whether continued railway service is economically justified. For this purpose, the railway's financial costs must be adjusted to reflect economic costs; also an analysis must determine whether the traffic which would divert to road transport if the line is closed can be carried at lower cost by the railway or by road (see "Economic Analysis").

Traffic

The railway has reduced its service on the branch line to three mixed trains a week in each direction. These trains now carry an average of twenty-five passengers each, 200 tons of ore from Y to X, and 5 tons of general cargo from X to Y. The annual traffic on the line is as follows: 7,500 passengers (560,000 passenger-miles), 750 tons of general cargo (56,000 ton-miles), and 30,000 tons of ore (2.25 million ton-miles).

The following volumes of branch-line traffic are carried annually beyond X on the main line to various destinations on it or originate on the main line and are carried to Y: 1,000 passengers (120,000 passenger-miles), 650 tons of cargo (130,000 ton-miles), and 30,000 tons of ore (7 million ton-miles). The entire ore traffic moves from Y to various points beyond X on the main line, most of the general cargo traffic originates beyond X on the main line, and most of the passenger traffic is local traffic between X and Y.

Closing the branch line means a loss to the railway of all traffic on that line, but the impact on the traffic originating from or destined for points on the main line depends on such factors as the distances involved, the comparative road and railway traffic, the relative transport speeds and quality of service, and the costs of loading and unloading at X. For example, traffic from Y moving only a few miles beyond X on the main line would not transfer to the railway at X if the branch line is closed, but continue by bus or truck. Bulk traffic continuing long distances on the main line and even traffic moving medium distances but destined for consumers with private railway sidings would not be lost to the railway after the branch line is closed; such traffic would be expected to continue by rail on the main line and to be transported to or from X by truck.

On the basis of detailed studies of the origin and destination of the traffic and the comparative rail and road distribution costs, the railway estimates that, of the traffic now destined for or originating from the branch line, 100 tons of general cargo (30,000 ton-miles) and 18,000 tons of ore (5 million ton-miles) would remain on the main line even if the

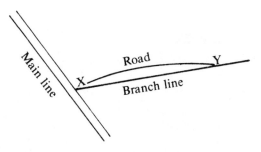

Figure 9-1. Location of Main and Branch Lines

Table 9-1. Volume of Traffic Shifted to Road Transport from Closure of Branch Rail Line

Traffic	Branch line	Main line	Total
Passengers (number)	7,500	1,000	n.a.[a]
Passenger-miles	560,000	120,000	680,000
General cargo (tons)	750	550	n.a.[a]
General cargo (ton-miles)	56,000	100,000	156,000
Ore (tons)	30,000	12,000	n.a.[a]
Ore (ton-miles)	2,250,000	2,000,000	4,250,000

a. The same passengers and cargo may move on the branch and main lines; thus there are no totals.

branch line is closed. All passenger traffic would be lost to the railway. Table 9-1 summarizes the annual volume of traffic that would shift from the railway (both branch line and main line) to road transport after closing the branch line.

Financial Analysis

Revenues

The financial analysis compares revenue and costs to the railway from operating the line. For this purpose, the revenue has been divided into revenue from the traffic on the branch line between X and Y and revenue from traffic from Y which continues beyond X to various points on the main line or which originates at such points and is destined to Y.

The railway has made a detailed study of its revenue. Current revenue is shown in table 9-2. The railway's earnings generated by the branch line traffic amount to Rs1.74 million of this amount, Rs. 480,000

Table 9-2. Current Railway Revenue

(thousands of rupees)

Traffic	Revenue on branch line	Revenue on main line	Total revenue
Passengers	60	15	75
Freight	405	1,245	1,650
Miscellaneous	15	0	15
Total	480	1,260	1,740

is from traffic which was carried on the branch line itself and Rs1.26 million from traffic on the main line which originated from or was destined for Y.

If the branch line is discontinued, the railway would lose the revenue from the branch line (Rs480,000) plus revenue from main-line traffic diverted to the roadway. The lost revenue from 100,000 ton-miles of general cargo and 2 million ton-miles of ore (see "Traffic") is estimated at Rs420,000; the lost revenue from 120,000 passenger-miles is Rs15,000.

The total loss of revenue to the railway from closing the line is all revenue on branch line, Rs480,000; passenger revenue on main line, Rs15,000; and freight revenue on main line, Rs420,000 for a total of Rs915,000. The railway would thus lose slightly more than half of current revenue from operating the line.

Costs

As with revenue, costs must be calculated separately for the branch line and the main line. The railway has made a detailed study of the current costs of operating the branch line (table 9-3).

Although the costs of some of the items, such as fuel, can readily be obtained, some of the others, such as the repair and maintenance of locomotives and rolling stock, are more difficult to determine and are based on systemwide averages which take into account the actual condition of the line. No allowance has been made for any staff reduction in the central and divisional headquarters because they are not likely to be affected. If a number of lines in the area are abandoned, however, the size of the divisional headquarters can be reduced. Depreciation is based on original costs and interest is set at 4 percent on the depreciated value of the assets; that is the interest rate paid by the railway to the government.

The calculation of costs on the main line is more difficult. As indicated, closing the branch line involves a loss of 120,000 passenger-

Table 9-3. Current Operating Costs of Branch Line
(thousands of rupees)

Item	Cost
Operations	2,040
Maintenance	1,650
Subtotal	3,690
Depreciation	600
Interest	720
Total	5,010

miles and 2.1 million ton-miles of freight on the main line. Since this is only a small part of the traffic on the main line, most of the operating costs on the line, such as maintenance of the permanent way and of buildings and structures, would be unaffected by closing the branch line. The annual long-run marginal costs of branch-line traffic are about Rs255,000.

Comparison of Revenue and Costs

Closing the line results in a Rs4.35 million saving: reduced revenue is Rs915,000 (Rs480,000, branch line; Rs435,000, main line), but costs are reduced by Rs5.26 million (Rs5 million, branch line; Rs225,000, main line).

Even though the traffic is highly profitable on the main line, with marginal costs only about 60 percent of revenue, the operation of the branch line is so expensive that its costs exceed its revenue by more than Rs4.5 million. Even if depreciation and interest are excluded from the costs of the branch line on the assumption that the assets will not be replaced and the line will be phased out gradually, or that interest payments on the existing assets will continue in any case, the costs of the branch line are still Rs3.7 million and the loss still exceeds Rs3 million. From the financial point of view, therefore, it is highly advantageous for the railway to close the line.

Economic Analysis

If the branch line is closed, traffic would divert to the road. The economic analysis of closing the line therefore consists in comparing the economic costs of transporting the traffic by railway and by road. Only after such an analysis can the government decide whether the interest of the country as a whole and that of the railway coincide.

The services provided by road and rail, however, differ in several important respects. While the railway provides only station-to-station service, road transport is usually door-to-door; a comparison of road and rail must therefore allow for the costs of pickup and delivery from and to the station as well as the additional loading and unloading costs at the station (except for traffic carried from or to private sidings). The quality of road service tends to be higher: it involves less time, less breakage, greater frequency, prompter settlement of claims, and so forth. These differences are important for passenger service and general cargo freight, though not for ore. To make the rail and road costs comparable, therefore, total distribution costs—door to door—must be estimated.

Railway Costs

ON THE BRANCH LINE.   To derive the economic costs from the financial costs of operating the line requires several adjustments. The tax component of operations and maintenance costs must be deducted and the foreign exchange component, primarily in fuel, must be adjusted by a shadow rate of 1.75 times the official rate; these two adjustments increase these costs by about Rs360,000. If the branch line is closed, some workers would be dismissed and would find it difficult to find other employment or might be underemployed. If one-quarter of the workers find themselves in that position, and one applies a shadow rate of 50 percent to their wages, the economic costs of wages are about Rs150,000 below the financial costs. Thus the economic costs of operation and maintenance are Rs3.9 million compared with financial costs of Rs3.69 million (see column 1 of table 9-4).

Depreciation and interest are not directly relevant for determining economic costs, but the investments which have alternative uses are relevant. Except for the rails which could be used on other lines, assets of the line, including land, bridges, and tunnels, have no significant economic value. The locomotives and rolling stock are old; they can be used for about another five years but then must be replaced. If replaced at that time, no further replacements are anticipated during the twenty-five-year period, nor is any salvage value allowed for at the end of the project life. The present value of the assets, as well as the periodic replacement costs, is shown in column 2 of table 9-4. These costs are net of taxes and reflect an adjustment for the foreign exchange component.

ON THE MAIN LINE.   The financial costs of transporting main-line traffic which would be diverted to road transport if the branch line is closed are estimated at Rs255,000 (see "Financial Analysis"). These costs, adjusted for taxes, foreign exchange costs, depreciation, and interest, are estimated at Rs210,000 (see column 3 of table 9-4).

Transport on the main line involves not only operating costs but also certain capital costs. Since the traffic originating on or destined for the branch line is only a minor part of the total traffic on the main line and since no new line investments are required, nor are any required earlier, the only relevant investments relate to locomotives and rolling stock. The value of these assets, as well as their replacement costs, is shown in column 4 of table 9-4.

Table 9-4. Comparison of Costs of Transport by Rail and by Road
(millions of rupees)

Year	Railway costs						Road transport costs				Present worth (discounted at 12 percent)	
	On branch line		On main line		Distribution to and from railway stations (5)	Total railway costs (6)	Capital cost of vehicles (7)	Vehicle operating costs (8)	Road costs (9)	Total road transport costs (10)	Railway costs (11)	Road transport costs (12)
	Operating costs (1)	Capital costs (2)	Operating costs (3)	Capital costs (4)								
1	3.90	8.40	0.21	1.80	0.21	14.52	5.10	2.76	0.09	7.95	14.52	7.95
2	3.90	0	0.21	0	0.21	4.32	0	2.76	0.09	2.85	3.86	2.55
3	3.90	0	0.21	0	0.21	4.32	0	2.76	0.09	2.85	3.44	2.27
4	3.90	0	0.21	2.40	0.21	6.72	0	2.76	0.09	2.85	4.78	2.03
5	3.90	0	0.21	0	0.21	4.32	0	2.76	0.09	2.85	2.75	1.81
6	3.90	25.20	0.21	0	0.21	29.52	0	2.76	0.09	2.85	16.74	1.62
7	3.90	0	0.21	0	0.21	4.32	0	2.76	0.09	2.85	2.19	1.44
8	3.90	0	0.21	4.80	0.21	9.12	0	2.76	0.09	2.85	4.12	1.29
9	3.90	0	0.21	0	0.21	4.32	5.10	2.76	0.09	7.95	1.75	3.21
10	3.90	0	0.21	0	0.21	4.32	0	2.76	0.09	2.85	1.56	1.03

											11	12
11	3.90	0	0.21	0	0.21	4.32	0	2.76	0.09	2.85	1.39	0.92
12	3.90	0	0.21	0	0.21	4.32	0	2.76	0.09	2.85	1.24	0.82
13	3.90	0	0.21	0	0.21	4.32	0	2.76	0.09	2.85	1.11	0.73
14	3.90	0	0.21	0	0.21	4.32	0	2.76	0.09	2.85	0.99	0.65
15	3.90	0	0.21	0	0.21	4.32	0	2.76	0.09	2.85	0.89	0.58
16	3.90	0	0.21	0	0.21	4.32	0	2.76	0.09	2.85	0.79	0.52
17	3.90	0	0.21	0	0.21	4.32	5.10	2.76	0.09	7.95	0.70	1.30
18	3.90	0	0.21	0	0.21	4.32	0	2.76	0.09	2.85	0.63	0.42
19	3.90	0	0.21	0	0.21	4.32	0	2.76	0.09	2.85	0.56	0.37
20	3.90	0	0.21	0	0.21	4.32	0	2.76	0.09	2.85	0.50	0.33
21	3.90	0	0.21	0	0.21	4.32	0	2.76	0.09	2.85	0.45	0.30
22	3.90	0	0.21	0	0.21	4.32	0	2.76	0.09	2.85	0.40	0.27
23	3.90	0	0.21	0	0.21	4.32	0	2.76	0.09	2.85	0.36	0.24
24	3.90	0	0.21	0	0.21	4.32	5.10	2.76	0.09	7.95	0.32	0.59
25	3.90	0	0.21	0	0.21	4.32	0	2.76	0.09	2.85	0.29	0.19
26	0	0	0	0	0	0	−3.60	0	0	−3.60	0	−0.21
Total											66.33	33.22

Note: Net present worth equals Rs33.11 million; this is the difference between columns 11 and 12.

OTHER DISTRIBUTION COSTS.   An estimate of the total distribution costs door to door, and not merely station to station, must include costs of bringing the freight to the railway station and loading it on the train as well as the costs of unloading it at the final station and delivering it to the destination. The 750 tons of general cargo on the branch line are delivered and picked up by truck an average distance of ten miles at each end, for an annual total of 15,000 ton-miles. The economic costs of this are estimated at Rs0.9 a ton-mile (including an allowance for additional road maintenance costs), or a total of Rs13,500. Loading and unloading costs are each about Rs6 a ton, or Rs7,800 for the 650 tons which shift to road. The nonrailway distribution costs for general cargo are thus Rs21,300.

The ore is transported to the railway station by truck an average distance of eight miles, or 240,000 ton-miles; at Rs0.68 a ton-mile, the cost is Rs163,000. Loading costs are about Rs1.5 a ton, or Rs18,000 for the 12,000 tons of ore which shift to the road. Since the ore is delivered by the railway to plants with private sidings, no additional distribution costs are involved at that end. The marginal costs of maintaining the roads involved are about Rs12,000. The nonrailway distribution costs for ore are thus Rs193,000, or Rs214,300 for all freight (see column 5 of table 9-4). Additional distribution costs are not taken into account for passengers since the distances from origin and destination to bus and railway stations are similar. The total distribution costs by railway are shown in column 6.

Road Transport Costs

As indicated, the annual traffic which would shift to road transport if the railway line is closed amounts to 680,000 passenger-miles, 156,000 ton-miles of general cargo, and 4.25 million ton-miles or ore (see "Traffic"). Based on the traffic and operational studies, such a shift of traffic to the roads is estimated to involve economic costs (net of taxes and shadow priced for foreign exchange components) shown in table 9-5.

Replacements for these vehicles will be required every eight years (see column 7 of table 9-4). For the vehicles procured two years before the end of the project life, a salvage value of two-thirds of their costs has been assumed. Vehicle operating costs are shown in table 9-6. These vehicle operating costs are shown in column 8 of table 9-4.

ROAD COSTS.   The addition of forty-one trucks and one bus to the existing road traffic is not expected to require additional, or earlier, road investments. The additional road maintenance costs each year from the

Table 9-5. Capital Costs of Traffic Shift from Rail to Road

Vehicle	Mileage conversion	Equivalent number of vehicles	Costs (thousands of rupees)
Bus	680,000 passenger-miles = 20,000 bus-miles	1	150
General cargo truck	156,000 ton-miles = 40,000 truck-miles	1	120
Ore trucks	4.25 million ton-miles = 1.2 million truck-miles	40	4,830
Total			5,100

additional vehicles are estimated at Rs900 per mile, or Rs60,000 on the road paralleling the branch line and Rs30,000 on the road along the main line, for a total annual cost of Rs90,000 (see column 9 of table 9-4). The total costs of carrying the traffic by road are shown in column 10.

Comparison of Rail and Road Costs

As shown in columns 11 and 12 of table 9-4, the net present costs of carrying the traffic by railway for the next twenty-five years amount to about Rs66.3 million, compared with costs by road of Rs33.2 million, with all costs discounted at 12 percent. Distribution by rail is thus almost twice as expensive as by road. At an 8 percent discount rate, the relative costs of railway transport are even greater: Rs39.3 million instead of Rs33.1 million. There can be no question therefore that the railway line should be closed.

Table 9-6. Vehicle Operating Costs Incurred by Traffic Shift from Rail to Road

Vehicle	Volume of traffic	Unit cost (rupees)	Annual cost (thousands of rupees)
Bus	680,000 passenger-miles	0.14	95.20
General cargo truck	156,000 ton-miles	0.74	115.44
Ore truck	4,250,000 ton miles	0.60	2,550.00
Total			2,760.64

Sensitivity of Conclusion

Because of the one-sidedness of the conclusion, from both a financial and an economic point of view, that the branch line should be closed, no change in any single factor is likely to lead to a different conclusion. Nevertheless, several considerations deserve careful investigation. The most important is the volume of traffic. If, for example, additional ore is found in the area, the costs by road transport would increase more or less proportionally; that is, a tripling of traffic would triple road costs. The marginal costs of carrying the additional ore by rail, however, might be less than 50 percent on the branch line and perhaps 65 percent on the main line. With large increases in traffic, the conclusion might change.

The case study might also take into account the possibilities of reducing railway costs. The efficiency of road transport, however, is also likely to increase with better roads, larger trucks, and so forth, so that the net changes in relative efficiency might not necessarily favor the railway. When the conclusion is less one-sided, it may be important to make separate analyses for discontinuing passenger and freight services. Furthermore, although the case study referred to qualitative differences in the service between road and rail, the calculations made no allowance for these, primarily because they do not apply to the ore shipment, which accounts for most of the traffic; for other traffic, however, these differences are likely to be quite important.

Other Considerations

Even if road transport costs are much lower than railway costs, the users of the railway are likely to object to the discontinuance of the railway service, primarily because the present rates and fares on the branch line cover only about one-tenth of the costs of the line and are thus even lower than road transport costs. The users are in effect receiving a substantial subsidy which would be eliminated if the line is abandoned, unless the government provides a subsidy in another form. If the railway had set tariffs at a level to cover costs, the traffic would have diverted to the road long ago. The case study thus illustrates one of the distortions which arise if rates and fares do not reflect costs properly.

According to studies in Europe and Africa, a railway line is likely to be unprofitable if the annual traffic is less than 250,000 tons per mile; in the United States, the figure is at least 350,000 tons. In these studies, 3 passenger-miles are generally treated as 1 ton-mile (the ratio differs for individual railways). The critical density depends on such factors as the type of commodity carried, seasonal changes, topography and climate, and availability of other transport alternatives. But since a railway train can readily carry 1,000 tons of revenue freight, one train a day has a capacity of 365,000 tons a year. African studies indicate that at 250,000 tons, revenue can cover operating expenses but not capital costs. Operation of a line at 250,000 tons might be justified until major investments are needed. To construct a new line requires an annual traffic of at least 300,000 tons a mile.

Construction of an Oil Pipeline

Proposed Project and Costs

THE PROPOSED PROJECT consists of the construction of a sixteen-inch pipeline from the location of a refinery to a consuming center about 525 miles away. The pipeline would carry white oil products—primarily kerosene, motor spirit, and aviation fuel. For the most part, the present distribution is by railway; trucks, however, carry almost all of the traffic within a radius of 150 miles of the refinery and some traffic to even more distant consumption centers since the railway is not always able to provide sufficient tankwagons. Black oil would continue to be moved by railway.

Capital Costs

The capital costs of the project are estimated at Rs900 million. They consist primarily of the pipeline (Rs300 million), the transportation and laying of the pipeline (Rs300 million), pumps, including adequate standby capacity (Rs90 million), and terminal tankage and railway facilities (Rs105 million). Additional pumping capacity will be required nine years after completion of the project to handle the growing traffic (see "Traffic"). Construction of the project is estimated to take two years. The life of the pipeline is estimated at thirty years and that of the pumps at fifteen years, when replacements for pumps will be required.

To calculate the economic costs, two adjustments are needed. First, duties and other taxes amounting to Rs75 million must be deducted. Second, the foreign exchange component is estimated at about Rs412 million. At a shadow rate for foreign exchange of 1.75 times the official rate, these costs amount to Rs721 million, or Rs309 million more than the financial costs. The total economic costs are thus Rs1,134 million (Rs900 million − Rs75 million + Rs309 million). These economic costs, as well as the costs of additional pumps in year 11 and of replacements in years 17 and 26, are shown in column 1 of table 10-1. The salvage value at the end of the project's life of the pumps installed in year 26 is estimated at Rs30 million.

Operating Costs

The annual operating costs of the pipeline (excluding depreciation) are estimated at Rs27 million in the first year of operation, rising gradually with the growth of traffic and reaching Rs40.8 million after additional pumps are added and full capacity is reached. The costs consist primarily of fuel, repair and maintenance, and administration. The economic costs, adjusted for taxes and foreign exchange costs, are estimated to be 10 percent higher. They are shown in column 2 of table 10-1 for the life of the project.

Value of Surplus Rolling Stock

If the pipeline is built, about 2,500 tankwagons and thirty-three diesel locomotives become surplus (see "Economic Justification"), and their economic value must be deducted from the costs of the pipeline. The value of the locomotives can be determined readily since they can be used by the railway immediately to replace steam locomotives and overage diesel locomotives or to handle the increase in traffic. As explained more fully in "Economic Justification," the economic value of the thirty-three locomotives is estimated at Rs138.6 million.

To estimate the economic value of 2,500 tankwagons is more difficult because the railway has no immediate use for them. Their economic value is determined by the best alternative for which they can be used, which includes sale to other countries, use of the underframes for other wagons, transport of white oil products in other parts of the country, transport of all black oil, and scrapping them. After reviewing these and other alternatives, the railway estimates that the best alternative is to dispose of 1,000 tankwagons for about Rs60,000 each, bringing total revenues of Rs60 million, and to hold the remainder to meet the increased requirements for the transport of other petroleum products as well as for replacements. These requirements are estimated to rise gradually from 150 tankwagons in year 4 to 310 in year 9; with the disposition of an additional 140 wagons in year 11, the total surplus would be absorbed (see table 10-2). Taking into account their age, condition, and replacement costs, the value of these tankwagons is estimated at Rs75,000 each. An amount of Rs300,000 annually has been deducted for storage costs. The total number of the surplus locomotives and tankwagons and their value (minus storage costs) is shown in table 10-2.

Table 10-1. Comparison of Transport Costs via Oil Pipeline and Railway
(millions of rupees)

Year	Cost of pipeline				Cost of railway transport							Present worth (discounted at 12 percent)	
					Capital costs			Operating costs					
	Capital costs (1)	Operating costs (2)	Value of surplus rolling stock (3)	Total costs (4)	Tank-wagons (5)	Locomotives (6)	Yard & line capacity (7)	Tank-wagons (8)	Locomotives (9)	Other (10)	Total costs (11)	Pipeline costs (12)	Railway costs (13)
1	510.0	0	0	510.0	0	0	0	0	0	0	0	510.0	0
2	624.0	0	0	624.0	0	0	0	0	0	0	0	557.2	0
3	0	30.0	−198.6	−168.6	96.9	159.4	19.2	7.2	42.1	11.0	335.8	−134.4	267.6
4	0	30.9	−11.0	19.9	41.8	20.8	0	7.8	45.6	12.0	128.0	14.2	91.1
5	0	31.8	−13.2	18.6	56.3	34.7	0	8.7	51.5	13.2	164.4	11.8	104.6
6	0	33.0	−15.5	17.5	52.4	27.7	0	9.3	56.2	14.6	160.2	9.9	90.8
7	0	34.2	−17.7	16.5	66.9	34.7	0	10.5	62.0	15.9	190.0	8.4	96.3
8	0	35.4	−20.0	15.4	69.2	34.7	0	11.4	67.9	17.6	200.8	7.0	90.8
9	0	36.6	−23.0	13.6	90.7	41.6	19.2	12.6	74.9	19.2	258.2	5.5	104.3
10	0	38.1	−10.2	27.9	77.9	41.6	0	14.1	81.9	21.2	236.7	10.1	85.4
11	75.0	39.6	0	114.6	67.7	83.2	0	15.3	90.1	23.3	279.6	36.9	90.0
12	0	43.5	0	43.5	80.0	55.4	0	16.8	99.5	25.5	277.2	12.5	79.6
13	0	45.0	0	45.0	80.0	124.7	0	18.4	108.8	28.1	360.0	11.6	92.5
14	0	45.0	0	45.0	6.2	0	0	18.4	108.8	28.1	161.5	10.3	37.0
15	0	45.0	0	45.0	6.2	69.3	0	18.4	108.8	28.1	230.8	9.2	47.3

16	0	45.0	0	45.0	6.2	0	0	18.4	108.8	28.1	161.5	8.2	29.6
17	144.0	45.0	189.0	45.0	12.3	0	0	18.4	108.8	28.1	167.6	30.8	27.3
18	0	45.0	0	45.0	12.3	0	0	18.4	108.8	28.1	167.6	6.6	24.5
19	0	45.0	0	45.0	18.5	55.4	0	18.4	108.8	28.1	229.2	5.9	29.8
20	0	45.0	0	45.0	18.5	0	0	18.4	108.8	28.1	173.8	5.2	20.2
21	0	45.0	0	45.0	18.5	0	0	18.4	108.8	28.1	173.8	4.7	18.1
22	0	45.0	0	45.0	18.5	0	0	18.4	108.8	28.1	173.8	4.2	16.2
23	0	45.0	0	45.0	24.6	20.8	0	18.4	108.8	28.1	200.7	3.7	16.7
24	0	45.0	0	45.0	24.6	20.8	0	18.4	108.8	28.1	200.7	3.3	14.9
25	0	45.0	0	45.0	24.6	34.7	0	18.4	108.8	28.1	214.6	3.0	14.2
26	75.0	45.0	120.0	45.0	24.6	27.7	0	18.4	108.8	28.1	207.6	7.1	12.2
27	0	45.0	45.0	45.0	30.8	34.7	0	18.4	108.8	28.1	220.8	2.4	11.7
28	0	45.0	45.0	45.0	30.8	34.7	0	18.4	108.8	28.1	220.8	2.1	10.4
29	0	45.0	45.0	45.0	36.9	41.6	0	18.4	108.8	28.1	233.8	1.9	9.8
30	0	45.0	45.0	45.0	30.8	41.6	0	18.4	108.8	28.1	227.7	1.7	8.4
31	0	45.0	45.0	45.0	43.1	83.2	0	18.4	108.8	28.1	281.6	1.5	9.3
32	0	45.0	45.0	45.0	36.9	55.4	0	18.4	108.8	28.1	247.6	1.4	7.4
33	-30.0	0	-30.0	0	-390.0	-360.0	0	0	0	0	-750.0	-0.8	-20.3
Total												1,173.1	1,537.7

Note: Net present worth equals Rs364.6 million; this is the difference between columns 12 and 13.

155

Table 10-2. Number and Value of Surplus Locomotives and Tankwagons

	Locomotives		Tankwagons		
Year	Number	Value (millions of rupees)	Number	Value (millions of rupees)	Total value (millions of rupees)
3	33	138.6	1,000	60.0	198.6
4	0	0	150	11.0	11.0
5	0	0	180	13.2	13.2
6	0	0	210	15.5	15.5
7	0	0	240	17.7	17.7
8	0	0	270	20.0	20.0
9	0	0	310	23.0	23.0
10	0	0	140	10.2	10.2
Total			2,500		

The value of the surplus locomotives and wagons is shown as a negative cost in column 3 of table 10-1. The total cost of the pipeline, minus the value of the surplus rolling stock, is shown in column 4.

Traffic

To prepare a forecast of white oil traffic for the pipeline, separate estimates have been made for the different types of petroleum, consisting primarily of kerosene, motor spirit, and aviation fuel. In addition, the area served by the pipeline has been divided into four separate zones of consumption. Since zone 1 is within a radius of 150 miles of the refinery, however, petroleum is distributed in the zone by truck; this is expected to continue even after the construction of the pipeline since trucks can provide direct distribution to many points, thus avoiding an additional transfer for most of the traffic. Taking into account such factors as the past growth of consumption, the growth in income in these zones, the specific sources of demand for each product, the availability of alternative sources of energy, and the likelihood of oil being discovered or refineries being established in other areas, the pipeline traffic has been projected to reach 1.65 million tons, or about 730 million ton-miles, in the opening year of the pipeline (year 3). Thereafter, it is expected to grow at an annual rate of 10 percent until year 13, when the traffic amounts to 4.25 million tons or 1,870 million ton-miles. No in-

Table 10-3. Estimate of Traffic and of Tankwagon and Locomotive Requirements

Year	Traffic Tons (1)	Traffic Ton-miles (million) (2)	Tankwagon Total fleet (3)	Tankwagon Annual increase (4)	Tankwagon Annual replacements (5)	Locomotive Total fleet (6)	Locomotive Annual increase (7)	Locomotive Annual replacements (8)
3	1.65	730	2,800	300	0	36	3	0
4	1.80	800	3,050	250	0	39	3	0
5	2.00	880	3,400	350	0	44	5	0
6	2.20	970	3,700	300	0	48	4	0
7	2.40	1,060	4,100	400	0	53	5	0
8	2.65	1,170	4,500	400	0	58	5	0
9	2.90	1,280	5,000	500	50	64	6	0
10	3.20	1,410	5,500	500	50	70	6	0
11	3.50	1,550	6,000	500	50	77	7	5
12	3.85	1,700	6,600	600	50	85	8	0
13	4.25	1,870	7,200	600	50	93	8	10
14	4.25	1,870	7,200	0	50	93	0	0
15	4.25	1,870	7,200	0	50	93	0	10
16	4.25	1,870	7,200	0	50	93	0	0
17	4.25	1,870	7,200	0	100	93	0	0
18	4.25	1,870	7,200	0	100	93	0	0
19	4.25	1,870	7,200	0	150	93	0	8
20	4.25	1,870	7,200	0	150	93	0	0
21	4.25	1,870	7,200	0	150	93	0	0
22	4.25	1,870	7,200	0	150	93	0	0
23	4.25	1,870	7,200	0	200	93	0	3
24	4.25	1,870	7,200	0	200	93	0	3
25	4.25	1,870	7,200	0	200	93	0	5
26	4.25	1,870	7,200	0	200	93	0	4
27	4.25	1,870	7,200	0	250	93	0	5
28	4.25	1,870	7,200	0	250	93	0	5
29	4.25	1,870	7,200	0	300	93	0	6
30	4.25	1,870	7,200	0	250	93	0	6
31	4.25	1,870	7,200	0	350	93	0	12
32	4.25	1,870	7,200	0	300	93	0	8

crease in traffic is allowed for thereafter since the capacity of the pipeline is then fully utilized (see columns 1 and 2 of table 10-3).

Economic Justification

The economic justification for a pipeline requires a number of investigations. For example, alternative locations of the pipeline may have to be compared. The size of the pipeline is important since a larger one, able to handle a greater traffic volume, involves higher capital costs but lower costs for pumps and operations. This case study assumes that these other studies have been undertaken and is therefore limited to a comparison of pipeline costs with the next best alternative, transport by railway. The costs by railway consist of capital costs for tankwagons, locomotives, yard facilities, and line capacity as well as operating costs.

Capital Costs

TANKWAGONS. Although most of the railway's tankwagons have a capacity of 18 tons, others have a capacity of 40 tons; the following estimates are therefore presented in terms of 18-ton wagon equivalents. Under present operations, the turnaround time per tankwagon for the average return trip of almost 900 miles is about ten days, thus permitting thirty-six trips a year. The annual capacity of a tankwagon is therefore 650 tons. To carry the estimated 1.65 million tons in the opening year of the pipeline thus requires about 2,500 tankwagons, plus a 10 percent allowance for repair time, for a total of 2,800 wagons. Thereafter, new tankwagons are required to handle the growth in traffic. For example, as shown in column 1 of table 10-3, traffic is expected to grow between years 3 and 4 from 1.65 to 1.8 million tons, an increase of 150,000 tons; this requires about 250 new wagons. The total requirements and annual increases are shown in columns 3 and 4 of the table.

As for replacement requirements, assuming an average life of twenty-five years for a tankwagon and taking into account the age composition of the 2,500 wagons existing at the beginning of year 3, replacement does not begin until year 9 since the existing fleet is relatively new. Between year 9 and year 28, 2,500 wagons must be replaced. Thereafter, replacements are identical to the annual increases in the fleet twenty-five years earlier. The annual replacement requirements are shown in column 5 of table 10-3.

To calculate the economic cost of the tankwagons, it is useful to distinguish between the value of the fleet of 2,500 wagons existing at the beginning of year 3, on the one hand, and the cost of additional wagons, including replacement requirements, on the other hand. As for the 2,500 tankwagons which the railway already owns, their value was previously determined (see "Proposed Project and Costs"). The financial cost of a new tankwagon is estimated at Rs96,000. After deducting Rs25,500 for duties and taxes and shadow pricing the foreign exchange component of Rs70,500 by 1.75 times the official exchange rate, the economic cost of a wagon amounts to about Rs123,000. For the 300 additional wagons required in year 3, this is an investment of Rs36.9 million. The value of the existing fleet and the costs of additional wagons, including replacements, are shown in column 5 of table 10-1. The salvage value of the fleet of 7,200 wagons at the end of the project life, taking into account such factors as their average age and the likelihood of technological improvements, is shown as a negative cost of Rs390 million in year 33.

LOCOMOTIVES.   One locomotive is required to haul about seventy-five tankwagons. The annual haulage capacity of a locomotive for thirty-six trips is thus 50,000 tons. In year 3 the railway requires thirty-six locomotives (including three spares) to haul the 1.65 million tons of petroleum. To carry the increase in traffic thereafter, the railway needs three new locomotives in year 3 to haul the additional 150,000 tons, an additional three in year 4, and so forth (see columns 6 and 7 of table 10-3). In addition, periodic replacements are required both for the fleet existing at the beginning of year 3 and for subsequent additions. Assuming an average life of twenty years for a diesel locomotive and taking into account the age composition of the existing fleet, these requirements begin in year 11; they are shown in column 8 of the table.

The value of the thirty-three locomotives existing at the beginning of year 3, taking into account their age and replacement costs, is estimated at Rs4.2 million each, or a total of Rs138.6 million. The capital cost of a new locomotive is estimated at Rs5.58 million. Deducting Rs1.37 million for duties and taxes and shadow pricing the foreign exchange component of Rs3.63 million make the economic costs Rs6.93 million. In year 3, therefore, capital costs of Rs20.8 million are incurred and in year 4, the same amount. The value of the existing fleet plus the costs of additional locomotives, including replacements, is shown in column 6 of table 10-1. The salvage value of the fleet of ninety-five locomotives at the end of the project life, taking into account such factors as their average life at that time, is shown as a negative cost of Rs360 million in year 33.

YARD FACILITIES AND LINE CAPACITY.   The yard and line capacity of the railway requires expansion if the railway is to carry the additional petroleum traffic. The railway estimates that the economic costs of the expansion are Rs19.2 million in year 3 and a further Rs19.2 million in year 9 (see column 7 of table 10-1).

Operating Costs

TANKWAGONS.   The direct operating costs of a tankwagon, especially repair and maintenance, amount to Rs2,400 annually. With an allowance for taxes and duties and for the foreign exchange component, the economic costs are about Rs2,555. For the 2,800 tankwagons in year 3, the operating costs are thus Rs7.2 million; they rise to Rs18.4 million in year 13 in line with the increase in the fleet (see column 8 of table 10-1).

LOCOMOTIVES.   For the distances involved, the direct operating costs of a diesel locomotive, including primarily fuel and maintenance, amount to Rs1.35 million annually. With adjustments for taxes and foreign exchange costs, the economic costs amount to Rs1.7 million. For the thirty-six locomotives required in year 3, the operating costs are thus Rs42.1 million; they rise to Rs108.8 million in year 13 in line with the increase in the locomotive fleet (see column 9 of table 10-1).

OTHER COSTS.   In addition to the direct costs as estimated, the railway incurs other costs such as the maintenance of track, the operation of signaling and communication equipment, and adminstrative expenses. The railway estimates these costs at Rs0.027 a ton-mile. These costs, however, do not vary directly with the volume of traffic. Taking into account the fact that the petroleum traffic lost to the railway if the pipeline is built is not an insignificant proportion of total traffic on the particular line, the railway estimates that the marginal costs—that is, the amount that could be saved—are 55 percent of the average cost or Rs0.015 a ton-mile. For the 730 million ton-miles carried in year 3 (see column 2 of table 10-3), this means a cost of Rs11.0 million; it rises to Rs28.1 million in year 13, in line with the growth of traffic (see column 10 of table 10-1).

The total costs of carrying the petroleum by railway, including both capital and operating costs, are shown in column 11 of table 10-1.

Comparison of Pipeline and Rail Costs

As shown in columns 12 and 13 of table 10-1, the net present costs of carrying the petroleum traffic by railway for the next thirty years amount to about Rs1,537.7 million compared with pipeline costs of only Rs1,173.1 million, with both costs discounted at 12 percent; the net present worth of the pipeline is Rs364.6 million.

Transport by railway is thus about 30 percent more expensive than by pipeline, and the pipeline project seems well justified. At an 8 percent discount rate, the net present worth of the pipeline is even greater, at Rs852.3 million. The internal rate of return is then about 17 percent.

In view of the pipeline's large net present worth, the conclusion is not particularly sensitive to changes in any one of the costs involved. A number of items, however, deserve attention.

The railway's competitive position would be enhanced greatly if it could improve its operating efficiency. If, for example, the turnaround time of tankwagons could be reduced from ten days to seven and one-half days, the number of wagons and locomotives required would be reduced by 25 percent, though the reduction in operating costs would be less. Since the average round trip is almost 900 miles, this implies a daily movement of about 165 miles, allowing one day each for loading and unloading. Such an improvement in efficiency reduces net present railway costs from Rs1,538 million to about 1,260 million. At the same time it increases the net costs of the pipeline since the size of the surplus rolling stock, the value of which has been credited to the pipeline, is also reduced by 25 percent; the amount involved (discounted) is about Rs51 million. The pipeline costs thus go up to about Rs1,224 million, compared with Rs1,260 million for the railway, and the advantage of the pipeline is sharply reduced, although is is still justified.

The valuation of the fleet of 2,500 tankwagons and thirty-three locomotives which become surplus if the pipeline is built also influences the conclusion. If, for example, the opportunities for disposal are less favorable and the value of the rolling stock to be disposed of in year 3 is only Rs99.3 million instead of Rs198.6 million, the total discounted costs of the pipeline rise to about Rs1,252 million and those of railway transport decline to about Rs1,459 million. The net present worth of the pipeline still is Rs207 million. This consideration and the improved efficiency are not fully additive, however, since the reduction in the turn-around time from ten to seven and one-half days reduces the surplus fleet by 25 percent.

The capital costs of the pipeline account for more than 90 percent of total discounted pipeline costs so that errors in the estimate of operating expenses can hardly influence the conclusion. If capital costs are 25 percent higher than estimated, the net present worth of the pipeline is sharply reduced to about Rs85 million.

A major item when not discounted is the salvage value of the rolling stock (Rs750 million) in year 33. Although the margin of error in estimating this value is large, the impact on the conclusion is slight since its discounted value is only Rs20.3 million.

Two items which are difficult to estimate are the reduction in indirect railway operating costs if the pipeline is built and the requirements for additional yard and line capacity if it is not built. In both cases it is necessary to forecast the railway's total traffic; if traffic declines, for example, additional line capacity is not needed. Fortunately both items have relatively little importance in this project.

The level of traffic affects railway costs almost proportionally while pipeline costs are largely fixed and have little relation to traffic. The case for a pipeline thus becomes stronger the greater the traffic. In view of the large net present worth of the pipeline, construction of the pipeline is justified even at a lower traffic level.

An important point which is not fully reflected in the estimates is the reliability of service provided by the two alternatives. It seems likely that the pipeline can provide more reliable service than the railway and thus reduce the need for storage capacity. The pipeline is less flexible, however, and therefore involves a greater risk. But a pipeline provides an alternative transport mode if the railway is incapacitated.

Case Study 11

Construction
of Additional Berths

Proposed Project and Costs

TRAFFIC AT A SMALL OCEAN PORT with two berths has been growing, and the port authority wants to determine the proper time to construct one or more additional berths. They would be medium-draft, multipurpose, and dry-cargo-handling berths, each about 550 feet long and designed for a dredged depth of 30 feet, with an allowance of 2 feet for siltation and another 2 feet for overdredging. The project would include the necessary cargo-handling facilities such as forklift trucks, tractors, trailers, and mobile cranes as well as related facilities such as transit-handling and storage areas, a truck-parking terminal, operational buildings, access and transit roads and rail tracks, freshwater mains, fuel oil bunker and discharge mains, telephone connections, electricity cables, and fire-fighting equipment.

The financial costs of a berth are estimated at Rs45 million, including Rs27 million for berth construction, Rs4.5 million for roads and pavements, and a similar amount for cargo-handling equipment. Replacement requirements are estimated at Rs4.5 million in the eighth year and Rs9 million in the sixteenth year. Construction is expected to take three years. The economic life of a berth is estimated at twenty-five years; this is less than its physical life, but a competitive port will probably be built by that time or innovations in containerization might make some of the berths obsolete.

To estimate the economic costs, several adjustments are necessary. First, an allowance must be made for the foreign exchange costs, which are estimated at Rs21 million; at a shadow price for foreign exchange of 1.75 times the official rate, this involves economic costs of about Rs36.9 million, or Rs15.9 million more than the financial costs. The estimate includes customs duties and sales taxes amounting to Rs4.5 million and interest during construction of Rs3 million; these charges of Rs7.5 million must be deducted. The economic costs per berth are thus Rs53.4 million (Rs45 million + Rs15.9 million − Rs7.5 million). These costs,

Table 11-1. Comparison of Project Costs and Benefits of Construction of Berths
(millions of rupees)

	Costs of berth			Benefits		Present worth (discounted at 12 percent)				Present cost (if project postponed) (discounted at 12 percent)	
								Benefits of fourth berth			
Year	Capital costs (1)	Maintenance costs (2)	Total costs (3)	Third berth (4)	Fourth berth (5)	Costs of berth (6)	Benefits of third berth (7)	No traffic increase after year 11 (8)	Traffic increase after year 11 (9)	1-year postponement (10)	2-year postponement (11)
1	15.00	0	15.00	0	0	15.00	0	0	0	0	0
2	18.00	0	18.00	0	0	16.07	0	0	0	13.40	0
3	20.40	0	20.40	0	0	16.26	0	0	0	14.35	11.96
4	0	0.60	0.60	3.27	0.45	0.43	2.33	0.32	0.32	14.52	12.82
5	0	0.60	0.60	4.20	0.54	0.38	2.67	0.34	0.34	0.38	12.97
6	0	0.60	0.60	5.64	0.69	0.34	3.20	0.39	0.39	0.34	0.34
7	0	0.60	0.60	7.95	0.87	0.30	4.03	0.44	0.44	0.30	0.30
8	0	0.60	0.60	10.32	1.17	0.27	4.66	0.53	0.53	0.27	0.27
9	0	0.60	0.60	13.38	1.68	0.24	5.41	0.68	0.68	0.24	0.24
10	0	0.60	0.60	23.04	2.16	0.22	8.32	0.78	0.78	0.22	0.22
11	6.00	0.60	6.60	41.76	2.70[a]	2.13	13.45	0.87	0.87	0.19	0.19
12	0	0.60	0.60	41.76	3.54	0.17	11.99	0.77	1.02	1.89	0.17

13	0.60	0	0.60	41.76	4.62	0.15	10.73	0.69	1.19	0.15	1.70
14	0.60	0	0.60	41.76	5.88	0.14	9.56	0.62	1.35	0.14	0.14
15	0.60	0	0.60	41.76	7.80	0.12	8.56	0.55	1.60	0.12	0.12
16	0.60	0	0.60	41.76	10.26	0.11	7.64	0.49	1.88	0.11	0.11
17	0.60	0	0.60	41.76	15.33	0.10	6.81	0.44	2.50	0.10	0.10
18	0.60	0	0.60	41.76	23.04	0.09	6.10	0.39	3.36	0.09	0.09
19	0.60	0	0.60	41.76	43.56	0.08	5.43	0.35	5.66	0.08	0.08
20	12.60	12.00	12.60	41.76	43.56	1.46	4.84	0.31	5.05	0.07	0.07
21	0.60	0	0.60	41.76	43.56	0.06	4.34	0.28	4.53	1.31	0.06
22	0.60	0	0.60	41.76	43.56	0.06	3.88	0.25	4.05	0.06	1.17
23	0.60	0	0.60	41.76	43.56	0.05	3.47	0.22	3.62	0.05	0.05
24	0.60	0	0.60	41.76	43.56	0.04	3.09	0.20	3.22	0.04	0.04
25	0.60	0	0.60	41.76	43.56	0.04	2.76	0.18	2.87	0.04	0.04
26	0.60	0	0.60	41.76	43.56	0.04	2.46	0.16	2.57	0.04	0.04
27	0.60	0	0.60	41.76	43.56	0.03	2.21	0.14	2.31	0.03	0.03
28	0.60	0	0.60	41.76	43.56	0.03	1.96	0.13	2.05	0.03	0.03
29	0	0	0	0	0	0	0	0	0	0.03	0.03
30	0	0	0	0	0	0	0	0	0	0	0.02
Total						54.41[a]	139.90[a]	10.52[a]	53.18[a]	48.59[a]	43.40[a]

Note: Net present worth of a third berth equals Rs85.49 million (the difference between columns 6 and 7); of a fourth berth, −Rs43.89 million (columns 6 and 8); and −Rs1.23 million (columns 6 and 9), depending on traffic growth.

a. Figures indicate the benefits if traffic continues to increase; if it does not increase, the additional benefits of the fourth berth remain at the level of the eleventh year (Rs2.70 million) for the remaining life of the project.

as well as the economic costs of periodic replacements, are shown in column 1 of table 11-1.

The economic costs for annual maintenance and repair of each berth are estimated at Rs0.6 million (see column 2 of table 11-1).

Project Benefit

The benefit of an additional berth is the value of the reduced waiting time of ships. To calculate this benefit, information is required on the number of ships expected to arrive and their arrival time, the average servicing time at berth, and the value of ship time. This case study presents separate estimates to determine the justification for both a third and a fourth berth.

Number of Ships

On the basis of detailed estimates of the country's exports, imports, and coastal traffic and taking into account such other relevant factors as probable increases in the size of ships, the number of ships estimated to call at the port annually is expected to reach 117 in the first year after completion of the project (year 4). Thereafter, traffic is estimated to grow by 8 percent annually for eight years (years 5–12) and 6 percent thereafter (years 13–28). For the purpose of estimating the benefits of a third berth, no increase in traffic is allowed for after year 11 since the waiting time in year 12 would become so long that ships would divert to another port (see discussion on waiting time). For the purpose of estimating the benefits of a fourth berth, however, traffic is estimated to increase by 6 percent annually for a further eight years (years 12–19); then ship waiting times would again lead to diversion to other ports (see columns 1 and 2 of table 11-2).

The frequency distribution of the number of ships arriving daily is estimated to follow approximately a Poisson distribution, and the timing of the daily ship arrivals is estimated to be random during the period under consideration; that is, no relationship exists between the number of ships arriving on a certain day, the day before, or the day after.

Servicing Time

The servicing time for a ship at berth has averaged three days. The expected increase in the volume of cargo handled for each ship is projected to be offset by increased mechanization and operating efficiencies, so that the average servicing time remains approximately three days. The number of days the berths are occupied during the year, that is, the number of ships multiplied by the servicing time for each ship, is shown in columns 3 and 4 of table 11-2.

Waiting Time

Given the preceding information, the waiting time of ships can be estimated on the basis of queuing theory for any number of berths. (The data used in this case study are merely illustrative. For an explanation of the mathematics involved, see de Weille and Ray 1968.) These waiting times are shown for two, three, and four berths in columns 5, 6, and 7, respectively, of table 11-2. The columns show, for example, that when 177 ships arrive annually and a total service time of 351 days is required (3 days per ship), the total annual waiting time is 105 days for a port with two berths, 14 days for one with three berths, and only 2 days with four berths. The average waiting time per ship thus declines from about 1 day with two berths to about three hours with three berths and to about twenty-five minutes with four berths.

Cost of Annual Waiting Time

An estimate of the type of ships expected to arrive at the port indicates that the economic cost of a ship waiting for a berth is about Rs36,000 a day; this allows for the fact that most of the cost is in foreign exchange. The costs of the annual ship waiting time when there are two, three, or four berths are shown in columns 8, 9, and 10, respectively, of table 11-2; in these columns the waiting times shown in columns 5, 6, and 7, respectively, are multiplied by Rs36,000

The savings from reduction in waiting time with a third berth—that is, the difference between columns 8 and 9 of table 11-2—are the benefits of such a berth; these benefits are shown in column 4 of table 11-1. The additional benefits of a fourth berth—that is, the difference between columns 9 and 10 of table 11-2—are shown in column 5 of table 11-1.

Comparison of Costs and Benefits

As shown in the note to table 11-1, the net present value of a third berth is Rs85.5 million with both costs and benefits discounted at 12 percent, and the cost-benefit ratio is 1 : 2.6. At an 8 percent discount rate, the net present worth is about Rs175 million. The net present

Table 11-2. Annual Ship Traffic, Berth Occupancy, and Ship Waiting Time and Costs by Number of Berths

Year	Number of ships per year		Total annual berth occupancy (days)		Total annual ship waiting time (days)			Cost of annual ship waiting time (millions of rupees)		
	Two berths (1)	Three or more berths (2)	Two berths (3)	Three or more berths (4)	Two berths (5)	Three berths (6)	Four berths (7)	Two berths (8)	Three berths (9)	Four berths (10)
1	0	0	0	0	0	0	0	0	0	0
2	0	0	0	0	0	0	0	0	0	0
3	0	0	0	0	0	0	0	0	0	0
4	117	117	351	351	105	14	2	3.78	0.51	0.06
5	127	127	381	381	135	18	3	4.86	0.66	0.12
6	137	137	411	411	180	23	4	6.48	0.84	0.15
7	148	148	444	444	250	29	5	9.00	1.05	0.18
8	160	160	480	480	325	38	6	11.70	1.38	0.21
9	173	173	519	519	425	53	7	15.30	1.92	0.24
10	187	187	561	561	710	70	10	25.56	2.52	0.36

11	202	202	606	606	1,250	90[a]	14[a]	45.00	3.24[a]	0.5[a]
12	202	214	606	642	1,250	115	17	45.00	4.14	0.60
13	202	226	606	678	1,250	150	22	45.00	5.40	0.78
14	202	239	606	717	1,250	190	27	45.00	6.84	0.96
15	202	253	606	759	1,250	250	33	45.00	9.00	1.20
16	202	268	606	804	1,250	325	40	45.00	11.70	1.44
17	202	284	606	852	1,250	475	49	45.00	17.10	1.77
18	202	301	606	903	1,250	700	60	45.00	25.20	2.16
19	202	319	606	957	1,250	1,300	90	45.00	46.80	3.24
20	202	319	606	957	1,250	1,300	90	45.00	46.80	3.24
21	202	319	606	957	1,250	1,300	90	45.00	46.80	3.24
22	202	319	606	957	1,250	1,300	90	45.00	46.80	3.24
23	202	319	606	957	1,250	1,300	90	45.00	46.80	3.24
24	202	319	606	957	1,250	1,300	90	45.00	46.80	3.24
25	202	319	606	957	1,250	1,300	90	45.00	46.80	3.24
26	202	319	606	957	1,250	1,300	90	45.00	46.80	3.24
27	202	319	606	957	1,250	1,300	90	45.00	46.80	3.24
28	202	319	606	957	1,250	1,300	90	45.00	46.80	3.24

a. The figures below this indicate ship waiting time and their costs if traffic continues to increase; if the traffic does not increase, the waiting times and their costs remain at the level of the eleventh year for the remaining life of the project.

worth of a fourth berth is a negative Rs43.9 million if the traffic does not increase after the eleventh year; if the traffic continues to increase, it is a negative Rs1.2 million (see note to table 11-1). At an 8 percent discount rate, the net present worth is a negative Rs43 million with no further traffic increase but becomes nearly Rs47 million if traffic continues to increase. The decision to build a fourth berth depends, therefore, primarily on the traffic forecast, but appears questionable, depending somewhat on the appropriate discount rate.

Optimum Timing of Project

Although a third berth appears well justified, an analysis of the optimum timing for its construction indicates that it is premature to start the berth now and have it ready in the fourth year.

To calculate the optimum time for starting the project, the costs of delay—that is, the loss of benefits as a result of the postponement—must be compared with the benefits—that is, the reduction in discounted costs. On the assumption that the project life continues to be twenty-five years and that it will not be replaced thereafter, a postponement of one year reduces present discounted costs from Rs54.41 million to Rs48.59 million, or by Rs5.82 million (see columns 6 and 10, table 11-1). At an 8 percent discount rate, the cost reduction is Rs4.5 million. The delay affects the benefits in two ways. First, the benefit of Rs2.33 million in the first year is lost. Second, a further benefit would materialize in the additional year at the end of the project life; its present discounted value is Rs1.75 million. The net loss in benefits is thus only Rs0.58 million, compared with a reduction in costs of Rs5.82 million. A postponement of at least one year is therefore well justified. Postponing the project a second year reduces costs by an additional Rs5.19 million (the difference between the totals of columns 10 and 11) while the net loss in benefits would be Rs1.12 million (that is, a loss of 2.67 million in the second year minus additional benefits of Rs1.55 million at the end of the project life). A postponement of at least two years is thus justified. The reduction in discounted costs and benefits for each of the first seven years is shown in table 11-3.

This year-by-year analysis indicates that the project should be started in about five years. Postponing it an additional year is not justified since in that year the loss of benefits exceeds the reduction in costs by Rs1.2 million. In this calculation, it has been assumed that the berth will not be replaced at the end of its life. If it is to be replaced, however, there is a further saving in costs from the delay in replacement, although the only impact on benefits is the loss in the early years. (For a

**Table 11-3. Reduction in Discounted Costs
and Benefits because of Postponement**
(millions of rupees)

Postponement (year)	Reduction in costs	Reduction in benefits	Net benefits (+) or costs (−)
1	5.8	0.6	+5.2
2	5.2	1.1	+4.1
3	4.5	1.8	+2.7
4	4.2	2.7	+1.5
5	3.6	3.6	0
6	3.3	4.5	−1.2
7	3.0	7.5	−4.5

more detailed discussion, see "Optimum Timing of Projects," chapter 5.)

Although a precise estimate of the optimum time for the berth requires the preceding calculation, an approximation is possible in this case since the initial capital costs account for a very large proportion of total costs. At an opportunity cost of 12 percent, a one-year postponement reduces the initial capital costs of Rs53.4 million by about Rs6.4 million. The net benefits in the third year after completion of the project are only Rs5 million (gross benefits of Rs5.6 million minus maintenance costs of Rs0.6 million), so that a postponement of at least three years appears justified. This is, however, only a rough guide since it does not allow for some of the other relevant factors.

Sensitivity of Conclusion

The conclusion could be sensitive to such factors as the capital costs of the project, future traffic, the distribution of ship arrivals, the servicing time at berth, and the congestion level at which traffic would move to another port.

Even a substantial increase in capital costs leaves a positive net present worth and does not affect the timing of the project significantly. For example, an increase of 33 percent in capital and replacement costs increases the savings of a seven-year postponement to Rs39 million, or by Rs8.4 million. But because of the large benefits of Rs13.4 million in the ninth year, a further postponement reduces benefits even more. It is quite possible that the construction of two berths at the same time reduces costs so that the additional costs of a fourth berth are relatively less. In the present case, however, this can hardly be sufficient to justify the simultaneous construction of two additional berths.

Traffic growth is important because of the sharp rise in ship waiting time with the growth in traffic. If the annual rate of traffic increase is 12 percent rather than 8 percent, the level of benefits in the early years rises much more sharply. For example, the undiscounted benefit of the third berth of Rs41.8 million in year 11 (column 4) is reached about two and one-half years earlier at a 12 percent traffic increase, which justifies earlier construction.

The distribution of ship arrivals is a crucial assumption, but there is some evidence that the Poisson distribution does reflect the situation in many ports. If a port is confronted with unusually strong seasonal traffic peaks, for example, the total waiting time increases and additional capacity is required earlier.

The servicing time is particularly important; if it can be reduced by better operations and greater mechanization, more ships can be handled without increasing the number of berths. If in the case study the time at berth had averaged 4 days per ship instead of 3 days, the annual ship waiting time with two berths would have been about 300 days in year 4, or three times as long as with a 3-day servicing time. Since the service time can be drastically reduced by containerization, it is likely to have a major impact on port capacity requirements in the future.

This case study assumes that beyond a certain congestion level traffic will move to another port. The case is not intended to illustrate the issue of competing ports (which is covered in case study 12), but the availability and capacity of other ports can nevertheless be crucial for estimating future traffic at the port under study. Furthermore, is is also relevant whether other ports have excess capacity and can therefore handle the additional traffic without new investments, or at what cost their capacity can be expanded.

Other Considerations

The case study illustrates that it is not correct to appraise two new berths jointly. Had this been done, it would have mistakenly appeared that two new berths would be justified; the extra benefits of the first berth would have hidden the inadequate benefits of the second.

The case study makes no allowance for generation of traffic by the reduction in waiting time or for a slower growth of traffic with an increase in waiting time. The amount of traffic depends on the elasticity of demand for the commodities involved. For example, increased shipping costs can be an important factor in the competitive position of bulk commodity exports. For imports, increased costs may stimulate domestic production. For a port handling relatively few commodities, it may be possible to make different traffic forecasts for different congestion costs.

The case study deals with only one type of berth. If a port has separate general cargo, oil, or bulk berths, individual calculations must be made for such berths. If there is interchangeability between the berths—for example, if a general cargo ship can be handled at a bulk berth—the problem can be solved by the Monte Carlo routine which provides probability distributions of the waiting time involved for specific numbers of different berths.

Although the case study refers to an ocean port, the methodology is identical for inland ports, provided the access channel to the port is not a separate bottleneck. If it is, separate calculations are needed for the optimum channel width. This might also apply to some ocean ports.

The case study estimates the benefits of the project but does not distinguish between various types of beneficiaries. This matter is discussed more fully in the beginning of chapter 4.

Construction of an Ocean Port

Proposed Project and Costs

THE PROJECT CONSISTS of the construction of an ocean port about fifty miles from an existing port. The existing port suffers from serious limitations of depth, with only about thirty-three feet of water available on most days of the year. Large, modern vessels cannot use the port at all and others only when partly loaded. Ships are delayed many days waiting for a berth because of congestion.

Consideration is being given to two alternatives: enlarging the existing port and constructing another port. The new port would have a depth of about forty to forty-two feet, which would permit larger ships. Much of the traffic, however, would have to be carried an additional forty miles for inland distribution by road and rail.

The additional capacity required for the future traffic (see "Traffic") consists of three general cargo berths; four bulk berths primarily for iron ore, coal, wheat, and fertilizer; and an offshore oil terminal. The berths would be equipped with modern general cargo- and bulk-handling facilities and have adequate covered and open storage areas. Although the new port requires forty miles of new road and rail connections, an expanded port also requires certain inland transport improvements, primarily a new acess road.

The estimated capital costs of the two alternatives are shown in table 12-1. The land costs for the new port are less than one-half those for expanding the existing port, which is surrounded by a large city. Although the land in the existing port is already owned by the port authority and therefore does not involve financial expenditure, the land can readily be sold and therefore does involve economic costs. The cost estimates for the seven berths include all related fixed installations, such as railway and crane tracks, roads, sheds, and other storage space, and fuel and water lines. A coal- and ore-loading plant account for almost half of the mechanical equipment costs; other items include loco-

**Table 12-1. Comparison of Estimated Capital Costs
of Expansion of Port and Construction of Port**

Item	Expansion of port (millions of rupees)	Construction of port (millions of rupees)	Foreign exchange component of both (percent)
Port			
Land	300	120	0
Breakwater	—	540	20
Seven berths	285	285	40
Offshore oil terminal	60	60	55
Mechanical equipment	210	210	70
Floating craft	270	270	80
Dredging and other costs	240	420	30
Engineering services, supervision, and contingencies	300	450	30
Customs, duties, and taxes	90	105	0
Subtotal	1,755	2,460	
Inland transport			
Railroad connection	—	360	30
Road connection	150	180	30
Subtotal	150	540	
Total	1,905	3,000	

— Not applicable.

motives and rolling stock, grain-handling equipment, and cranes. The
floating craft include tugs, launches, dredgers, and a floating crane.

As shown in table 12-1, the capital costs of construction exceed those
of expansion by Rs1,095 million, or by 60 percent. This is accounted for
primarily by the breakwater (Rs540 million), the railroad connection
(Rs360 million), and more dredging (Rs180 million). The land costs at
the new port are less (Rs180 million).

To calculate economic costs, customs duties and other taxes must be
deducted from the estimates of financial costs. In the absence of large-
scale unemployment in the area, no adjustment has been made for the

**Table 12-2. Comparison of Economic Capital Costs
of Expansion and Construction**
(millions of rupees, rounded)

	Costs	
Item	*Port expansion*	*New port construction*
Port		
Land	300	120
Breakwater	—	630
Seven berths	375	375
Offshore oil terminal	90	90
Mechanical equipment	330	330
Floating craft	435	435
Dredging and other costs	300	510
Engineering services, supervision, and contingencies	360	555
Subtotal	2,190	3,045
Inland transport		
Railroad connection	—	435
Road connection	180	210
Subtotal	180	645
Total	2,370	3,690

— Not applicable.

price of labor, but an allowance must be made for the substantial foreign exchange component (indicated in table 12-1). When a rate of 1.75 times the official rate is applied to the foreign exchange costs to reflect is scarcity value properly, the economic capital costs of the two alternatives are as shown in table 12-2.

The economic costs exceed the financial costs in both alternatives by slightly less than one-quarter. The absolute difference in costs, which is Rs1,095 million for financial costs, becomes Rs1,320 million for the economic ones.

Because of the different nature of the construction in the two alternatives, the phasing of expenditure is different. Most important, construction is expected to take five years, compared with three years for expansion. The annual phasing of economic costs is shown in columns 1 and 2 of table 12-3.

Traffic

Detailed studies of the future traffic at the new port forecast imports and exports of major commodities as well as the allocation of traffic between the country's ports, with consideration of such factors as the origin and destination of the traffic and relative transport costs both overseas and inland. Estimates of the following traffic at the new port in the opening year and five years later are shown in table 12-4.

The table indicates that in the opening year 30 percent of the estimated traffic is accounted for by petroleum which is handled at the offshore terminal and piped to storage tanks; about 65 percent is accounted for by commodities (other than petroleum) which can be more efficiently handled in bulk; and only 5 percent is general cargo. This traffic composition reflects the advantages of greater depth at the new port.

Project Benefits

The economic analysis of the new port was preceded by a separate economic study of whether additional port capacity is justified at all (for an example see case study 11); this study revealed that congestion at the existing port justifies further capacity. The economic issue here is therefore whether it is better to expand the existing port or construct a new one. The decongestion at the existing port from additional capacity is the same whether the port is expanded or a new one built; although decongestion was the main reason in deciding on additional capacity, it is therefore no longer relevant.

A new port has both advantages and disadvantages over an expanded one. Its major advantages are that it will be able to handle larger ships and that the average time in port per ship will be about one day less. The major disadvantages are the larger capital costs, the longer construction period (see "Proposed Project and Costs"), and the additional inland transport costs since much of trafic would have to be transported an additional forty miles. The operating costs at the two ports are about the same and the differences in ocean distances for ships are insignificant.

Reduced Shipping Costs

The benefits from the use of larger ships must be calculated separately for each commodity. The calculations for iron ore illustrate the

Table 12-3. Comparison of Costs and Benefits of Construction and Expansion of an Ocean Port

(millions of rupees)

| | Costs | | Benefits | | | Present worth (discounted at 12 percent) | | Internal rate of return (discounted at 18 percent) | |
| | Cost of construction (1) | Cost of expansion (2) | Reduction in shipping costs (3) | Additional inland transport costs (4) | Total benefits (5) | Costs (6) | Benefits (7) | Costs (8) | Benefits (9) |
Year									
1	600	0	0	0	0	600	0	600	0
2	750	0	0	0	0	670	0	635	0
3	750	600	0	0	600	598	478	539	431
4	750	810	0	0	810	534	577	457	493
5	840	960	0	0	960	534	611	433	495
6	0	0	219	−6	213	0	121	0	93
7	0	0	300	−9	291	0	148	0	108
8	0	0	390	−12	378	0	171	0	119
9	0	0	480	−15	465	0	188	0	124
10	0	0	588	−18	570	0	206	0	128
11	0	0	588	−18	570	0	184	0	109
12	0	0	588	−18	570	0	164	0	92
13	0	0	588	−18	570	0	146	0	78
14	0	0	588	−18	570	0	131	0	66
15	0	0	588	−18	570	0	117	0	56

16	0	0	588	−18	570	0	104	0	48
17	0	0	588	−18	570	0	93	0	40
18	0	0	588	−18	570	0	83	0	34
19	0	0	588	−18	570	0	74	0	29
20	0	0	588	−18	570	0	66	0	25
21	0	0	588	−18	570	0	59	0	21
22	0	0	588	−18	570	0	53	0	18
23	0	0	588	−18	570	0	47	0	15
24	0	0	588	−18	570	0	42	0	13
25	0	0	588	−18	570	0	38	0	11
26	0	0	588	−18	570	0	34	0	9
27	0	0	588	−18	570	0	30	0	8
28	0	0	588	−18	570	0	27	0	6
29	0	0	588	−18	570	0	24	0	6
30	0	0	588	−18	570	0	21	0	5
31	0	0	588	−18	570	0	19	0	4
32	0	0	588	−18	570	0	17	0	3
33	0	0	588	−18	570	0	15	0	3
34	0	0	588	−18	570	0	14	0	2
35	0	0	588	−18	570	0	12	0	2
Total						2,936	4,114	2,664	2,694

Note: Net present worth equals Rs1,178 million; this is the difference between columns 6 and 7.

179

Table 12-4. Estimated Traffic at New Port in Opening and Fifth Years of Operation
(millions of tons)

Commodity	Opening year	Fifth year
Petroleum	3.0	4.5
Iron ore	2.0	2.8
Coal	1.5	2.0
Food grains	2.0	2.5
Fertilizer	1.0	1.5
General cargo	0.5	0.7
Total	10.0	14.0

methodology which is similar for other commodities. As shown in table 12-5, the size of ship which can use the new port is about 40,000 tons, compared with only 11,500 tons at the expanded port. The estimated iron ore shipments of 2 million tons in the opening year require only 56 trips instead of 190 via the existing port. Two major benefits result: reduced ship costs in port and reduced sailing costs.

REDUCED SHIP COSTS IN PORT.   Because of the more difficult conditions in the existing port even after expansion, the turnaround time would be reduced only from three and one-half to two and one-half days (see table 12-5). The daily cost in port is about Rs37,500 (with adjustments for the foreign exchange cost) for the type of ship using the expanded port and Rs72,000 for the much larger ships using the new port. The total ship costs at port in the opening year are thus Rs24.9 million at the expanded port compared with Rs10.1 million at the new port, a saving of Rs14.8 million.

REDUCED SAILING COSTS.   The average sailing time per round-trip from the existing port is about thirty days; for the larger ships using the new port, this would be reduced to twenty-five days (see table 12-5). Although the daily cost per ship is nearly twice as great for the larger ships, the number of trips required is less than one-third, so that the estimated total sailing costs are reduced from Rs265 million to Rs118 million in the opening year, a saving of Rs147 million.

The total benefit for iron ore shipments is thus Rs162 million in the opening year (see line 13, table 12-5). This benefit, however, is unlikely to materialize immediately upon the opening of a new port. The use of larger ships tends to be a gradual process, and the reduction in costs may not be fully passed on to the developing country in the form of

Table 12-5. Comparison of Costs of Shipping Iron Ore via Expanded Port and New Port

	Existing port	New port
Basic data		
1. Size of ship (dwt)	11,500	40,000
2. Average load (tons)	10,500	36,000
3. Quantity of ore (millions of tons)	2.0	2.0
4. Number of trips required	190	56
Ship costs at port		
5. Average days in port	3.5	2.5
6. Total ship-days in port	665	140
7. Cost per ship-day in port (rupees)	37,500	72,000
8. Total ship cost at port (millions of rupees)	24.9	10.1
Sailing costs		
9. Average sailing time per round-trip (days)	30	25
10. Total sailing days	5,700	1,400
11. Cost per ship sailing day (rupees)	46,500	84,000
12. Total sailing costs (millions of rupees)	265.2	117.6
Shipping costs		
13. At port (line 8) plus sailing costs (line 12) (millions of rupees)	290.1	127.8
14. Per ton (rupees)	145.1	63.9
Inland transport costs		
15. Miles	400	440
16. Railway freight cost per ton (rupees)	69.3	76.2
17. Total freight costs (millions of rupees)	138.6	152.4
Total transport costs		
18. Per ton (lines 14 + 16) (rupees)	214.4	140.1
19. Total costs (lines 13 + 17) (millions of rupees)	428.7	280.2

lower rates to the extent that the freight is carried in foreign ships. The benefit in the initial year is therefore assumed to be only half of that estimated; the country would not obtain the full benefits for five years. On this assumption, the benefit in the opening year has been reduced to Rs81 million.

A summary of similar calculations for all commodities at the new port is given in table 12-6. The savings per ton differ sharply for individual commodities and depend primarily on the size of ships suitable for each commodity and the sailing distances involved. There is no

Table 12-6. Reduction in Shipping Costs at New Port by Commodity

		Reduction in shipping costs	
Commodity	Reduction per ton (rupees)	Reduction for opening year traffic (millions of rupees)	Reduction for fifth year traffic (millions of rupees)
Petroleum	0	0	0
Iron ore	81.0	162	228
Coal	36.6	54	72
Food grains	86.4	174	216
Fertilizer	42.6	42	63
General cargo	12.6	6	9
Total		438	588
Adjusted total		219	588

difference in shipping costs for petroleum products because the offshore facilities at both ports could handle tankers of equal size. The benefits for general cargo are also slight because only a minor part of the general cargo traffic is likely to be carried in ships above 11,500 deadweight tons and the economies of scale for larger general cargo ships are much smaller than those for ships carrying bulk commodities. As explained in the discussion of iron ore, the benefits are expected to materialize fully in five years. No increase in benefits is allowed for thereafter since new investments would be required (see "Conclusion" for a discussion of the sensitivity of the decision to this assumption). The annual benefits from reduction in shipping costs are shown in column 3 of table 12-3 for thirty years, which is the weighted average life of the items in the project.

Changes in Inland Transport Costs

In order to calculate the impact of the port on inland transport costs, origin and destination studies have been made for each major commodity. The proportions of the traffic carried by road and rail have been determined, with relative distribution costs taken into account.

As shown in table 12-5, the inland transport distance for iron ore is forty miles longer to the new port than to the existing one and all of it is carried by rail. The resultant increase in freight costs is Rs13.8 million in the opening year. The results of similar studies for all commodities are summarized in table 12-7.

The reduction in shipping costs at the new port is offset to a small degree by higher inland transport costs. The change in inland transport costs per ton for each commodity is a weighted average since the origin and destination points vary for each commodity. The higher unit costs of general cargo arise primarily because much of it is carried by road transport. The additional inland transport costs are shown in column 4 of table 12-3. The total benefits of the new port are shown in column 5.

Comparison of Costs and Benefits

As shown in columns 6 and 7 of table 12-3, the net present worth of the project is Rs1,178 million, with both costs and benefits discounted at 12 percent, and the cost-benefit ratio is 1 : 1.4. The internal rate of return is almost 18 percent (see columns 8 and 9).

Although the project therefore seems justified, the preceding global calculations hide the fact that some of its parts may not be justified. This is particularly true for the offshore oil terminal. Because a terminal at either port could handle tankers of equal size, shipping costs via the two ports are the same. But because the inland shipping costs are higher at the new port (see table 12-7), total distribution costs for petroleum are lower at the existing port. For general cargo, the difference between the two alternatives is small, with the reduction in

Table 12-7. Impact of New Port on Inland Transport Costs, Opening and Fifth Years

Commodity	Change in inland transport costs		
	Increase (+) or decrease (−) per ton (rupees)	*Increase (+) or decrease (−) for opening year traffic (millions of rupees)*	*Increase (+) or decrease (−) for fifth year traffic (millions of rupees)*
Petroleum	+1.2	+3.6	+5.4
Iron ore	+6.9	+13.8	+19.2
Coal	+5.7	+8.4	+11.4
Food grains	−6.3	−12.3	−15.9
Fertilizer	−6.9	−6.9	−10.2
General cargo	+11.4	+5.7	+8.1
Total		+12.3	+18.0
Adjusted total		+6.2	+18.0

shipping costs of Rs12.6 per ton at the new port almost offset by an increase in inland transport costs of Rs11.4. Because this difference is small and the benefits from reduced shipping costs accrue only in time, while inland transport costs increase at once, this matter deserves fuller study.

The conclusion is sensitive to the capital costs of the alternatives. The margin of error in the estimates is likely to be greater in the construction of an entirely new port than in the expansion of an existing port, but some allowance has been made for this in the larger contingency. If this margin is inadequate and the cost of construction (excluding equipment and craft) of the new port is 25 percent higher than estimated, its net present worth declines from Rs1,178 million to Rs549 million, but it is still justified. The switching value for these construction costs—that is, the percentage increase in costs which equalize costs and benefits at a 12 percent discount rate—is about 50 percent.

Errors in the traffic forecast affect both alternatives but not identically. A smaller volume of traffic would have a greater adverse effect on the new port since even at lower traffic levels large investments such as the breakwater and the railway would have to be undertaken. Expansion of the existing port could be geared more closely to the traffic growth. If, however, the traffic is greater than forecast or if allowance is made for traffic growth beyond the fifth year after completion of the project, the relative advantage of a new port is even greater.

There seems little doubt that larger ships would be used for bulk traffic, though it is less certain for general cargo. The major uncertainty concerns the timing and the extent to which the full benefits accrue to the developing country. The calculation assumes that this takes five years, but it depends on such factors as the proportion of traffic carried by foreign ships and the impact of conference rates. In any case, the country could make certain that it receives most of the benefits by appropriate port charges.

Cargo-Handling Equipment for a Port

Proposed Project and Costs

THE PROJECT CONSISTS of the acquisition of cargo-handling equipment for a general cargo berth. The cargo, which amounts to about 140,000 tons annually, is now handled largely by labor. Estimates of capital costs, annual operating costs (primarily for maintenance and fuel for tractors and forklifts but not depreciation), and economic life of the required equipment are given in table 13-1.

The capital costs are entirely in foreign exchange and have been shadow priced at 1.75 times the official exchange rate. A similar adjustment has been made for the foreign exchange component of operating costs. All costs are net of taxes. Labor costs are not included because no increase in labor is anticipated (see "Benefits"). No salvage value is allowed for except for the forklifts acquired in the ninth year. The costs of the project, including periodic replacement requirements over twelve years, are shown in columns 1 to 3 of table 13-2.

Project Benefits

The benefits of the equipment are faster unloading of ships—which reduces their turnaround time and permits greater utilization of the berth—and reductions in labor costs.

Reduced Ship Turnaround Time

The actual increase in the handling rate, although improved by the equipment, depends on the type of cargo. Although the rate increase could theoretically be as high as 60 percent, for some types of cargo handled at a particular berth an improvement of 25 percent might be reasonable. This does not lead, however, to an equivalent reduction in the time of ships in the port because ships work only sixteen hours a

**Table 13-1. Costs and Economic Life
of Cargo-Handling Equipment**

Equipment	Costs (thousands of rupees)		Economic life (years)
	Capital costs	Annual operating costs	
Forklifts (10)	1,650	255	8
Tractors (7)	600	120	12
Trailers (54)	750	15	12
Pallets (2,375)	2,100	90	4
Total	5,100	480	

day, six days a week, and time is lost in bringing ships alongside, opening and closing hatches, starting work late and quitting early, and so forth. The savings in turnaround time are therefore estimated at half the 25 percent rate, or 12.5 percent.

The present average turnaround time at berth is 94 hours per ship. A saving of 12.5 percent is 11.7 hours per ship. The average number of ships at the berth per year, at a 77 percent occupancy rate, as in the past, is about seventy-five. The total annual saving is thus about 880 hours. For the type of ship involved, and because most of the cost is in foreign exchange, the value per hour is about Rs1,500, so that the annual benefit is Rs1.32 million (see column 4 of table 13-2).

Increased Berth Capacity

The reduction in turnaround time also permits more ships to be handled at the berth. The value of this additional capacity depends on the port situation as a whole. If the port has excess capacity, the additional berth capacity has no value until traffic growth requires capacity expansion of the port. At that time, the value depends on the costs of expanding port capacity. Additional capacity of any form is not required for about two years; because of the additional capacity which the new equipment has made available, the physical expansion can be postponed one year. Since the additional berth is estimated to cost Rs18 million, a delay of one year at an opportunity cost of capital of 12 percent gives a benefit of about Rs2.16 million in the third year (see column 5 of table 13-2).

Table 13-2. Comparison of Costs and Benefits of Cargo-Handling Equipment
(thousands of rupees)

| Year | Costs of equipment | | | Benefits | | | | Present worth (discounted at 12 percent) | | Internal rate of return (discounted at 30 percent) | |
	Capital costs (1)	Operating costs (2)	Total costs (3)	Reduced ship time (4)	Increased berth capacity (5)	Labor saving (6)	Total benefits (7)	Costs (8)	Benefits (9)	Costs (10)	Benefits (11)
1	5,100	480	5,580	1,320	0	368	1,688	5,580	1,688	5,580	1,688
2	0	480	480	1,320	0	368	1,688	429	1,507	369	1,298
3	0	480	480	1,320	2,160	368	3,848	383	3,067	284	2,278
4	0	480	480	1,320	0	368	1,688	342	1,202	218	768
5	2,100	480	2,580	1,320	0	368	1,688	1,641	1,074	903	591
6	0	480	480	1,320	0	368	1,688	272	957	129	454
7	0	480	480	1,320	0	368	1,688	243	856	99	349
8	0	480	480	1,320	0	368	1,688	217	763	76	268
9	3,750	480	4,230	1,320	0	368	1,688	1,709	682	520	208
10	0	480	480	1,320	0	368	1,688	173	609	45	159
11	0	480	480	1,320	0	368	1,688	155	544	35	123
12	0	480	480	1,320	0	368	1,688	138	484	27	95
13	-600	0	-600	0	0	0	0	-154	0	-26	0
Total								11,128	13,433	8,259	8,279

Note: Net present worth equals Rs2,305 million; this is the difference between columns 8 and 9.

187

Reduction in Labor Costs

The cargo-handling equipment might theoretically lead to a reduction in the existing labor force, although this is difficult to achieve in practice. Moreover, any reduction in the size of the labor force would probably be offset by increased pay of operators. Thus the estimated 25 percent increase in cargo handled as a result of the mechanization would be undertaken with the same labor force.

The labor cost of handling cargo is about Rs21 a ton. For the increased annual output of 35,000 tons (25 percent of 140,000 tons), this is a saving of Rs735,000, Since such labor is generally unskilled and would otherwise remain largely unemployed, however, a shadow wage of 50 percent of the actual wage has been applied; this makes the economic benefit about Rs368,000 a year (see column 6 of table 13-2). The total benefits are shown in column 7.

Comparison of Costs and Benefits

As shown in columns 8 and 9 of table 13-2, the benefits of the project exceed its costs—both discounted at 12 percent—by about Rs2.3 million. The ratio of costs to benefits is 1 : 1.2, and the internal rate of return is 30 percent (see columns 10 and 11). The project is therefore justified.

This conclusion is, however, subject to an important reservation. Most of the ships which benefit from the lower turnaround time are foreign ships, while the costs are incurred by the developing country. If, for example, two-thirds of the ships are foreign, they receive almost Rs900,000 of the annual benefits (two-thirds of Rs1.32 million), or about half of the project benefits. Whether this is worthwhile for the developing country depends on a number of considerations. The reduced turnaround time could lead to lower shipping rates and thus benefit the country's exports and imports. These adjustments, however, may not take place promptly, especially for ships moving under conference rates. It is therefore desirable to impose a charge for the use of the equipment to cover its costs (including a rate of return of 12 percent). In this way, some of the benefits can be recaptured for the developing country, although the foreign ships also benefit.

Although the internal rate of return of the project is a high 30 percent, the net present worth and the cost-benefit ratio are relatively modest. This difference arises because large replacement costs are incurred periodically while the benefits remain constant after the third year. In such a project, the internal rate of return is not an appropriate guide in determining priorities (see "Methods of Comparison," chapter 5, for a more detailed discussion).

Although the costs of the major items can be determined with considerable certainty, their effective utilization depends on organizational arrangements and may therefore vary considerably; for example, the operators may not be sufficiently skilled, or maintenance may take longer because spare parts may have to be imported. If, as a result of such factors, 15 percent more equipment is needed to handle the estimated volume of traffic and operating costs are 15 percent higher, the present worth of the project is reduced quite sharply from Rs2.3 million to Rs683,000. If capital and operating costs are 21 percent higher than estimated, the net present worth of the project is zero. It is therefore important to make sure that the utilization of the equipment is as effective in practice as assumed in these calculations.

On the benefit side, about two-thirds of the benefits are accounted for by reduced ship time. Although the value of ship time can be measured reasonably well since the costs of ships are known, achieving the time savings depends on the various steps in the operation. If, for example, the reduction in turnaround time is only 10 percent instead of the estimated 12.5 percent, the annual benefit for reduced ship time drops from Rs1.32 million to Rs1.06 million, the increase in berth capacity is less, and the present worth of the project is virtually eliminated. This factor therefore deserves careful review.

Because the saving in labor cost accounts for about one-fifth of the total benefits, the justification for the project is sensitive to the assumption concerning the shadow price of labor. If the cost of labor is not shadow priced but assumed to be equal to wages paid, the benefits from laborsaving double and the net present worth of the project rises to Rs4.9 million.

Laborsaving can present considerable difficulties, however. Port labor is frequently well organized and may object to the use of the equipment and delay its effective utilization. This factor is minimized somewhat in this case since it has been assumed that the existing labor force would not be reduced, but would be utilized more efficiently. Expansion of the labor force, however, would not take place. If the increased productivity is shared with the labor force in increased wages, acceptance may also be improved.

Case Study 14

Construction of a Grain Silo in a Port

Proposed Project and Costs

TANKERS UNLOAD grain at a port by blowing it out of ships onto open concrete; the grain is then bagged and the bags are carried by stevedores to the railroad wagons on a nearby siding. To speed the unloading of ships and provide better temporary storage for the grain, the construction of a 30,000-ton silo is proposed.

The capital costs of the silo are estimated at Rs78 million, with a foreign exchange component of Rs66 million. With a shadow rate for foreign exchange of 1.75 times the official exchange rate, the economic cost of the silo is Rs127.5 million. Construction is estimated to take two years. The annual maintenance and operating costs are estimated at Rs1.26 million; after allowance for some foreign exchange costs, the economic cost is Rs1.5 million. The estimated life of the project is fifteen years with no salvage value thereafter. Capital and operating costs are shown in columns 1 and 2 of table 14-1.

Traffic

The volume of grain imports expected to be handled by the port is estimated at 800,000 tons in the first year of operation (year 3) of the silo. As a result of the increased domestic production, imports are expected to decline gradually to 300,000 tons in the fifteenth year of operation (year 17).

Project Benefits

The benefits of the proposed silo are primarily savings in the turnaround time of ships and in berth space and a reduction in spoilage.

Table 14-1. Comparison of Costs and Benefits of Construction of a Grain Silo in a Port

(millions of rupees)

Year	Costs Capital costs (1)	Operating costs (2)	Total costs (3)	Benefits Reduced turnaround time (4)	Reduced spoilage (5)	Total benefits (6)	Present worth (discounted at 12 percent) Costs (7)	Benefits (8)
1	51.0	0	51.0	0	0	0	51.00	0
2	76.5	0	76.5	0	0	0	68.31	0
3	0	1.5	1.5	19.8	11.0	30.8	1.20	24.55
4	0	1.5	1.5	18.3	9.9	28.2	1.07	20.08
5	0	1.5	1.5	17.1	9.3	26.4	0.95	16.79
6	0	1.5	1.5	15.6	8.4	24.0	0.85	13.61
7	0	1.5	1.5	14.1	7.8	21.9	0.76	11.10
8	0	1.5	1.5	13.2	7.2	20.4	0.68	9.22
9	0	1.5	1.5	12.6	6.9	19.5	0.61	7.88
10	0	1.5	1.5	11.1	6.0	17.1	0.54	6.17
11	0	1.5	1.5	9.9	5.4	15.3	0.48	4.93
12	0	1.5	1.5	9.6	5.1	14.7	0.43	4.22
13	0	1.5	1.5	8.7	4.8	13.5	0.39	3.47
14	0	1.5	1.5	7.8	4.2	12.0	0.34	2.75
15	0	1.5	1.5	7.5	4.1	11.6	0.31	2.38
16	0	1.5	1.5	7.5	4.1	11.6	0.27	2.12
17	0	1.5	1.5	7.5	4.1	11.6	0.24	1.89
Total							128.43	131.16

Note: Net present worth equals Rs2.73 million; this is the difference between columns 7 and 8.

Savings in Ship Turnaround Time and Berth Space

The present unloading rate is about 1,200 tons of grain a day. Since most of the grain arrives in ships with a capacity of 12,000 tons, it takes on the average ten days to unload a ship. The silo, equipped with an elevator, would reduce this to five days and save five days per ship. The 800,000 tons of grain in the opening year (year 3) would be carried by about sixty-six ships (800,000 tons divided by 12,000 tons); this would decline to twenty-five ships in the last year (year 17) in line with the decrease in grain imports to 300,000 tons.

The cost of a ship waiting in port is about Rs36,000 a day; this figure allows for most of the cost being in foreign exchange. The capital cost of the berth taken up by the ship and the grain piles is estimated at Rs24,000 a day; this allows for a foreign exchange component of 40 percent. It assumes that the berth will be utilized for other traffic after construction of the silo and that there would be no excess berth capacity. The total saving, including berth and ship, thus amounts to about Rs60,000 a day. Since in the opening year sixty-six ships each save 5 days, or a total of 330 ship-days, the total benefit is Rs19.8 million. This declines to Rs7.5 million in the last year, in line with the decrease in traffic (see column 4 of table 14-1).

Reduction in Spoilage

Losses in the handling of grain amount to about 5 percent of its value, but this loss rate is not entirely because of port operations. The fact that the grain now lies in an open, uncovered area definitely contributes to the loss, however; an elevator that would clean and fumigate the grain as well as eliminate handling in the open would substantially reduce loss. A reasonable estimate of savings from this is 1 percent, or about Rs13.8 per ton of grain. The total annual saving is thus Rs11 million in the first year of operation (Rs13.8 × 800,000 tons), declining to Rs4.1 million in the last year (see column 5 of table 14-1).

Benefits may arise from lower cargo-handling costs. Whether the grain is pumped onto the open concrete or directly into the silo, however, does not eliminate the need to bag it and to transport it to railroad wagons on a nearby siding. No benefits have therefore been allowed for lower cargo-handling costs since this part of the overall operation will continue.

Comparison of Costs and Benefits

As shown in columns 7 and 8 of table 14-1, the benefits of the proposed project exceed the costs by about Rs3 million when both are discounted at 12 percent. The cost-benefit ratio is 1 : 1.02, and the internal rate of return is 12.5 percent. The project therefore appears justified.

Since the net present worth of the project is small, the conclusion that the project is justified is highly sensitive to any adverse factors. As usual, one of the most important considerations is the capital costs of the project. If, for example, the capital costs are 25 percent higher than estimated, the net present worth of the project is sharply reduced from about Rs3 million to a negative Rs27 million. The project should therefore be reviewed after firm bids have been received.

A change in the traffic forecast could also significantly alter the justification for the project. If, for example, domestic production of grain does not increase as rapidly as anticipated, so that import requirements decline from 800,000 tons in year 3 to 500,000 tons in year 17, instead of 300,000 tons as assumed, the benefits of the silo increase correspondingly and the net worth of the project is about Rs34 million. There is also the possibility that the silo could in the more distant future be used for exports.

Another factor which affects the viability of the silo is an extension of its life from fifteen to twenty years; this increases the net worth of the project to about Rs9 million, if the traffic level continues as in the fifteenth year. The project is also sensitive to the discount rate. At a discount rate of 8 percent, the net present worth is nearly Rs30 million.

Case Study 15

Construction of an Airport

Proposed Project

THE PROJECT CONSISTS of the construction of an airport in a fast-growing industrial and commercial city. The airport will include one runway 5,500 feet long by 75 feet wide, an aircraft parking and service apron, an apron access taxiway, a terminal building, utilities, fire and crash rescue facilities, and communications and navigation aids. Scheduled service will be provided by an aircraft with about forty seats.

The city of 130,000 is the hub of a series of population centers closely connected by economic and commercial interests. The entire area is situated in a delta region with few ground transportation facilities. An interwoven network of river and canal systems makes the area relatively inaccessible, particularly during the rainy season, when travel to other areas of the country becomes virtually impossible except by air or water.

Railway connections are provided from the city (point A in figure 15-1) to points north, but the trip from A to C, the country's major city,

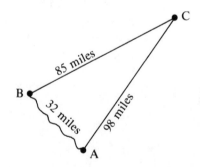

Figure 15-1. Configuration of Cities A, B, and C

194

takes approximately twenty-four hours. Passenger transportation by road to points outside the area is relatively insignificant; many of the rivers lack bridges and the continual changing of riverbeds makes road construction expensive.

The city is served by an airport located approximately thirty-two miles to the northwest at B, a smaller town (see figure 15-1). Two round-trip flights a day are provided between C and B. Passengers going to or departing from A use bus transportation between A and B before or after a flight. About 75 percent of the passenger volume handled at B is destined for or originates at A. Studies indicate that after the construction of the airport at A, continued operation of the airport at B is no longer justified. After the new airfield has ben constructed at A and direct air services provided between A and C, 25 percent of the passengers would have to use bus transport between A and B (compared with 75 percent now).

The economic analysis of the project primarily compares the costs of continuing the present mode of travel between A, B, and C with the costs of constructing and operating a new airport at A, the costs of additional flight time between A and C, the benefits of reduced bus-operating costs between A and B, and savings in time for passengers. (Almost no freight is carried on the route.)

Project Costs

The capital costs of constructing an airport at A are estimated at Rs33 million, net of taxes; the foreign exchange component is Rs12 million, primarily for the purchase of airport equipment. With a shadow rate for foreign exchange of 1.75 times the official exchange rate, the economic costs of the airport are Rs42 million. Construction is expected to take two years (see column 1 of table 15-1). The life of the project is an estimated twenty years with no salvage value thereafter. The salvage value of the old airport, including the value of equipment, is shown in column 1 as a negative cost (Rs15 million), however.

The annual maintenance and operating costs of the new airport would be about the same as those of the old airport at B. Because these costs in effect cancel each other, they can be excluded from the economic appraisal.

In addition to the capital costs, the new airport at A will involve the costs of additional flight time since the distance between A and C is thirteen miles longer than between B and C. The flight time between B and C is forty minutes; between A and C, forty-four. The economic

Table 15-1. Comparison Costs and Benefits of Construction of an Airport
(millions of rupees)

Year	Costs			Benefits			Present worth (discounted at 12 percent)		Internal rate of return (discounted at 4 percent)	
	Capital costs (1)	Additional flight costs (2)	Total costs (3)	Time savings (4)	Reduced bus costs (5)	Total benefits (6)	Costs (7)	Benefits (8)	Costs (9)	Benefits (10)
1	12.60	0	12.60	0	0	0	12.60	0	12.60	0
2	29.40	0	29.40	0	0	0	26.25	0	28.28	0
3	-15.00	0.27	-14.73	0.79	0.04	0.83	-11.74	0.66	-13.63	0.77
4	0	0.30	0.30	0.90	0.06	0.96	0.21	0.68	0.27	0.85
5	0	0.30	0.30	1.17	0.06	1.23	0.19	0.78	0.26	1.05
6	0	0.30	0.30	1.26	0.06	1.32	0.17	0.75	0.25	1.09
7	0	0.54	0.54	1.41	0.06	1.47	0.27	0.75	0.43	1.16
8	0	0.54	0.54	1.50	0.06	1.56	0.24	0.71	0.41	1.19
9	0	0.54	0.54	1.68	0.06	1.74	0.22	0.70	0.39	1.27
10	0	0.63	0.63	1.86	0.09	1.95	0.23	0.70	0.44	1.37

11	0	0.63	0.63	1.98	0.09	2.07	0.20	0.67	0.43	1.40
12	0	0.68	0.68	2.22	0.09	2.31	0.20	0.66	0.44	1.50
13	0	0.78	0.78	3.03	0.12	3.15	0.20	0.81	0.49	1.97
14	0	0.78	0.78	3.33	0.12	3.45	0.18	0.79	0.47	2.07
15	0	0.90	0.90	3.66	0.12	3.78	0.18	0.77	0.52	2.18
16	0	1.05	1.05	4.02	0.13	4.15	0.19	0.76	0.58	2.30
17	0	1.08	1.08	4.41	0.13	4.54	0.18	0.74	0.58	2.42
18	0	1.17	1.17	5.52	0.13	5.65	0.17	0.82	0.60	2.90
19	0	1.17	1.17	5.76	0.13	5.89	0.15	0.77	0.58	2.91
20	0	1.29	1.29	6.09	0.14	6.23	0.15	0.72	0.61	2.96
21	0	1.29	1.29	6.36	0.14	6.50	0.13	0.68	0.59	2.96
22	0	1.35	1.35	6.66	0.14	6.80	0.13	0.63	0.59	2.99
Total						30.71		14.55	36.18	37.31

Note: The net present worth equals −Rs16.2 million; this is the difference between columns 7 and 8.

costs of operating the aircraft used on the route average Rs4,200 an hour. The marginal costs of an additional four minutes of flight time, however, are estimated to be only about two-thirds of the average costs, or Rs185 for the additional four minutes. The 1,460 trips estimated in the first year after the airport opens (see "Traffic"), cost Rs0.27 million; this cost increases to Rs1.35 million in the last year of the project, in line with the increase in the frequency of service between A and C (see column 2 of table 5-1).

Traffic

The air traffic potential of a community is determined by such factors as the size of its population, its economic character, and the availability of other transport alternatives. The two return flights between C and B have an average daily passenger load of 66, which is about 28,000 passengers yearly. In the opening year of the airport (year 3), the daily number of passengers is expected to reach 130. The estimated annual increase in passengers is 20 percent for the first five years of operation (years 3–7), 10 percent for the following ten years (years 8–17), and 5 percent thereafter. The volume of traffic would thus reach 275,000 passengers in the last year of the project (see table 15-2).

No allowance is made for any generated or diverted traffic in this forecast since the additional time savings from the new project are slight compared with the existing time differential on air service via B relative to rail and road service.

As indicated, 75 percent of the traffic is accounted for by A and 25 percent by B. Since A is growing at a more rapid rate than B, A's proportion of traffic is estimated to increase gradually to 85 percent, while B's declines.

Table 15-2. Estimated Passenger Traffic by Selected Years

Year	Passengers a day	Passengers a year	Round-trip flights a day
3	130	48,000	2
7	230	83,000	4
12	370	134,000	5
17	590	216,000	8
22	750	275,000	10

Project Benefits

The benefits of the proposed airport are primarily time savings for passengers and reduced road transport costs.

Time Savings

FOR PASSENGERS FROM A TO C. As shown in table 15-3, the total travel time between A and C is about three hours. Construction of an airport at A would reduce total travel time between A and C to about two hours. Time savings in the opening year would thus be 1 hour per trip for each

Table 15-3. Current and Future Travel Time between A and C and between B and C (in minutes)

Activity	Current schedule	Activity	Future schedule
		Between A and C	
Journey from point of origin to bus terminal at A	15	Journey from point of origin to air terminal at A	20
Baggage handling at A	10	Loading at A	20
Journey between A and B by road	60	Flight between A and C	49
Loading at B	20	Baggage handling at C	10
Flight between B and C	45	Journey from airport to destination at C	20
Baggage handling at C	10	Total	119
Journey from airport to destination at C	20		
Total	180		
		Between B and C	
Journey from point of origin to airport at B	15	Journey from point of origin to bus terminal at B	10
Loading at B	20	Baggage handling at B	10
Flight between B and C	45	Travel time between B and A by road	60
Baggage handling at C	10	Loading time at A	20
Journey from airport to destination at C	20	Flight time between A and C	49
Total	110	Baggage handling at C	10
		Journey from airport to destination at C	20
		Total	179

of the 36,000 passengers (75 percent of 48,000 passengers) destined for or originating at A. This is expected to increase to 233,000 hours (85 percent of 275,000) in the last year of the project, in line with the increase in traffic.

TIME LOSSES FOR PASSENGERS FROM B TO C VIA A. Passengers between B and C now have a direct air connection and their total travel time is about one hour and fifty minutes. When the airport at B is abandoned, these persons will in fact suffer time losses of one hour and ten minutes per trip. The annual time loss increases from 14,000 hours in the first year (one hour and ten minutes for 12,000 passengers) to 48,000 hours in the last year, in line with the traffic increase. The net gain for all passengers is 22,000 hours in the opening year (year 3) and rises to 185,000 hours in the last year of the project.

VALUE OF TIME. The valuation of time is related to the income of the passengers carried on the route. An estimated one-third of the passengers are government servants with an average income of Rs27 an hour (Rs4,500 a month) and one third are businessmen with an income of Rs75 an hour (Rs15,000 a month). The travel of the remaining one-third passengers is unrelated to their work. The valuation of time for this group is related to the extra amount they are willing to pay to travel by air compared with the next best alternative, rail. The fare differential indicates that the value of time to them is about Rs5 an hour. The weighted average value of time per passenger is Rs36 an hour. No allowance is made for increases in income and in the value of time during the life of the project.

Based on these assumptions, the value of time savings is estimated at Rs0.79 million (Rs36 × 22,000 hours) in the first year of the project (year 3); this increases to Rs6.66 million in the last year, in line with the increase in traffic (see column 4 of table 15-1).

Reduced Road Transport Costs

The economic cost of operating bus services between A and B, a distance of thirty-two miles, is estimated at Rs1.76 a bus-mile. At four trips a day (that is, two round-trips), total operating costs are Rs225 a day, or about Rs82,000 a year. As traffic increases, however, the number of bus trips increases gradually to sixteen (that is, eight round trips) in the last year of the project, and total operating costs rise to Rs329,000 in that year.

With the construction of the airport at A and the operation of direct air services between A and C, 75 percent of the passengers (increased gradually to 85 percent) will be flown directly between A and C and will no longer need to undertake the bus journey between A and B. However, 25 percent of the passengers (gradually declining to 15 percent)—those who had direct service between B and C—will have to use road transport between B and A. The costs involved in transporting these persons, however, are substantially less since the smaller volume of traffic could be handled by a microbus. The estimated economic cost of operating microbus services is Rs0.99 a mile, compared with Rs1.76 for regular bus service. The saving of Rs0.77 a mile amounts to about Rs49 a round-trip, or Rs36,000 for the 730 round-trips required in the opening year. This saving grows in line with the frequency in service (see column 5 of table 15-1).

Comparison of Costs and Benefits

As shown in columns 7 and 8 of table 15-1, the costs of the proposed airport exceed the benefits—both discounted at 12 percent—by Rs16.2 million during the life of the project, and the cost-benefit ratio is about 1 : 0.5. As shown in columns 9 and 10, the internal rate of return is 4 percent.

In view of the disparity between costs and benefits, the decision is not likely to be changed because of changes in any single factor. For example, if the use of lower design standards can reduce capital costs by 25 percent the project still has a negative net worth of about Rs6 million.

As emphasized in this manual, the valuation of time is highly speculative. But even if the value of time is 50 percent greater than assumed in the appraisal, the net worth is still a negative Rs9 million. If capital costs can be reduced by 25 percent and if the value of time is 50 percent greater, however, the project becomes justified, with a net worth of Rs2.4 million when discounted at 12 percent.

This case study also illustrates a situation in which a project may not be economic in a developing country but may well be justified in a more developed country. In the United States, for example, where the value of time of passengers in commercial aircraft has been estimated at $18 (about Rs150) an hour, or about four times the average used in this study, and where the opportunity cost of capital is lower, this project would deserve favorable consideration.

Appendix Table. Discount Rates

(present value of Rs1,000)

	Discount rate (percent)							
Year	*2*	*3*	*4*	*5*	*6*	*7*	*8*	*9*
1	980	971	962	952	943	935	926	917
2	961	943	925	907	890	873	857	842
3	942	915	889	864	840	816	794	772
4	924	884	855	823	792	763	735	708
5	906	863	822	784	747	713	681	650
6	888	837	790	746	705	666	630	596
7	871	813	760	711	665	623	583	547
8	853	789	731	677	627	582	540	502
9	837	766	703	645	592	544	500	460
10	820	744	676	614	558	508	463	422
11	804	722	650	585	527	475	429	388
12	788	701	625	557	497	444	397	356
13	773	681	601	530	469	415	368	326
14	758	661	577	505	442	388	340	299
15	743	642	555	481	417	362	315	275
16	728	623	534	458	394	339	292	252
17	714	605	513	436	371	317	270	231
18	700	587	494	416	350	296	250	212
19	686	570	475	396	331	277	232	194
20	673	554	456	377	312	258	215	178
21	660	538	439	359	294	242	199	164
22	647	522	422	342	278	226	184	150
23	634	507	406	326	262	211	170	138
24	622	492	390	310	247	197	158	126
25	610	478	375	295	233	184	146	116
26	598	464	361	281	220	172	135	106
27	586	450	347	268	207	161	125	098
28	574	437	333	255	196	150	116	090
29	563	424	321	243	185	141	107	082
30	552	412	308	231	174	131	099	075
31	541	400	296	220	164	123	092	069
32	531	388	285	210	155	115	085	063
33	520	377	274	200	146	107	079	058
34	510	366	264	190	138	100	073	053
35	500	355	253	181	130	094	068	049
36	490	345	244	173	123	088	063	045
37	481	335	234	164	116	082	058	041
38	471	325	225	157	109	076	054	038
39	462	316	217	149	103	071	050	035
40	453	307	208	142	097	067	046	032

	Discount rate (percent)							
Year	*10*	*11*	*12*	*13*	*14*	*15*	*16*	*17*
1	909	901	893	885	877	870	862	855
2	826	812	797	783	769	756	743	731
3	751	731	712	693	675	658	641	624
4	683	659	636	613	592	572	552	534
5	621	593	567	543	519	497	476	456
6	564	535	507	480	456	432	410	390
7	513	482	452	425	400	376	354	333
8	467	434	404	376	351	327	305	285
9	424	391	361	333	308	284	263	243
10	386	352	322	295	270	247	227	208
11	350	317	287	261	237	215	195	178
12	319	286	257	231	208	187	168	152
13	290	258	229	204	182	163	145	130
14	263	232	205	181	160	141	125	111
15	239	209	183	160	140	123	108	095
16	218	188	163	141	123	107	093	081
17	198	170	146	125	108	093	080	069
18	180	153	130	111	095	081	069	059
19	164	138	116	098	083	070	060	051
20	149	124	104	087	073	061	051	043
21	135	112	093	077	064	053	044	037
22	123	101	083	068	056	046	038	032
23	112	091	074	060	050	040	033	027
24	102	082	066	053	043	035	028	023
25	092	074	059	047	038	030	024	020
26	084	066	053	042	033	026	021	017
27	076	060	047	037	029	023	018	014
28	069	054	042	033	026	020	016	012
29	063	048	037	029	022	017	014	011
30	057	044	033	026	020	015	012	009
31	052	040	030	023	017	013	010	008
32	047	035	027	020	015	011	009	007
33	043	032	024	018	013	010	007	006
34	039	029	021	016	012	009	006	005
35	036	026	019	014	010	008	006	004
36	032	023	017	012	009	007	005	004
37	029	021	015	011	008	006	004	003
38	027	019	013	010	007	005	004	003
39	024	017	012	009	006	004	003	002
40	022	015	011	008	005	004	003	002

(Table continues on the following page.)

Appendix Table (*continued*)

Year	Discount rate (percent)							
	18	19	20	22	24	26	28	30
1	847	840	833	820	806	794	781	769
2	718	706	694	672	650	630	610	592
3	609	593	579	551	524	500	477	455
4	516	499	482	451	423	397	373	350
5	437	419	402	370	341	315	291	269
6	370	352	335	303	275	250	227	207
7	314	296	279	249	222	198	178	159
8	266	249	233	204	179	157	139	123
9	225	209	194	167	144	125	108	094
10	191	176	162	137	116	099	085	073
11	162	148	135	112	094	079	066	056
12	137	124	112	092	076	062	052	043
13	116	104	093	075	061	050	040	033
14	099	088	078	062	049	039	032	025
15	084	074	065	051	040	031	025	020
16	071	062	054	042	032	025	019	015
17	060	052	045	034	026	020	015	012
18	051	044	038	028	021	016	012	009
19	043	037	031	023	017	012	009	007
20	037	031	026	019	014	010	007	005
21	031	026	022	015	011	008	006	004
22	026	022	018	013	009	006	004	003
23	022	018	015	010	007	005	003	002
24	019	015	013	008	006	004	003	002
25	016	013	010	007	005	003	002	001
26	014	011	009	006	004	002	002	001
27	011	009	007	005	003	002	001	001
28	010	008	006	004	002	002	001	001
29	008	006	005	003	002	001	001	000
30	007	005	004	003	002	001	001	000
31	006	005	004	002	001	001	000	000
32	005	004	003	002	001	001	000	000
33	004	003	002	001	001	000	000	000
34	004	003	002	001	001	000	000	000
35	003	002	002	001	001	000	000	000
36	003	002	001	001	000	000	000	000
37	002	002	001	001	000	000	000	000
38	002	001	001	001	000	000	000	000
39	002	001	001	000	000	000	000	000
40	001	001	001	000	000	000	000	000

References

Adler, Hans A. 1967. *Sector and Project Planning in Transportation.* World Bank Occasional Paper 4. Baltimore, Md.: Johns Hopkins University Press.

Ahmed, Sadiq. 1983. *Shadow Prices for Economic Appraisal of Projects: An Application to Thailand.* World Bank Staff Working Paper 609. Washington, D.C.

Anand, Sudhir. 1975. *Appraisal of a Highway Project in Malaysia.* World Bank Staff Working Paper 213. Washington, D.C.

Beenhakker, Henri L., and A. M. Lago. 1982. *Economic Appraisal of Rural Roads.* World Bank Staff Working Paper 610. Washington, D.C.

Bell, Clive, Peter Hazell, and Roger Slade. 1982. *Project Evaluation in Regional Perspective.* Baltimore, Md.: Johns Hopkins University Press.

Bovill, D. I. N. 1978. *Rural Roads Appraisal Methods for Developing Countries.* Transport and Road Research Laboratory Supplementary Report 395. Crowthorne, Eng.

Bruce, Colin. 1976. *Social Cost-Benefit Analysis.* World Bank Staff Working Paper 239. Washington, D.C.

Carapetis, S., H. L. Beenhakker, and J. D. F. Howe. 1984. *The Supply and Quality of Rural Transport Services in Developing Countries.* World Bank Staff Working Paper 654. Washington, D.C.

Carnemark, Curt, Jaime Biderman, and David Bovet. 1976. *The Economic Analysis of Rural Road Projects.* World Bank Staff Working Paper 241. Washington, D.C.

Coukis, Basil, and others. 1984. *Labor-Based Construction Programs.* New Delhi: Oxford University Press.

Devres, Inc. 1980. *Socio-Economic and Environmental Impacts of Low-Volume Roads: A Review of the Literature.* AID Program Evaluation Discussion Paper 7. Washington, D.C.: U.S. Agency for International Development.

de Weille, Jan, and Anandarup Ray. 1968. *The Optimum Number of Berths of a Port.* World Bank Staff Working Paper 29, Washington, D.C.

Dickey, J. W., and L. H. Miller. 1984. *Road Project Appraisal for Developing Countries.* New York: Wiley.

Edmonds, G. A. 1982. "Towards More Rational Rural Road Transport Planning." *International Labor Review* 121(1): 55–65.

Gittinger, J. Price. 1982. *Economic Analysis of Agricultural Projects.* Baltimore, Md.: Johns Hopkins University Press.

Great Britain. Department of Transport. 1978. *Report of the Advisory Committee on Trunk Road Assessment.* London: Her Majesty's Stationery Office.

_____. 1981. *Traffic Appraisal Manual.* London: Department of Transport.

Great Britain. Ministry of Overseas Development. 1977. *A Guide to the Economic Appraisal of Projects in Developing Countries.* London: Her Majesty's Stationery Office.

Harberger, A. C. 1984. "Basic Needs versus Distributional Weights in Social Cost-Benefit Analysis." *Economic Development and Cultural Change* 32(3): 455–74.

Harral, Clell G. 1968. *Preparation and Appraisal of Transport Projects.* Washington, D.C.: U.S. Department of Transportation.

Harral, Clell G., and P. E. Fossberg. 1977. *Evaluating the Economic Priority of Highway Maintenance.* United Nations Economic Commission for Africa, Pan-African Conference on Highway Maintenance and Rehabilitation. Ghana.

Harrison, A. J. 1974. *The Economics of Transport Appraisal.* New York: Wiley.

Heggie, Ian G. 1972. *Transport Engineering Economics.* Maidenhead, Eng.: McGraw-Hill.

———. 1976. "Practical Problems of Implementing Accounting Prices." In I. M. D. Little and M. FG. Scott, eds., *Using Shadow Prices.* London: Heinemann.

Hills, Peter J., and Michael Jones-Lee. N.d. "The Costs of Traffic Accidents and the Valuation of Accident-Prevention in Less-Developed Countries." A report to the Transportation Department,World Bank. Washington, D.C. Processed.

Hine, J. L. 1975. "The Appraisal of Rural 'Feeder' Roads in Developing Countries." In *Transport Planning in Developing Countries.* London: Planning and Transport Research and Computation Co.

Howe, J. D. G. F. 1976. "Valuing Time Savings in Developing Countries." *Journal of Transport Economics and Policy* 10(2): 113–25.

Howe, John. 1981. *The Impact of Rural Roads on Poverty Alleviation: A Review of the Literature.* International Labour Organisation Working Paper. Geneva.

Howe, John, and Peter Richards, eds. 1984. *Rural Roads and Poverty Alleviation.* London: Intermediate Technology Publications.

Hylland, Aanund, and Richard Zeckhauser. 1981. "Distributional Objectives Should Affect Taxes but Not Program Choice or Design." In Steinar Strom, ed., *Measurement in Public Choice.* London: Macmillan.

Jansson, Jan O., and Dan Shneerson. 1982. *Port Economics.* Cambridge, Mass.: MIT Press.

Kresge, David T., and Paul O. Roberts. 1971. *Systems Analysis and Simulation Models.* Vol. 2 of *Techniques of Transport Planning.* Washington, D.C.: Brookings Institution.

Lal, Deepak. 1980. *Prices for Planning.* London: Heinemann.

Little, I. M. D., and J. A. Mirrlees. *Project Appraisal and Planning for the Developing Countries.* London: Heinemann.

Little, I. M. D., and M. FG. Scott, eds. 1976. *Using Shadow Prices.* London: Heinmann.

MacArthur, J. D., and G. A. Amin, eds. 1978. "Cost-Benefit Analysis and Income Distribution in Developing Countries: A Symposium." *World Development* 6(2): entire issue.

McDiarmid, Orville John. 1977. *Unskilled Labor for Development.* Baltimore, Md.: Johns Hopkins University Press.

Marglin, Stephen, Amartya Sen, and Partha Dasgupta. 1972. *Guidelines for Project Evaluation.* Vienna: United Nations.

Mashayekhi, Afsaneh. 1980. *Shadow Prices for Project Appraisal in Turkey.* World Bank Staff Working Paper 392. Washington, D.C.

Mayworm, Patrick D., and Armando M. Lago. 1982. "The Value of Time: A Review with Recommendations for the Valuation of Travel Time Savings in Rural Road Projects in Developing Countries." Ecosometrics, Inc. Processed.

Miller, Fred. 1973. "Highway Improvements and Agricultural Production: An Argentine Case Study." In B. S. Hoyle, ed., *Transport and Development.* London: Macmillan.

O'Connor, A. M. 1973. "Recent Railway Construction in Tropical Africa." In B. S. Hoyle, ed., *Transport and Development.* London: Macmillan.

Okano, Y. 1983. "Model Split, Efficiency and Public Policy." In T. S. Khachaturov and P. B. Goodwin, eds., *The Economics of Long-Distance Transportation.* New York: St. Martin's.

Page, John M., Jr. 1982. *Shadow Prices for Trade Strategy in Investment Planning in Egypt.* World Bank Staff Working Paper 521. Washington, D.C.

Pearce, David W. 1983. *Cost-Benefit Analysis.* New York: St. Martin's.

Pearce, David W., and C. A. Nash. 1981. *The Social Appraisal of Projects.* New York: Wiley.

Pouliquen, L. Y. 1970. *Risk Analysis in Project Appraisal.* World Bank Occasional Paper 11. Washington D.C.

Powers, Terry, ed. 1981. *Estimating Accounting Prices for Project Appraisal.* Washington, D.C.: Inter-American Development Bank.

Ray, Anandarup. 1984. *Cost-Benefit Analysis.* Baltimore, Md.: Johns Hopkins University Press.

Sharp, C. H. 1983. "Time in Transport Investment." In K. J. Button and A. D. Pearman, eds. *The Practice of Transport Investment Appraisal.* Aldershot, Eng.: Gower.

Sharp, Clifford, and T. Jennings. 1976. *Transport and the Environment.* Leicester, Eng. Leicester University Press.

Squire, Lyn, and I. M. D. Little, 1979. *Application of Shadow Pricing to Country Economic Analysis with an Illustration from Pakistan.* World Bank Staff Working Paper 330. Washington, D.C.

Squire, Lyn, and Herman van der Tak. 1975. *Economic Analysis of Projects.* Baltimore, Md.: Johns Hopkins University Press.

U.S. Department of Transportation. 1981. *Economic Values for Evaluation of Federal Aviation Administration Investment and Regulatory Programs.* Federal Aviation Administration Report FAA-APO-81-3. Washington, D.C.

Watanatada, Thanat, Koji Tsunokawa, William D. O. Paterson, Anil Bhandari, and Clell G. Harral. Forthcoming. The Highway Design and Maintenance Standards Study. Vol. 4, *The Highway Design and Maintenance Standards Model.* Washington, D.C.: World Bank.

Williams, A. 1977. "Income Distribution and Public Expenditure Decisions." In Michael Posner, ed. *Public Expenditure: Allocation between Competing Ends.* New York: Cambridge University Press.

Willoughby, C. R. 1983. "Road Safety Components in World Bank Projects: Informal Guidelines." Washington, D.C.: Transportation Department, World Bank. Processed.

Yucel, N. C. 1975. *A Survey of the Theories and Empirical Investigations of the Value of Travel Time Savings.* World Bank Staff Working Paper 199. Washington, D.C.

Bibliography

The bibliography is organized as follows:

I. The economics of transportation
II. Project appraisal: general
III. Project appraisal: transport
    A. All transport modes
    B. Roads
    C. Railways
    D. Ports
    E. Aviation
    F. Urban transport

The bibliography is not intended to be all-embracing. Many of the items listed contain extensive bibliographies, often of special aspects of the subject area covered.

I. The Economics of Transportation

Baron, Paul. 1980. "The Impact of Transport on the Social and Economic Development in Less-Developed Countries." *Transport Policy and Decision Making* 1:47–53.
    The author suggests that since transport is an important, but not the only, requirement for development, transport planning should be part of a comprehensive approach toward regional development.

Brown, Robert T. 1966. *Transport and the Economic Integration of South America*. Washington, D.C.: Brookings Institution.
    A study of the contribution improved transport could make to closer integration of South America.

Button, K. J. 1982. *Transport Economics*. London: Heinmann.
    A good introduction, including chapters on cost-benefit analysis, transport planning and forecasting, external costs, transport, and economic development. Each chapter has a useful bibliography.

Button, K. J., and A. D. Pearman. 1981. *The Economics of Urban Freight Transport*. London: Macmillan.
    An introduction to the economic, operational, and public policy aspects of urban freight movement.

Campbell, T. C. 1972. "Transport and Its Impact in Developing Countries." *Transportation Journal,* Fall, pp. 15–22.
The author warns that "the importance of transportation can easily be exaggerated" and that there tends to be a "disproportionate investment in the transport sector."

Foster, Christopher D. 1963. *The Transport Problem.* London: Blackie.
A good introduction to transport investment and pricing.

Fromm, Gary, ed. *Transport Investment and Economic Development.* Washington, D.C.: Brookings Institution.
A series of essays on various aspects of transportation economics.

Glaister, Stephen. 1981. *Fundamentals of Transport Economics.* New York: St. Martin's.
Requires familiarity with quantitative and mathematical methods.

Gwilliam, K. M., and P. J. Mackie. 1975. *Economics and Transport Policy.* London: Allen and Unwin.
A good introduction, with emphasis on transport in the United Kingdom.

Haefele, Edwin T., ed. 1969. *Transportation and National Goals.* Washington, D.C.: Brookings Institution.
A series of essays by authors such as Mason (India), Weisshoff (Columbia), Hughes (Malaysia), and Owen (transport and food).

Hoyle, B. S., ed. 1973. *Transport and Development.* London: Macmillan.
Twelve essays, mostly by geographers; half of them deal with transport in Africa. Of special interest are the essays by Miller on transport and agriculture and O'Connor on railways in Africa (see references in section IIIB and C).

Hunter, Holland. 1968. *Soviet Transport Experience: Its Lessons for Other Countries.* Washington, D.C.: Brookings Institution.
The book reviews lessons from Soviet transport policies; particularly for developing countries.

Khachaturov, T. S. and P. B. Goodwin, eds. 1983. *The Economics of Long-Distance Transportation.* New York: St. Martin's Press.
These proceedings of an international conference contain a number of papers on transport in socialist countries.

Kirkpatrick, C. H. 1975. "Public Sector Transport Pricing in Developing Countries." In *Transport Planning in Developing Countries.* London: Planning and Transport Reasearch and Computation Co.
The paper emphasizes the important relation between transport pricing and investment decisions.

Mohring, Herbert. 1976. *Transportation Economics.* Cambridge, Mass.: Ballinger.
Has some discussion of cost-benefit analysis.

Nash, C. A. 1976. *Public versus Private Transport.* London: Macmillan.
The book reviews the social costs of different modes of transport, particularly in Great Britain, and concludes that there is a strong case for promoting public rather than private transport, especially in urban areas and for intercity freight transport.

Owen, Wilfred. 1964. *Strategy for Mobility.* Washington, D.C.: Brookings Institution.
An old but still valid description of the importance of transportation in developing countries.

_____. 1968. *Distance and Development.* Brookings Institution. Washington, D.C.:
The relation of transport and communications to economic development in India, with emphasis on agriculture, urban congestion, and so forth.

Prest, Alan R. 1969. *Transport Economics in Developing Countries.* New York: Praeger.
The major focus is on the correct pricing of roads and railways to ensure transport coordination.

Stubbs, P. C., W. J. Tyson, and M. O. Dalvi. 1980. *Transport Economics.* London: Allen and Unwin.
A particularly useful introduction to key issues in the economics of transport; includes a good bibliography.

Tripathi, P. C. 1972. *Rural Transport and Economic Development.* Delhi: Sultan Chand.
A study of road and rail transport in Rajasthan and its relation to economic development.

Wilson, George W. 1980. *Economic Analysis of Intercity Freight Transportation.* Bloomington: Indiana University Press.
A clear and comprehensive analysis of the structure and problems of intercity freight including the nature of demand and costs, pricing and regulation, and cost-benefit analysis.

Winston, Clifford. 1985. "Conceptual Developments in the Economics of Transportation: An Interpretive Survey." *Journal of Economic Literature* 23(1): 57–94.
A survey of the literature in transportation economics in the United States with emphasis on regulation.

Wohl, Martin, and Chris Hendrickson. 1984. *Transportation Investment and Pricing Principles.* New York: Wiley.
This is an introductory, but sophisticated, text on the theory of transport pricing, financing, and investment planning.

II. Project Appraisal: General

Abouchar, Alan. 1985. *Project Decision Making in the Public Sector.* Lexington, Mass.: D.C. Heath.
An introductory text.

Ahmed, Sadiq. 1983. *Shadow Prices for Economic Appraisal of Projects: An Application to Thailand.* World Bank Staff Working Paper 609. Washington, D.C.
An interesting review of economic and social shadow prices.

Barish, Norman N. 1962. *Economic Analysis for Engineering and Managerial Decision Making.* New York: McGraw-Hill.
Part III deals with project appraisal.

Baum, W. C., and S. M. Tolbert. 1985. *Investing in Development.* New York: Oxford University Press.
The book presents the lessons of World Bank experience in financing development projects. Chapter 11 deals with transport projects.

Baumol, W. J. 1968. "On the Social Rate of Discount." *American Economic Review* 58 (4):788–803.
A clear exposition of the major issues involved in selecting an appropriate discount rate; see also Feldstein's articles listed below. There are a number of comments on this article in the *American Economic Review* 59(5).

Beenhakker, H. L. 1976. *Handbook for the Analysis of Capital Investments.* Westport, Conn.: Greenwood.

The handbook deals with the economic, financial, accounting, engineering economy, statistical, and operations research aspects of investment planning. Chapter 3 deals with project appraisal.

Bell, Clive, Peter Hazell, and Roger Slade. 1982. *Project Evaluation in Regional Perspective.* Baltimore, Md: Johns Hopkins University Press.
A sophisticated evaluation of an irrigational project in Malaysia, including indirect effects and social cost-benefit analysis.

Bridger, G. A., and J. T. Winpenny. 1983. *Planning Development Projects.* London: Overseas Development Administration.
A practical guide to project appraisal. Individual chapters deal with major sectors and give sector background, types of benefits, and checklists of main questions and further reading. Chapters 4–7 deal with roads, railways, ports, and airports.

Bruce, Colin. 1976. *Social Cost-Benefit Analysis.* World Bank Staff Working Paper 239. Washington, D.C.
Explains the derivation of national and project-specific perimeters for estimating economic and social accounting prices; methodology is applied to Thailand, Malaysia, and the Philippines.

Campen, James T. 1986. *Benefit, Cost and Beyond.* Cambridge, Mass.: Ballinger. A critical review, including a radical, Marxist perspective of benefit-cost analysis, especially as it is applied to social, environmental, and regulatory matters.

Chervel, Marc, and Michel Le Gall. 1978. *The Methodology of Planning: Manual of Economic Evaluation of Projects.* Paris: Ministry of Cooperation.
Describes the effects method for project appraisal. For a critique and a reply by Chervel, see Bela Balassa, "The 'Effects Method' of Project Evaluation," World Bank Reprint Series 55, 1977.

Eckstein, Otto. 1958. *Water Resource Development: The Economics of Project Evaluation.* Cambridge, Mass.: Harvard University Press.
This is a classic study on project appraisal; the first part deals with economic appraisal in general and is followed by chapters on flood control, navigation, irrigation, and electric power projects.

English, J. Marley. 1984. *Project Evaluation: A Unified Approach for the Analysis of Capital Investments.* New York: Macmillan.
An introductory textbook.

Feldstein, Martin S. 1964. "Opportunity Cost Calculations in Cost-Benefit Analysis." *Public Finance* 19(2): 177–39; "The Social Time Preference Discount Rate in Cost Benefit Analysis." *Economic Journal* 74 (June 1964): 360–79; and (with J. S. Flemming) "The Problem of Time-Stream Evaluation: Present Value versus Internal Rate of Return Rules." *Bulletin of the Oxford University Institute of Economics and Statistics* (February 1964): 79–85.
These three articles are a good illustration of the extensive literature on the appropriate discount rate. See also Baumol's article listed above.

Fiszel, Henryk. 1966. *Investment Efficiency in a Socialist Economy.* New York: Pergamon.
This is a Polish book (in English translation) on project appraisal methods in a socialist economy.

Fitzgerald, E. V. K. 1978. *Public Sector Investment Planning for Developing Countries.* London: Macmillian.
An introductory text, dealing both with project appraisal and the relation between projects and development plans. With case studies, exercises, and test questions.

Gittinger, J. Price. 1982. *Economic Analysis of Agricultural Projects.* Baltimore, Md.: Johns Hopkins University Press.
A lucid description of the basic financial and economic concepts of project appraisal.

Great Britain. Ministry of Overseas Development. 1977. *A Guide to the Economic Appraisal of Projects in Developing Countries.* London: Her Majesty's Stationery Office.
The guide is based largely on the analytical framework suggested by I. M. D. Little and J. A. Mirrlees. About half of the guide consists of checklists, including nine for various aspects of transport projects.

Harberger, Arnold C. 1972. *Project Evaluation.* Chicago: University of Chicago Press.
A collection of essays, including one on transport projects.

———. 1984. "Basic Needs versus Distributional Weights in Social Cost-Benefit Analysis." *Economic Development and Cultural Change* 32(3): 455–74.
The author concludes that the use of distributional weights in measuring costs and benefits is inconsistent with and less efficient than addressing basic needs indirectly.

Helmers, F. L. C. 1979. *Project Planning and Income Distribution.* Boston: Martinus Nijhoff.
A study with particular reference to developing countries.

Hirschman, Albert O. 1967. *Development Projects Observed.* Washington, D.C.: Brookings Institution.
A thought-provoking study of sociological, psychological, and economic aspects of projects based on a review of completed World Bank projects.

Hirshleifer, Jack, James C. Dehaven, and Jerome M. Milliman. 1969. *Water Supply: Economics, Technology and Policy.* Chicago: University of Chicago Press.
This classic study covers most major aspects of project evaluation.

Hylland, Aanund, and Richard Zeckhauser. 1981. "Distributional Objectives Should Affect Taxes but Not Program Choice or Design." In Steinar Strom, ed., *Measurement in Public Choice.* London: Macmillan.
Suggests that under reasonable assumptions, goverment projects should be designed without taking distributional aspects into account; redistribution should be accomplished solely through the tax system.

Ireson, W. Grant. 1982. *Principles of Engineering Economy.* New York: Wiley.
A good introduction.

Irvin, George. 1978. *Modern Cost-Benefit Methods.* New York: Barnes and Noble.
A useful introduction to the financial, economic, and social appraisal of projects, with exercises for students and a discussion of the literature.

King, John Andrews. 1967. *Economic Development Projects and Their Appraisal.* Baltimore, Md.: Johns Hopkins University Press.
An early book of case studies of World Bank projects, including transport projects.

Lal, Deepak. 1974. *Methods of Project Analysis: A Review.* World Bank Staff Occasional Paper 16. Baltimore, Md.: Johns Hopkins University Press.
A good review of different approaches to shadow pricing.

———. 1980. *Prices for Planning.* London: Heinemann.
Summarizes the results of studies of the Indian Planning Commision on shadow prices.

Lee, James A. 1985. *The Environment, Public Health, and Human Ecology: Considerations for Economic Development.* Baltimore, Md.: Johns Hopkins University Press.
Chapter 7 deals with transportation projects.

Lind, Robert C., and Kenneth V. Arrow. 1982. *Discounting for Time and Risk in Energy Policy.* Baltimore, Md.: Johns Hopkins University Press.
   The book addresses the question of the appropriate rate of discount for evaluating the present value of benefits from a national or social perspective. Much of the discussion has general application to investment decisions in sectors other than energy.

Little, I. M. D., and J. A. Mirrlees. 1974. *Project Appraisal and Planning for Developing Countries.* London: Heinemann.
   A classic study of the subject.

Little, I. M. D., and M. FG. Scott, eds. 1976. *Using Shadow Prices.* London: Heinemann.
   A series of case studies applying shadow prices in Trinidad, Kenya, Ghana, Mauritius, and elsewhere. Of special interest is the essay by I. G. Heggie on "Practical Problems of Implementing Accounting Prices" (chapter 8).

MacArthur, J. D., and G. A. Amin, ed. 1978. "Cost-Benefit Analysis and Income Distribution in Developing Countries: A Symposium." *World Development* 6(2): 123–24.
   A series of articles by Mirrlees, Amin, Stewart, MacArthur, and others.

McDiarmid, Orville John. 1977. *Unskilled Labor for Development.* Baltimore, Md.: Johns Hopkins University Press.
   A study of the economic costs of unskilled agricultural labor in Korea, Taiwan, the Philippines, and Indonesia.

Marglin, Stephen, Amartya Sen, and Partha Dasgupta. 1972. *Guidelines for Project Evaluation.* Vienna: United Nations.
   A basic book on the subject.

Mashayekhi, Afsaneh. 1980. *Shadow Prices for Project Appraisal in Turkey.* World Bank Staff Working Paper 392. Washington, D.C.
   A study of both economic and social accounting prices in Turkey.

Nwaneri, V. C. 1973. "Income Distribution Criteria for the Analysis of Development Projects." *Finance and Development* 10(1): 16–19, 37.
   This is an excellent article on how to allow for income distribution in project appraisal. See also Nwaneri 1970 (section IIIE) for application of a new airport.

Organisation for Economic Co-operation and Development. 1968. *Manual of Industrial Project Analysis in Developing Countries.* Paris: OECD Development Centre.
   Although this manual deals primarily with industrial projects, much of it is also useful for projects in transportation; volume 2, in particular, deals with major economic issues in project appraisal.

Page, John M., Jr. 1982. *Shadow Prices for Trade Strategy in Investment Planning in Egypt.* World Bank Staff Working Paper 521. Washington, D.C.
   An excellent application of estimating shadow prices, for both efficiency and social rate of return calculations.

Pearce, David W., ed. 1978. *The Valuation of Social Cost.* London: Allen and Unwin.
   A series of essays on various aspects of social costs, including air pollution and the value of life and pain.

Pearce, David W. 1983. *Cost-Benefit Analysis.* New York: St. Martin's.
   An excellent introduction to the basic concepts of cost-benefit analysis.

Pearce, David W., and Nash, C. A. 1981. *The Social Appraisal of Projects.* New York: Wiley.
   An excellent text in cost-benefit analysis; has a chapter on developing countries and one on transport.

Posner, Michael, ed. 1977. *Public Expenditure: Allocation between Competing Ends.* New York: Cambridge University Press.

Interesting essays, including Harrison on transport, Heather on the third London air-port, and Rees on the Channel tunnel.

Pouliquen, L. Y. 1970. *Risk Analysis in Project Appraisal.* World Bank Staff Occasional Paper 11. Washington, D.C.
Applies formal risk analysis techniques primarily to transport and public utility projects.

Powers, Terry, ed. 1981. *Estimating Accounting Prices for Project Appraisal.* Washington, D.C.: Inter-American Development Bank.
A study of economic and social accounting prices in several Latin American countries.

Prest, Alan R., and R. Turvey. 1965. "Cost-Benefit Analysis: A Survey." *Economic Journal* 75(300): 683–735.
The article reviews the status of cost-benefit analysis in different fields, including transportation.

Ray, Anandarup. 1984. *Cost-Benefit Analysis.* Baltimore, Md.: Johns Hopkins University Press.
This book consolidates much of the work done on cost-benefit analysis by Little and Mirrlees, Squire and van der Tak, and others; it focuses on controversial issues.

Reutlinger, Shlomo. 1970. *Techniques for Project Appraisal under Uncertainty.* World Bank Occasional Paper 10. Baltimore, Md.: Johns Hopkins University Press.
Recommends that judgments about the factors underlying cost and benefit estimates be recorded in terms of probability distributions and that these be aggregated to yield a probability distribution of the rate of return (or net present worth) of the project.

Squire, Lyn, and Herman van der Tak. 1975. *Economic Analysis of Projects.* Baltimore, Md.: Johns Hopkins University Press.
A basic study, with emphasis on economic and social accounting prices.

Squire, Lyn, and I. M. D. Little. 1979. *Application of Shadow Pricing to Country Economic Analysis with an Illustration from Pakistan.* World Bank Staff Working Paper 330. Washington, D.C.

Sugden, Robert, and Alan Williams. 1978. *The Principles of Practical Cost-Benefit Analysis.* New York: Oxford University Press.
An excellent introduction.

United Nations Industrial Development Organization. 1972. *Guidelines for Project Evalua-tion.* New York: UNIDO.
A basic book on the subject.

———. 1978. *Guide to Practical Project Appraisal: Social Benefit-Cost Analysis in Developing Countries.* New York: UNIDO.

Wood, Adrian. 1984. *Economic Evaluation of Investment Projects.* World Bank Staff Work-ing Paper 631. Washington, D.C.
A clear and simple description of economic cost-benefit analysis, with a discussion of its applicability to project appraisal in China. It is concerned mainly with estimating shadow prices in China.

III. Project Appraisal: Transport

A. All Transport Modes

Adler, Hans A. 1967. *Sector and Project Planning in Transportation.* World Bank Occasional Paper 4. Baltimore, Md.: Johns Hopkins University Press.

The first of two essays deals with the preparation of a transport sector program. The second, on project appraisal, is, with major modifications, the basis of Part I of this manual.

Bruzelius, Nils. 1979. *The Value of Travel Time.* London: Croom Helm.
Provides a theoretical basis for determining the value of travel time, especially leisure time; extensive bibliography.

Burns, Robert E. 1969. "Transport Planning: Selection of Analytical Techniques." *Journal of Transport Economics and Policy* 3(3): 306–21.
Discusses several major approaches to transport planning, such as the bottleneck approach, project analysis, linear programming, integer programming, and simulation models, and their applicability to a developing country like Pakistan.

Button, K. J., and A. D. Pearman, eds. 1983. *The Practice of Transport Investment Appraisal.* Aldershot, Eng.: Gower.
Essays by transport planners and economists on the application, rather than the theory, of project appraisal. Of special interest are essays on airports, the Channel tunnel, risk and uncertainty, the valuation of time savings, and port appraisal in developing countries. Each essay includes references to the literature.

Cohen, Benjamin I. 1966. *Capital Budgeting for Transportation in Under-developed Countries.* Harvard Transportation and Economic Development Seminar, Discussion Paper 39. Cambridge, Mass. Processed.
A good introduction.

Georgi, Hanspeter. 1973. *Cost-Benefit Analysis and Public Investment in Transport: A Survey.* London: Butterworths.
An introductory survey, translated from the German edition published in 1970.

Gronau, Reuben. 1970. "The Effect of Traveling Time on the Demand for Passenger Transportation." *Journal of Political Economy* 78(2): 377–94.
A clear presentation, relating the value of time to the price travelers are paying for time savings and their income level.

Harberger, Arnold C. 1967. *Cost-Benefit Analysis of Transportation Projects.* Paper prepared for a conference on Engineering and the Building of Nations, August 27-September 1. Estes Park, Colo. Processed.
A good theoretical introduction.

Harral, Clell G. 1968. *Preparation and Appraisal of Transport Projects.* Washington, D.C.: U.S. Department of Transportation.
A useful introduction.

Harrison, A. J. 1974. *The Economics of Transport Appraisal.* New York: Wiley.
An introduction with emphasis on urban transport and time savings.

Heggie, Ian G. 1969. "Are Gravity and Interactance Models a Valid Technique for Planning Regional Transport Facilities?" *Operational Research Quarterly* 20(1): 93–111.
This article concludes that these models cannot yet be used for explaining existing or future traffic flows.

_____. 1972. *Transport Engineering Economics.* Maidenhead, Eng.: McGraw-Hill.
An excellent survey of major issues in the appraisal of transport projects.

_____, ed. 1976. *Modal Choice and the Value of Travel Time.* Oxford, Eng.: Clarendon.
Six essays by different authors dealing primarily with urban transport. Of special interest is the essay by A. Jennings and C. Sharp, "The Value of Travel Time Savings and Transport Investment Appraisal."

Hills, Peter J., and Michael Jones-Lee. N.d. "The Costs of Traffic Accidents and the

Valuation of Accident-Prevention in Less-Developed Countries." A report to the Transportation Department, World Bank. Washington, D.C. Processed.
A comprehensive review, with extensive bibliography.

Houel, B. J. 1979. *National Transportation Planning in Developing Countries.* Institute of Transportation Studies, University of California, Research Report UCB-ITS-RR-79-4. Berkeley.
A critical review of the methodologies used in transport sector planning, based primarily on nine case studies of transport plans undertaken between 1962 and 1975.

Howe, J. D. G. F. 1976. "Valuing Time Savings in Developing Countries." *Journal of Transport Economics and Policy* 10(2): 113–25.
After reviewing the methods for valuing time savings, the author concludes that the evidence is insufficient to permit use of the resultant values; suggests that willingness to pay may be a more reliable criterion.

Jones-Lee, M. W. 1976. *The Value of Life.* Chicago: University of Chicago Press.
Chapter 2 provides a useful survey and evaluation of the literature.

Jones-Lee, M. W., M. Hammerton, and P. R. Philips. 1985. "The Value of Safety: Results of a National Sample Survey." *The Economic Journal,* 95: 49–72.
A study, based on a questionnaire, of willingness to pay for reductions in the risk of death or injury in the United Kingdom.

Kanafani, Adif, and Dan Sperling. 1982. *National Transportation Planning.* The Hague: Martinus Nijhoff.
The book presents a detailed methodology and procedure for conducting a national transportation plan; with an extensive bibliography.

Kobe, Susumu. 1967. *Transport Problems in West Africa.* Paris: OECD Development Centre.
This early book presents many interesting insights into aspects of project appraisal that are still appropriate for parts of Africa.

Lago, Armando M. 1966. "Cost Functions for Inter-city Transportation Systems in Underdeveloped Countries: A Model of Optimum Technology." Ph.D diss. Harvard University.
Interesting study.

Lee, N., and M. Quasim Dalvi. 1969. "Variations in the Value of Travel Time." *Manchester School of Economic and Social Studies* 37(3): 213–36.
The article reviews major factors determining the value of travel time and presents the results of a study involving travel to work in Manchester, England.

Mahayni, R. G. 1977. "Reorienting Transportation Planning Rationale in Developing Countries." *Traffic Quarterly* 31(2): 351–65.
Planning should consider transport as an integrated system rather than as an aggregation of projects and modes. Because traditional cost-benefit analysis does not include all costs and benefits and is exclusively oriented toward economic efficiency, decisionmakers should be presented with indexes that summarize the advantages and disadvantages of alternative transport proposals.

Martin, Brian V., and Charles N. Warden. 1965. *Transportation Planning in Developing Countries.* Washington, D.C.: Brookings Institution.
This pamphlet emphasizes systems analysis in project appraisal.

Meyer, J. R., ed. 1971. *Techniques of Transport Planning.* Vol. 2, *Systems Analysis and Simulation Models.* Washington, D.C.: Brookings Institution.
Development of a large-scale computer macroeconomic transport simulation model,

with submodels, for transport planning, and an application to Colombia.

Moses, Leon, and Harold Williamson, Jr. 1963. "Value of Time, Choice of Mode and the Subsidy Issue in Urban Transportation." *Journal of Political Economy* 71(3): 247-65. Useful on measuring the value of time.

Oort, Conrad J. 1967. "Criteria for Investment in the Infrastructure of Inland Transport." In *Second International Symposium on Theory and Practice in Transport Economics.* Munich: European Conference of Ministries of Transport. A good introduction to the cost-benefit analysis of transport projects.

Organisation for Economic Co-operation and Development. 1971. *Problems of Environmental Economics.* Paris. A collection of essays. Of special interest is that by D. Pearce on noise abatement.

Roberts, Paul O., and David T. Kresge. 1968. "Simulation of Transport Policy Alternatives for Columbia." *American Economic Review* 58(2): 311-60. Describes the application of a model developed at Harvard University for appraising projects (see Meyer, 1971, above).

Sharp, Clifford. 1979. "The Environmental Impact of Transport and the Public Interest." *Journal of Transport Economics and Policy* 13(1): 88-101. Examines some of the fundamental problems raised by action intended to reduce the level of environmental pollution produced by transport, with illustrations from decisions on speed limits, accident reduction, and noise reduction.

_____. 1981. *The Economics of Time.* Oxford, Eng.: Martin Robertson. An introduction. Chapter 5 deals with the valuation of time in transport projects; chapter 7 with the valuation of present and future satisfaction in determining appropriate discount rates.

_____. 1983. "Time in Transport Investment." In K. J. Button and A. D. Pearman, eds., *The Practice of Transport Investment Appraisals.* Aldershot, Eng.: Gower. A review of the theory and its practical application in the United Kingdom.

Sharp, Clifford, and T. Jennings. 1976. *Transport and the Environment.* Leicester, Eng.: Leicester University Press. A comprehensive survey of the environmental costs of transport, including noise, air pollution, vibration, accidents, delays, road wear, visual intrusion, and the severance of communities. Each chapter has an excellent summary and bibliography. The emphasis is on the United Kingdom.

Soberman, Richard M. 1966. *Transport Technology for Developing Regions.* Cambridge, Mass.: MIT Press. Although primarily a study of road transportation in Venezuela, the methodology has general application.

Stairs, Sonia. 1968. "Selecting a Traffic Network." *Journal of Transport Economics and Policy* 2(2): 218-32. Describes the use of systems analysis and computers in the selection of projects.

Starkie, D. N. M., and D. M. Johnson. 1975. *The Economic Value of Peace and Quiet.* Lexington, Mass.: D.C. Heath. A study of the economic evaluation of measures to reduce noise, particularly aircraft noise.

Stein, Martin. 1977. "Social Impact Assessment Techniques and Their Application to Transportation Decisions." *Traffic Quarterly* 31(2). Deals with social impact assessment methodologies; primarily related to urban transport.

Stokes, C. J. 1968. *Transportation and Economic Development in Latin America.* New York: Praeger.

An examination of three major transport investments: a highway in Venezuela, the freight transport system of Colombia, and a highway along the eastern edge of the Andes.

Thomas, S. 1975. "The Relevance of the Value of Time Savings to Developing Countries." In *Transport Planning in Developing Countries.* London: Planning and Transport Research and Computation Co.

The paper suggests that time savings tend to be neglected and that savings of leisure time should not necessarily be excluded.

Turvey, Ralph. 1976. *Analysis of Economic Costs and Expenses in Road and Rail Transport.* Commission of the European Communities, Transport Series 4. Brussels.

Describes the differences between economic costs and financial expenses.

United Nations Economic Commission for Asia and the Far East. 1967. *Introduction to Transport Planning.* New York.

Old, but still contains a great deal of useful information about the process of transport planning.

Yucel, N. C. 1975. *A Survey of the Theories and Empirical Investigations of the Value of Travel Time Savings.* World Bank Staff Working Paper 199. Washington, D.C.

An excellent survey of the entire field but does not include the value of time savings for freight.

B. Roads

Abaynayaka, S. W., H. Hide, G. Morosiuk, and R. Robinson. 1976. *Tables for Estimating Vehicle Operating Costs on Rural Roads in Developing Countries.* Transport and Road Research Laboratory Report 723. Crowthorne, Eng.

Tables for estimating vehicle operating costs on free-flowing, low-volume rural roads in developing countries.

Ableson, P. W., and A. D. J. Flowerdew. 1975. "Models for the Economic Evaluation of Road Maintenance." *Journal of Transport Economics and Policy* 9(2): 93–114.

Useful on road maintenance evaluation; based on work in Jamaica.

Ahmed, Yusuf, Patrick O'Sullivan, Sujono, and Derek Wilson. 1976. *Road Investment Programming for Developing Countries: An Indonesian Example.* Evanston, Ill.: Northwestern University.

Purpose of study is to develop a practical model for investment planning which may be applied to transport problems in developing countries at the regional level. The approach is based on regionwide optimization of road transport by means of mathematical programming.

Allal, Moise, and G. A. Edmonds. 1977. *Manual on the Planning of Labour-Intensive Road Construction.* Geneva: ILO.

A manual for the planning, evaluation, and design of road projects, with emphasis on labor-intensive technology.

American Association of State Highway Officials. 1960. *Road User Benefit Analyses for Highway Improvements.* Washington, D.C.: AASHO.

This report has been used extensively in the United States but must be used with caution, especially in developing countries.

Anand, Sudhir. 1975. *Appraisal of a Highway Project in Malaysia.* World Bank Staff Working Paper 213. Washington, D.C.
The paper presents the application of the Little-Mirrlees approach to project appraisal to a highway project.

Barwell, I. J., and J. D. G. F. Howe. 1979. *Appropriate Transport Facilities for the Rural Sector in Developing Countries.* Geneva: ILO.
The authors suggest that there should be a shift of emphasis from costly rural roads to more appropriate transport technologies including freight movement by man, more efficient animal transport, and cheap motorized transport.

Beenhakker, Henri L., and A. Chammari. 1979. *Identification and Appraisal of Rural Roads Projects.* World Bank Staff Working Paper 362. Washington, D.C.
Describes an approach to the appraisal of projects consisting of both rural roads and complementary agricultural investments.

Beenhakker, Henri L., and A. M. Lago. 1982. *Economic Appraisal of Rural Roads.* World Bank Staff Working Paper 610. Washington, D.C.
Suggests methods to simplify the screening and appraisal of rural road projects, particularly when many roads are being considered. Annex K provides information on costs of construction and vehicle operation for different road surfaces in several countries.

Bhandari, A. S., and Sinha, K. C. 1979. "Optimal Timing for Paving Low-Volume Gravel Roads." In *Low-Volume Roads: Second International Conference.* Transportation Research Record 702. Washington, D.C.: National Academy of Sciences.
The article suggests a method for determining the optimal timing for paving a gravel road, including the opportunity cost of capital.

Botham, R. W. 1980. "The Regional Development Effects of Road Investment." *Transportation Planning and Technology* 6(2): 97–108.
Britain's postwar road investment program had relatively little impact on the spatial distribution of employment.

Bovill, D. I. N. 1978. *Rural Roads Appraisal Methods for Developing Countries.* Transport and Road Research Laboratory Supplementary Report 395. Crowthorne, Eng.
Reviews appraisal methods for rural roads and suggests techniques for incorporating both economic and social objectives.

Bovill, D. I. N., I. G. Heggie, and J. L. Hine. 1978. *A Guide to Transport Planning within the Roads Sector For Developing Countries.* London: Ministry of Overseas Development.
A useful survey, including an extensive bibliography.

Brademayer, B., F. Moavenzadeh, M. J. Markow, M. El-Hawary, and M. Owais. 1979. "Road Network Analysis for Transportation Investment in Egypt." In *Low-Volume Roads: Second International Conference.* Transportation Research Record 702. Washington, D.C.: National Academy of Sciences.
An application of the MIT road investment analysis model to planning highway investments in Egypt.

Brazil Ministry of Transportation and United Nations Development Programme. *Research on the Interrelationships between Costs of Highway Construction, Maintenance and Utilization.* 12 vols. Brasilia.
An extensive study, part of a more general study by the World Bank.

Carapetis, Steve, H. L. Beenhakker, and J. D. G. F. Howe. 1984. *The Supply and Quality of Rural Transport Services in Developing Countries.* World Bank Staff Working Paper 654. Washington, D.C.

The study stresses that the supply and quality of rural transport frequently depends less on investments in rural roads than on use of a wider range of vehicles; more tracks, paths, and trails; availability of vehicles for rent; and less restrictive government regulation of transport.

Carnemark, Curt, Jaime Biderman, and David Bovet. 1976. *The Economic Analysis of Rural Road Projects.* World Bank Staff Working Paper 241. Washington, D.C.
Offers a general approach for the economic appraisal of rural roads, which extends beyond the quantification of road user savings to increased agricultural production.

Chesher, Andrew, and Robert Harrison. Forthcoming. *Vehicle Operating Costs: Evidence from Developing Countries.* Highway Design and Maintenance Standards Study. vol. 1. Washington, D.C.: World Bank.
A comprehensive study of transport costs on nonurban, noncongested highways and the relationships between these costs and highway characteristics such as surface condition and vertical and horizontal geometry. The data are based on road user cost studies in Kenya, the Caribbean, Brazil, and India.

Coburn, T. M., M. E. Beesley, and D. J. Reynolds. 1960. *The London-Birmingham Motorway: Traffic and Economics.* Road Research Technical Paper 46. London: Her Majesty's Stationery Office.
A pioneering study of a major expressway.

Coukis, Basil, and others. 1984. *Labor-Based Construction Programs.* New Delhi: Oxford University Press.
A practical guide for planning and management of labor-based construction programs, based on experience with labor-based road and irrigation projects in a number of countries. Pages 5–40 deal with economic issues.

Dawson, R. F. F. 1968. *The Economic Assessment of Road Improvement Schemes.* Road Research Technical Paper 75. London: Ministry of Transport.
A practical document on how to appraise road projects.

Devres, Inc. 1980. *Socio-Economic and Environmental Impacts of Low-Volume Roads: A Review of the Literature.* AID Program Evaluation Discussion Paper 7. Washington, D.C.: U.S. Agency for International Development.
An excellent survey of the literature of the socioeconomic and environmental impact of rural roads in developing countries.

de Weille, Jan. 1966. *Quantification of Road User Savings.* World Bank Occasional Paper 2. Baltimore, Md.: Johns Hopkins University Press.
A comprehensive study of vehicle operating costs on different road surfaces.

Dickey, J. W., and L. H. Miller. 1984. *Road Project Appraisal for Developing Countries.* New York: Wiley.
A comprehesive introduction to economic, financial, and institutional aspects of road project appraisal.

Dodgson, J. S. 1973. "External Effects and Secondary Benefits in Road Investment Appraisal." *Journal of Transport Economics and Policy* 7(2): 169–85.
Study finds that in developed economies few external effects from road investment are likely, and that secondary benefits (for example, to final consumers of goods transported) are already covered by the benefits to traffic.

Edmonds, G. A. 1982. "Towards More Rational Rural Road Transport Planning." *International Labor Review* 121(1): 55–65.
The article suggests that because it will not be possible to provide adequate rural roads in many developing countries for a long time, more emphasis should be placed on the

use of alternative forms of transport such as animal-drawn carts, bicycles, and simple mechanized transport.

Edwards, Chris. 1978. "Some Problems of Evaluating Investments in Rural Transport." In *Transport Planning in Developing Countries.* London: Planning and Transport Research and Computation Co. and Transport Research Board.
 Paper finds that in Bangladesh improvements in transport have only small effects on development relative to other factors, such as the provision of credit, land tenure, and other policies of the government.

Faiz, Asif, and Edgar Staffini. 1979. "Engineering Economics of the Maintenance of Earth and Gravel Roads." In *Low-Volume Roads: Second International Conference.* Transportation Research Record 702. Washington, D.C.: National Academy of Sciences.
 The paper presents a method for the economic evaluation of road maintenance programs for unpaved roads.

Fisher, N. W. F., and J. K. Stanley. 1970. "The Production Benefits from Investment in Road Construction in Rural Australia." In *Australian Road Research Board, Fifth Conference.* Canberra.
 Finds a low elasticity of demand for transport on Australian feeder roads.

Fossberg, P. E., A. S. Bhandari, and C. G. Harral. 1984. "Evaluating Economic Priorities in the Highway Sector." Paper presented at the Tenth International Road Federation Meeting. Rio de Janeiro.
 The paper presents a methodology for the economic evaluation of alternative maintenance policies for paved roads.

Friedlaender, Ann. F. 1963. *The Interstate Highway System: A Study in Public Investment.* Amsterdam: North-Holland.
 A cost-benefit study of the United States interstate highway system which suggests overbuilding in the rural areas and underbuilding in or near urban areas.

Great Britain. Department of Transport. 1978. *Report of the Advisory Committee on Trunk Road Assessment.* London.
 A thorough review and critique of the department's method of appraising trunk roads, including both economic and environmental factors. The report also summarizes road appraisal methods in the United States, France, and Germany and provides a comparison of appraisal methods for investments in other transport modes.

_____. 1980. *Report of the Inquiry into Lorries, People and the Environment.* London.
 A report to the minister of transport on the causes and consequences of the growth in the movement of freight by road and, in particular, of the impact of trucks on people and their environment.

_____. 1981. *Traffic Appraisal Manual.* London.
 A practical manual for forecasting traffic in the appraisal of trunk roads.

_____. 1985. *COBA 9 Manual.* London.
 COBA is a computer program which compares the costs and benefits of improvements for trunk roads. The program has been updated periodically.

_____. 1986. *Project Preparation and Appraisal in the Road Sector.* Crowthorne, Eng. Draft.
 A practical guide for technical and economic preparation and appraisal of roads in developing countries.

Great Britain. The Standing Advisory Committee on Trunk Road Assessment. 1979. *Forecasting Traffic on Trunk Roads: A Report on the Regional Highway Traffic Model Project.* (Leitch Report). London.

A critical evaluation of the Department of Transport's Regional Highway Model Project designed to assist in estimating traffic flows for use in the appraisal of trunk road investments; a useful report on the state of the art of traffic modeling.

Gwilliam, K. M. 1970. "The Indirect Effects of Highway Investment." *Regional Studies* 4, no. 2 (August): 167–76.
Finds that benefits to users are generally a correct measure for appraisal of transport projects; secondary benefits might be important in some situations.

Harral, Clell G., and P. E. Fossberg. 1977. *Evaluating the Economic Priority of Highway Maintenance.* United Nations Economic Commission for Africa, Pan-African Conference on Highway Maintenance and Rehabilitation, Ghana.
An extensive study of maintenance of roads with different surfaces, traffic levels, and so forth.

Hawkins, E. K. 1960. "Investment in Roads in Underdeveloped Countries." *Bulletin of the Oxford University Institute of Statistics* 22(4): 359–69.
A pioneer introductory article, growing out of Uganda experience.

Heggie, I. G. 1979. "Economics and the Road Program." *Journal of Transport Economics and Policy* 13(1): 52–67.
Interesting critique of cost-benefit analysis as applied in the United Kingdom in relation to traffic forecasting, valuation of time, and neglect of environmental factors.

Hide, Henry. 1982. *Vehicle Operating Costs in the Caribbean.* Department of the Environment, Transport and Road Research Laboratory Report LR 1031. Crowthorne, Eng.
A study of vehicle operating costs.

Hide, Henry, and S. W. Abaynayaka. 1975. "Some Vehicle Operating Cost Relationships for Developing Countries." In *Transport Planning in Developing Countries.* London: Planning and Transport Research and Computation Co.
The paper summarizes the results of an investigation of vehicle operating costs in Kenya.

Hide, Henry, S. W. Abaynayaka, I. Sayer, and R. J. Wyatt. 1975. *The Kenya Road Transport Cost Study: Research on Vehicle Operating Costs.* Transport and Road Research Laboratory Report 672. Crowthorne, Eng.
A major investigation of the effects of various road, vehicle, and environmental parameters on vehicle operating costs.

Hine, J. L. 1975. "The Appraisal of Rural 'Feeder' Roads in Developing Countries." In *Transport Planning in Developing Countries.* London: Planning and Transport Research and Computation Co.
The paper reviews various methodologies for appraising rural roads and finds none of them satisfactory.

Howe, John. 1981. *The Impact of Rural Roads on Poverty Alleviation: A Review of the Literature.* International Labour Organisation Working Paper, Geneva.
A review of more than 60 case studies on the impact of rural road construction and improvement on development in general and on income and income distribution in particular.

―――. 1984. *Rural Roads and Poverty Alleviation.* London: Intermediate Technology Publications.
Essays on the appraisal of rural road improvements, with emphasis on their impact on income distribution and poverty alleviation; case studies of Egypt, India, Botswana, and Thailand.

Howe, John, and Peter Richards, eds. 1984. *Rural Roads and Poverty Alleviation.* London:

Intermediate Technology Publications.
Essays on the appraisal of rural road improvements, with special emphasis on their impact on income distribution and poverty alleviation; case studies of Egypt, India, Botswana, and Thailand.

Hughes, William. 1969. "Social Benefits through Improved Transport in Malaya." In E. T. Haefele, ed., *Transport and National Goals.* Washington, D.C.: Brookings Institution.
A study of the impact of rural roads on such factors as education, health, and newspaper distribution in a rural area of Malaya.

India Central Road Research Institute. 1982. *Road User Cost Study in India.* Final Report. 8 vols. New Delhi.
A study of vehicle operating costs.

Irvin, G. W. 1975. *Roads and Redistribution.* Geneva: ILO.
A study of the social costs and employment benefits of labor-intensive road construction in Iran.

Israel, Arturo. 1970. *Appraisal Methodology for Feeder Road Projects.* World Bank Economics Department Working Paper 70 Washington, D.C.
A suggested methodology for measuring the benefits of feeder road investments in developing countries; with extensive bibliography.

Koch, J. A., F. Moavenzadeh, and K. S. Chew. 1979. "A Methodology for Evaluation of Rural Roads in the Context of Development." In *Low-Volume Roads: Second International Conference.* Transportation Research Record 702. Washington, D.C.: National Academy of Sciences.
The article suggests a multicriteria appraisal framework to account for various socioeconomic objectives of rural roads.

Mayworm, Patrick D., and Armando M. Lago. 1982. "The Value of Time: A Review with Recommendations for the Valuation of Travel Time Savings in Rural Road Projects in Developing Countries." Ecosometrics, Inc. Processed.
An excellent summary, prepared for the Transportation Department, World Bank, of the state of the art of valuing travel time; with a good bibliography.

Millard, R. S., and R. S. P. Bonney. 1965. "The Costs of Operating Buses and Trucks on Roads with Different Surfaces in Africa." *Road International,* June, pp. 18–23, 26–27.
Although this early study by the Road Research Laboratory (United Kingdom) gives out-of-date information on vehicle operating costs, the general discussion is still valuable.

Miller, Fred. 1973. "Highway Improvements and Agricultural Production: An Argentine Case Study." In B. S. Hoyle, ed., *Transport and Development.* London: Macmillan.
An interesting study of the impact of road improvements on agricultural production in a provice of Argentina; found "a surprising lack of benefits."

Mohring, Herbert, and M. Harwitz. 1962. *Highway Benefits: An Analytical Framework.* Evanston, Ill.: Northwestern University Press.
A basic study of major highway benefits.

Odier, Lionel. 1963. *The Economic Benefits of Road Construction and Improvements.* Paris: Publications ESTOUP.
A dated but still useful introduction by a French engineer-economist; available in English.

Plumbe, A. J. 1978. "Implications of Feeder Road Usage by the Farming Community of South-East Thailand." In *Transport Planning in Developing Countries.* London: Planning and Transport Research Computation Co. and Transportation Research Board.

The paper examines some aspects of the appraisal of feeder roads and suggests that increased passenger traffic may be the main result of feeder road improvements.

Pollack, E. E. 1964. "Methods Currently Used in Calculating Direct Savings in Transport Costs and the Indirect Social Economic Benefits Derived from Road Improvement Projects." Transport and Communications Bulletin 37. New York: United Nations Economic Commission for Asia and the Far East.

Roberts, Paul O., and Richard M. Soberman. 1966. *A Vehicle Performance Model for Highways in Developing Countries.* Harvard Transport Research Program Discussion Paper 46. Cambridge, Mass. Processed.
The paper presents an analysis of road costs and so forth in terms of a model (see Meyer 1971, section IIIB).

Robinson, R., H. Hide, J. W. Hodges, J. Rolt, and S. W. Abaynayaka. 1975. *A Road Transport Investment Model for Developing Countries.* Transport and Road Research Laboratory Report 674. Crowthorne, Eng.
The report describes a model for the appraisal of roads in developing countries, including construction, road deterioration, road user cost, and road maintenance, and applies the model to a road in Kenya.

Smith, Ian. 1968. "The Western Nigeria Road Development Survey." *Journal of Transport Economics and Policy* 2(1): 94–104.
Explains the application of cost-benefit techniques to many roads in Nigeria.

Squire, Lyn. 1973. "Optimal Feeder Roads in Developing Countries: The Case of Thailand." *Journal of Development Studies* 9(2): 279–90.
The article examines the economic theory underlying the possiblity of induced production benefits from feeder roads and applies the theory to feeder roads in Thailand.

Sychrava, Lev. 1968. "Some Thoughts on Feasibility Studies." *Journal of Transport Economics and Policy* 2(3): 332–49.
A thoughtful presentation of the difficulties of appraising feeder roads in Thailand. For a reply presenting somewhat different views, see Hans A. Adler, "Some Thoughts on Feasibility Studies," *Journal of Transport Economics and Policy* 3(2): 231–36.

United Nations Economic Commission for Asia and the Far East. 1973. *Guide to Highway Feasibility Studies.* Bangkok and New York.
A short introduction focusing on terms of reference, data collection, forecasting, evaluation, and analysis.

van der Tak, Herman G. and de Weille, Jan. 1969. *Reappraisal of a Road Project in Iran.* World Bank Occasional Paper 7. Baltimore, Md.: Johns Hopkins University Press.
An early effort at ex post evaluation of a road project.

van der Tak, Herman G., and Anandarup Ray. 1971. *The Economic Benefits of Road Transport Projects.* World Bank Occasional Paper 13. Baltimore, Md.: Johns Hopkins University Press.
A theoretical exposition of the major types of benefits.

Walters, A. A. 1968. *The Economics of Road User Charges.* World Bank Occasional Paper 5. Baltimore, Md.: Johns Hopkins University Press.
The case for short-run marginal cost pricing and its relation to investment decisions presented at a high level of economic sophistication.

Watanatada, Thanat, Koji Tsunokawa, William D. O. Paterson, Anil Bhandari, and Clell G. Harral. Forthcoming. *The Highway Design and Maintenance Standards Model.* The Highway Design and Maintenance Standards Study, vol. 4. Washington, D.C.: World Bank.
A description of the highway design model and a user's manual. HDM is a project and

sector planning model which permits a quantitative analysis of the cost tradeoffs in highway construction, maintenance, and an assessment of economic priorities.

Weiss, Willard D. 1974. *Manual on Highway Project Appraisal in Developing Countries.* Washington, D.C.: Economic Development Institute, World Bank.
An introduction that has been useful in training noneconomists.

Willoughby, C. R. 1983. "Road Safety Components in World Bank Projects: Informal Guidelines." Washington, D.C.: Transportation Department, World Bank. Processed.
Based on a study of road safety components in World Bank projects.

Wilson, George W., B. R. Bergman, L. V. Hirsch and M. S. Klein. 1966. *The Impact of Highway Investment on Development.* Washington, D.C.: Brookings Institution.
A review of the impact of a number of completed highway projects on economic development.

Winfrey, Robley. 1969. *Economic Analysis for Highways.* Scranton, Pa.: International Textbook.
A basic, somewhat traditional textbook. Appropriate for heavy traffic patterns.

World Health Organization. 1984. *Road Traffic Accidents in Developing Countries.* WHO Technical Report Series 703. Geneva.
Report of a WHO meeting summarizing a wide range of recommendations for reducing traffic accidents in developing countries.

C. Railways

Alston, L. L. 1984. *Railways and Energy.* World Bank Staff Working Paper 364. Washington, D.C.
Useful methodological approach to cost-benefit studies comparing railway electrification with dieselization.

Brown, Robert T. 1965. "The Railroad Decision in Chile." In Gary Fromm, ed., *Transport Investment and Economic Development.* Washington, D.C.: Brookings Institution.
This article reviews the decision to modernize the Chilean railway in 1959. It concludes that the investment was not justified and that abandonment of much of the system would have been better.

Else, P. K., and M. Howe. 1969. "Cost-Benefit Analysis and Withdrawl of Railway Services." *Journal of Transport Economics and Policy* 2(2): 178–94.
Application of cost-benefit analysis to two railway lines in Great Britain.

Foster, Christopher D., and M. E. Beesley. 1963. "Estimating the Social Benefit of Constructing an Underground Railway in London." *Journal of the Royal Statistical Society* 126(pt. I): 46–78.
A classic article of cost-benefit analysis in transport and an interesting case study.

O'Connor, A. M. 1973. "Recent Railway Construction in Tropical Africa." In B. S. Hoyle, ed., *Transport and Development.* London: Macmillan.
Finds little impact of new railway lines on agricultural development.

Pryke, R. W. S., and J. S. Dodgson. 1975. *The British Rail Problem: A Case Study in Economic Disaster.* Boulder, Colo.: Westview.
A vigorously argued proposal for a self-sufficient, profitable railway system. Of special interest are analyses of various types of railway investment (chapter 7); the social benefits of rail passenger services (chapter 9), including cost-benefit analyses of closing railway lines; an analysis of freight movements by road, including social costs (chapter 10), such as accidents, noise, congestion, air pollution, and vibration, and a comparison of these costs with road user charges.

World Bank, Transportation and Water Department (P. N. Taborga). 1979. "The Economic Role of Railways: Determinants of Railway Traffic." Washington, D.C.
The study defines practical methods for forecasting the role of railways by identifying key parameters determining the role of transport and the various transport modes.

D. Ports

Bennathan, Esra, and Alan A. Walters. 1978. *Port Pricing and Investment Policy for Developing Countries.* New York: Oxford University Press.
A major contribution to the intellectual foundations of appropriate pricing or tariff policy for ports.

de Weille, Jan, and Anandarup Ray. 1968. *The Optimum Number of Berths of a Port.* World Bank Working Paper 29. Washington, D.C.
———. 1974. "The Optimum Port Capacity." *Journal of Transport Economics and Policy* 8(3): 244–59.
The article considers the extent to which a port should install additional berths to cater for random arrival of ships.

Goss, R. O. 1968. "Port Investment." In Denys Munby, ed., *Transport.* Baltimore, Md.: Penguin.
A useful introduction.

Heggie, I. G., and C. B. Edwards. 1968. "Port Investment Problems: How to Decide Investment Priorities." *Conference on Civil Engineering Problems Overseas:* London: Institution of Civil Engineers.
The paper describes how an investment program was prepared for a port in Malaysia on the basis of a cost-benefit analysis using a computerized simulation model.

Holt, J. A. 1983. "Port Investment Appraisal in Developing Countries." In K. J. Button and A. D. Pearman, eds., *The Practice of Transport Investment Appraisal.* Aldershot, Eng.: Gower.
An introduction.

Jansson, Jan O., and Dan Shneerson. 1982. *Port Economics.* Cambridge, Mass.: MIT Press.
A good introduction, with emphasis on the application of queuing theory to investment decisions and on the economics of port pricing; with illustrations from Nigeria.

Klausner, Robert. 1969. "The Evaluation of Risk in Marine Capital Investments." *Engineering Economist* 14(4): 183–214.
A good exposition of the treatment of risk and uncertainty, including the application of probability analysis, with little emphasis, however, on marine investments.

Laing, E. T. 1977. "The Distribution of Benefits from Port Investment." *Maritime Policy and Management* 4(3): 141–54.
The author concludes that port investments that reduce ship costs are usually passed on in lower freight rates.

Oram, R. B., and C. C. R. Baker. 1971. *The Efficient Port.* New York: Pergamon.
An introduction to the technical, operational, and administrative aspects of port operations; does not deal with economic issues.

Plumlee, Carl H. 1966. "Optimum Size Seaport." In *Proceedings.* New York: Association of the American Society of American Engineers.
The article deals mainly with port capacity.

Shoup, Donald S. 1967. *Ports and Economic Development.* Washington, D.C.: Brookings Institution.

The study deals with such subjects as port organization, port charges, and the appraisal of port projects.

United Nations Conference on Trade and Development. 1968. *Establishment or Expansion of Merchant Marines in Developing Countries.* New York: United Nations.
A useful study indicating the type of economic and financial analysis needed to determine whether a developing country should establish its own shipping fleet.

United Nations Development Programme. 1978. *Port Development.* New York.
This is a useful reference manual for port planners in developing countries.

E. Aviation

Abouchar, Alan. 1970. "Air Transport Demand, Congestion Costs, and the Theory of Optimal Airport Use." *Canadian Journal of Economics,* August, pp. 463–75.
An attempt to develop a theory of optimum congestion at airports.

Carlin, Alan, and Rolla Edward Park. 1970. "A Model of Long Delays at Busy Airports." *Journal of Transport Economics and Policy* 4(1): 37–54.
An interesting cost-benefit study of improvements at Kennedy Airport, New York.

Carruthers, R. C., and D. A. Hensher. 1976. "Resource Value of Business Air Travel Time." In Ian G. Heggie, ed., *Modal Choice and the Value of Travel Time.* Oxford, Eng.: Clarendon.

de Neufville, Richard, and Ralph L. Keeney. 1971. "Use of Decision Analysis in Airport Development for Mexico City." In *Benefit Cost Analysis.* Hawthorne, N.Y.: Aldine.
An interesting article on a cost-benefit analysis of a new airport for Mexico City.

De Vany, Arthur. 1974. "The Revealed Value of Time in Air Travel." *Review of Economics and Statistics* 56(1): 77–82.
Finds that air travelers value their time at their wage.

Fordham, R. C. 1970. "Airport Planning in the Context of the Third London Airport." *Economic Journal* 80(318): 307–22.
Article addresses itself mainly to the terms of reference of the Royal Commission on the Third London Airport.

Fromm, Gary. 1962. *Economic Criteria for Federal Aviation Agency Expenditures.* Cambridge, Mass.: United Research.
A study on the appraisal of expenditures of the U.S. Federal Aviation Agency.

————. 1965. "Civil Aviation Expenditures." In Robert Dorfman, ed., *Measuring Benefits of Government Investments.* Washington, D.C.: Brookings Institution.
An interesting attempt to measure all benefits in monetary terms.

Great Britain. 1971. *Report of the Commission on the Third London Airport.* London: Her Majesty's Stationery Office.
This is a classic study of a major new airport. It includes both a cost-benefit analysis and an analysis of major environmental considerations.

Gronau, Reuben. 1970. *The Value of Time in Passenger Transportation: The Demand for Air Travel.* New York: Columbia University Press.
Finds that business travelers value time at approximately their hourly earnings.

Hettich, Walter, and C. Swoveland. 1983. *Benefit Cost Analysis for Air Transportation Projects.* Canadian Air Transportation Administration.
A clear, comprehensive, and practical guide, with case studies.

Mackie, P. J. 1983. "Appraisal of Regional Airport Projects." In K. J. Button and A. D. Pearman, eds., *The Practice of Transport Investment Appraisal*. Aldershot, Eng.: Gower.
Case study of a proposed runway extension at a regional airport in England; with extensive references.

Mishan, E. J. 1970. "What is Wrong with Roskill." *Journal of Transport Economics and Policy* 4(3): 221–34.
A critique of the third London airport report.

Noah, J. W., Associates. 1977. *Cost-Benefit Analysis and the National Aviation System.* Federal Aviation Adminstration Report FAA-AVP-77-15, Washington, D.C.: U.S. Department of Commerce.
A manual on the application of cost-benefit methodology to aviation projects.

Nwaneri, V. C. 1970. "Equity in Cost-Benefit Analysis." *Journal of Transport Economics and Policy* 4(3): 235–54.
An interesting attempt to recalculate the costs and benefits of the third London airport by taking into account equity, that is, the differential income of those who bear the costs and get the benefits. See also V. C. Nwaneri, "Income Distribution and Project Selection." *Finance and Development* 10(3): 27–29, 33.

Ody, J. G. 1969. "Application of Cost-Benefit Analysis to Airports." *Journal of Transport Economics and Policy* 3(3): 322–32.
An interesting attempt to measure the costs and benefits of lengthening a runway.

Paul, M. E. 1971. "Can Aircraft Noise Nuisance be Measured in Money?" *Oxford Economic Papers* 23(3): 297–322.
An interesting critique of the attempt in the study for the third London airport to measure the disbenefit of noise by changes in the value of housing.

U.S. Department of Transportation. 1981. *Economic Values for Evaluation of Federal Aviation Adminstration Investment and Regulatory Programs*. Federal Aviation Administration Report FAA-APO-81-3. Washington, D.C.
A clear discussion, with data, on the value of time of air travelers, the value of life, costs of aviation injuries, costs of aircraft damage, and aircraft variable operating costs. The data were updated in Report FAA-APO-84-3, 1984

Wood, Donald F. 1971. "Determining General Aviation Airport System Benefits." *Journal of Transport Economics and Policy* 5(3): 295–313.
An attempt at cost-benefit analysis in aviation, as applied to general aviation airports in Wisconsin.

F. Urban Transport

[Many aspects of urban transport, such as the value of time savings, also apply to other areas of transport; they are therefore covered in other sections of the bibliography.]

Barwell, I. J., and J. D. G. F. Howe. 1979. *Appropriate Transport Facilities for the Rural Sector in Developing Countries.* See section IIIB.

Bonsall, P., Q. Dalvi, and P. J. Hills, eds. 1977. *Urban Transport Planning.* Tunbridge Wells, Eng.: Abacus.
A series of articles on urban planning in the United Kingdom.

Domencich, Thomas A., and David McFadden. 1975. *Urban Travel Demand.* Amsterdam: North-Holland.
A behavioral analysis, that is, a model which represents the decision that consumers make when confronted with alternative choices.

Edwards, Chris. 1978. "Some Problems of Evaluating Investments in Rural Transport." See section IIIB above.

Gwilliam, K. M. 1972. "Economic Evaluation of Urban Transport Projects." *Transportation Planning and Technology* 1(2): 123–41.
An interesting critique of the state of the art, with suggestions for improvement.

Hall, J. W., R. B. Sawhill, and J. H. Matteson. 1970. "User Benefits in Economic Analysis of Metropolitan Freeway Construction." *Highway Research Record* 314: 32–40.
Time savings and accident reduction are found to be major benefits.

Haney, D. G. 1970. "Problems, Misconceptions and Errors in Benefit-Cost Analyses of Transit Systems." *Highway Research Record* 314: 98–113.
Presents a number of interesting ideas.

Hensher, D. A., ed. 1977. *Urban Transport Economics.* Cambridge, Eng.: Cambridge University Press.
A series of essays on various aspects of urban transport planning, including pricing, appraisal, demand analysis for passenger and freight traffic, and cost-benefit analysis of transport improvements.

Hide, Henry, and S. W. Abaynayaka. 1975. "Some Vehicle Operating Cost Relationships for Developing Countries." See section IIIB above.

Hine, J. L. 1975. "The Appraisal of Rural 'Feeder' Roads in Developing Countries." In *Transport Planning in Developing Countries.* See section IIIB above.

Hutchinson, B. G. 1970. "An Approach to the Economic Evaluation of Urban Transportation Investments." *Highway Research Record* 314: 72–86.
An interesting attempt to deal not only with economic efficiency but also with distributional and environmental effects.

Jones, I. S. 1977. *Urban Transport Appraisal.* New York: Wiley.
An introduction dealing with both traffic forecasting and economic appraisal of urban transport projects and policies.

Kuhn, Tillo E. 1965. "The Economics of Transportation Planning in Urban Areas." *Transportation Economics.* New York: National Bureau of Economic Research.
Useful on cost-benefit approach.

Meyer, J. R., and J. A. Gomez-Ibanez. 1981. *Autos, Transit and Cities.* Cambridge, Mass.: Harvard University Press.
A comprehensive review of urban transportation. Although the focus is on the United States, many of the issues, such as congestion, pricing, and environmental problems, have applicability to urban transport in developing countries.

Meyer, John, John F. Kain, and Martin Wohl. 1965. *The Urban Transportation Problem.* Cambridge, Mass.: Harvard University Press.
A good introduction to urban transport planning.

Mohring, Herbert. 1965. "Urban Highway Investments." In Robert Dorfman, ed., *Measuring Benefits of Government Investment.* Washington, D.C.: Brookings Institution.
Useful on urban highways.

Owen, Wilfred. 1966. *The Metropolitan Transportation Problem.* Washington, D.C.: Brookings Institution.

_____. 1972. *The Accessible City.* Washington, D.C.: Brookings Institution.
In urban transport, the planning of the city is an essential aspect of transport planning.

Plumbe, A. J. 1978. "Implications of Feeder Road Usage by the Farming Community of South-East Thailand." See section IIIB above.

Rothenberg, J. G., and I. G. Heggie, eds. 1974. *Transport and the Urban Environment.* New York: Wiley.
Part II of this volume of essays deals with urban transport. Of special interest are C. D. Foster, "Transport and the Urban Environment," and H. Levy-Cambert, "Cost Benefit Analysis of Urban Traffic Congestion: The Example of Paris."

Squire, Lyn. 1973. "Optimal Feeder Roads in Developing Countries: The Case of Thailand." See section IIIB above.

Thomas, C. T., and G. I. Thompson. 1970. "The Value of Time for Commuting Motorists as a Function of Their Income Level and Amount of Time Saved." *Highway Research Record* 314: 1–14.
A study of the value of commuter time.

Thomson, J. M. 1983. *Toward Better Urban Transport Planning in Developing Countries.* World Bank Staff Working Paper 600. Washington, D.C.
A critique of existing planning methods and suggestions for improvements. Appendix includes simple terms of reference for an urban transport study.

Watson, P. L. 1978. "Singapore's Area License Scheme: Results and Lessons." In *Transport Planning in Developing Countries.* London: Planning and Transport Research and Computation, and Transportation Research Board.
Discussion of an interesting effort to solve urban congestion problems by reducing the demand for transport through pricing and licensing, rather than by increasing the supply.

World Bank. 1985. *Urban Transport.* Washington, D.C.
The study focuses on urban transport policy and the Bank's experience with financing of urban transport projects.

Index

Accident reduction, economic benefit of, 41–44
Agricultural development, and road construction, 36–37, 103
Airport construction: benefits of, 199–201; cost-benefit comparison of, 201; costs of, 195, 198; description of, 194–95; traffic affected by, 198

Bell, Clive, 62n 1
Benefits: of additional port berths, 166–67; of airport construction, 199–201; of bridge construction, 109–14; of cargo-handling equipment, 186, 188; of development road, 102–04; discounting, 49–50; economic versus financial appraisal of, 57–58; of grain silo, 190–92; and Highway Design Model, 61–62; of highway maintenance, 119, 121; of major highway, 89–94; of modernizing marshaling yard, 134–35, 138; of ocean port, 177, 180–83; and optimum timing, 58–61; of paving gravel road, 72–75; of widening pavement, 79–81
Berth capacity: and cargo-handling equipment, 186; and construction, 163, 166–67, 170–73, 174; and silo construction, 190–92
Bridge construction: benefits of, 109–14; cost-benefit comparison of, 114–15; costs of, 106; traffic affected by, 106, 109, 114

Capital costs: of airport construction, 195; of cargo-handling equipment, 185; of development road, 97, 100, 101–02; of expanding water transport, 101–02; of grain silo, 190; of modernizing marshaling yard, 134; of ocean port, 174–75; of oil pipeline, 152–53, 158–60; of paving gravel road, 69; of rail dieselization, 130; of rail electrification, 129
Cargo-handling equipment for port: benefits of, 185–86, 188; cost-benefit comparison of, 188–89; costs of, 185
Contingencies, and economic costs, 15–16
Cost(s): of additional berths, 163, 166; of airport construction, 195, 198; of bridge construction, 106; of cargo-handling equipment, 185; of development road, 97, 100–01; of discontinuing railway service, 143–44, 145, 148–51; discounting of, 49–50; economic versus financial appraisal of, 57–58; of electrification versus dieselization of railway line, 128–32; of expanding water transport, 101–02; financial versus economic, 57; of forecasting, 23; of grain silo, 190; and Highway Design Model, 61–62; of highway maintenance, 118–21; of major highway, 84–85; of modernizing marshaling yard, 134; of ocean port, 174–76; of oil pipeline,

Cost(s) (*continued*)
  152–56, 161–62; and optimum tim-
    ing, 58–61; of paving gravel road,
    69, 71, 74–75; of risk and uncer-
    tainty, 54–57; versus wages, 12–14;
    of waiting time, 167; of widening
    pavement, 77. *See also* Capital
    costs; Economic costs; Labor
    costs; Operating costs; Opportun-
    ity cost; Road transport costs;
    Sailing costs; Shipping costs;
    Shunting costs; Vehicle operating
    costs
Cost-benefit comparison: of ad-
    ditional port berths, 167–73; of
    airport construction, 201; of
    bridge construction, 114–15; of
    cargo-handling equipment, 188–
    89; of development road, 104–05;
    of grain silo, 192–93; in Highway
    Design Model, 61–62; of highway
    maintenance, 121–22; of major
    highway, 94–95; of modernizing
    marshaling yard, 138–39; methods
    of, 49–53; of ocean port, 183–84;
    and optimum timing of projects,
    58–61; of paving gravel road, 76;
    of widening pavement, 82–83
Cost-benefit guidelines, 54
"Crossover" values in project ap-
    praisal, 55

Development road, 96; benefits of,
    102–04; cost-benefit comparison
    of, 104–05; costs of, 97, 100–02
Devres, Inc., 46n 4
Dickey, J. W., 19n 3, 47n 16
Dieselization of railway, 123–32
Discounting costs and benefits, 49–
    50, 51
Discount rates, 204–06; and interest
    during construction, 16
Diverted traffic: and highway con-
    struction, 90–91, 92; in forecasting,
    25–26; and reduced operating ex-
    penses, 32–33

Drivers: and cost saving, 112; educa-
    tion, and road accident reduction,
    41

Economic analysis of rail service,
    144–49
Economic appraisal: adjustments
    for, 15–18; bridge construction,
    109–10; versus financial, 57–58; of
    projects, 3. *See also* Cost-benefit
    comparison
Economic benefits, 27–29; of acci-
    dent reduction, 41–44; distribution
    of, 29–30; and economic develop-
    ment, 33–37; of reduced operating
    expenses, 30–33; secondary, 44–46;
    of time savings, 37–41
Economic costs: of additional port
    berths, 163–66; and contingencies,
    15–16; of development road,
    97–98; of forecasting traffic, 23–24;
    of foreign expenditures, 12;
    of foreign loans, 18; and inflation,
    15–16; of interest during construc-
    tion, 16–17; of modernizing mar-
    shaling yard, 134; of ocean port,
    175–76; of oil pipeline, 152; of
    paving gravel road, 69; and proj-
    ect scope, 17–18; of railway die-
    selization, 130; of railway elec-
    trification, 129; and shadow
    prices, 11–15; of tankwagons, 159;
    and transport prices, 9; of widen-
    ing pavement, 77
Edmonds, G. A., 46n 4
Electrification of railway, 123–32

Financial analysis, of rail service,
    142–44
Financial appraisal. *See* Economic
    appraisal (versus financial); Proj-
    ect analysis (aspects of)
Financial costs, 14, 97, 163
Fishing benefits, 103–04
Foreign loans, economic costs of, 18